Who Killed Precious?

Who Killed Precious?

How FBI special agents combine
high technology and psychology
to identify violent criminals

H. Paul Jeffers

PHAROS BOOKS
A SCRIPPS HOWARD COMPANY
NEW YORK, NEW YORK

LIBRARY OF CONGRESS CATALOGING-IN-PUBLICATION DATA
Jeffers, H. Paul (Harry Paul), 1934-
Who killed Precious? : how FBI special agents combine high
technology and psychology to identify violent criminals / H. Paul
Jeffers.
p. cm.
Includes bibliographical references (p. 215) and index.
ISBN 0-88687-538-2 : $17.95
1. Criminal investigation—United States—Case studies. 2. United
States. Federal Bureau of Investigation. I. Title.
HV8073.J44 1991
363.2'5—dc20   90-20743
CIP

Printed in the United States of America
Jacket design by Suzanne Reisel
Book design by Fritz Metsch

Pharos Books
A Scripps Howard Company
200 Park Avenue
New York, NY 10166

10 9 8 7 6 5 4 3 2 1

Pharos Books are available at special discounts on bulk purchases for
sales promotions, premiums, fundraising or educational use. For
details, contact the Special Sales Department, Pharos Books, 200
Park Avenue, New York, NY 10166.

This book is dedicated to my brother,
Judge John T. Jeffers

"The very point which appears to complicate a case is, when duly considered and scientifically handled, the one which is most likely to elucidate it."
—Sherlock Holmes, in
The Hound of the Baskervilles

Contents

Acknowledgments

With gratitude I recognize those in the FBI who cooperated in my research: Director William S. Sessions; Milt Ahleric, assistant director, Office of Public Affairs (OPA), when work on the book began; Robert B. Davenport and Thomas F. Jones, Inspectors in Charge, OPA, Ms. Bobbi Cotter of the OPA; and Special Agent Dr. Richard Ault of the Behavioral Sciences Unit of the National Center for the Analysis of Violent Crime (NCAVC).

For assistance in obtaining materials on the NCAVC's role in the investigation of "equivocal" mass death in Gun Turret No. 2 of the battleship *Iowa* I offer my thanks to Cathy Lipovack of the Investigations Subcommittee and Defense Policy Panel of the Committee on Armed Services, U.S. House of Representatives. I am indebted also to Senator Arlen Specter of the U.S. Senate's Committee on the Judiciary and Phil Shipman of its staff for providing a hard-to-get copy of the out-of-print 1983 report of the Subcommittee on Juvenile Justice of the Senate Judiciary Committee on its ground-breaking hearings on the subject of serial killers, which contributed greatly to the making of a national commitment to deal with violent crime by backing a plan for the Violent Criminal Apprehension Program (VICAP) that became integral to the work of the NCAVC.

Invaluable assistance in researching the 1990 murderers of prostitutes in the Washington, D.C., area in which a profile by the NCAVC became crucial was provided by Edward S. Rickards. He also helped in the researching of the New York Zodiac and the Dart Man, a descriptive phrase which Ed coined, adding yet another colorful appellation to the lexicon of crime.

Thanks also for the general support and counsel afforded by Sid Goldstein, president of Pace Publications, Inc., and publisher of *Criminal Justice Newsletter,* and his Washington, D.C., staff for their logistical help.

For guidance in shaping the concept of this book and advice on my other efforts as an author, I am indebted to Mel Berger, vice-president of William Morris Agency.

Special thanks go to Hana Umlauf Lane of Pharos Books, a gentle lady who overcame an abhorrence of violence to take on the task of editing another of my books on the subject that has enthralled me as a newsman and author for forty years—violent crime and bloody murder.

—H. Paul Jeffers

Who Killed
Precious?

Where Evil Lurks

Every Sunday afternoon years ago on the radio, the Shadow asked, "Who knows what evil lurks in the hearts of men?" Tuned in as a child, I certainly didn't.

Until I was eighteen, murder was something on radio and TV, on the movie screen or in the daily news—a distant event, an abstraction. Then someone I knew was murdered. A pretty high school student, she was grabbed off a street in my hometown, Phoenixville, Pennsylvania, raped, stabbed to death, and tossed into a well behind an abandoned schoolhouse in a lonely stretch of snowy countryside. As a journalism student and budding newsman working for a small radio station, I covered the case. It was the first corpse I'd ever seen. Unfortunately, the killer was never caught. This was in the early 1950s, when criminology had at its disposal very few of the dazzling scientific techniques that are routinely available to homicide investigators today. Criminal psychological profiling, which is the subject of this book, was but a distant dream.

Besides its savagery, what my first murder story impressed upon me was the terror and suspicion that grips a community when a killer is loose. I was to witness that phenomenon on a grander scale while working in television news in the 1960s when Boston was frozen with fear during a two-year period as a strangler methodically assaulted and brutally murdered thirteen women in their homes. With sickening regularity from 1962 to 1964, Boston newsrooms were alerted to the

1

discovery of another victim. Invariably, the crime scene took on a circus atmosphere as newsmen waited for someone in authority to come out to make a statement giving us the name of the victim, her age, when the body had been found, and under what circumstances—enough sketchy details to confirm that this was a genuine "Strangler" crime and not a look-alike copycat killing. Although most of the Boston Strangler's victims were elderly, one of the victims was Patricia Bissette, a neighbor of mine—a pleasant, fresh-faced twenty-three-year-old-secretary who met a horrible death at Christmastime.

The questions asked by the journalists covering the Boston Strangler's deeds were the same ones being asked by the police: Who? What? Where? When? Why?

In this case the "who" turned out to be Albert DeSalvo. An incarnation of banality, he stemmed from a family in which beatings of his mother, his siblings, and himself were commonplace. By the age of seventeen, Albert had a record of breaking-and-entering arrests. Married to a German girl he met in the Army, he became an abusive husband when his wife rebuffed what she considered his outrageous sexual demands. In 1955 while stationed in New Jersey he was charged with molesting a nine-year-old girl, but the mother dropped the case. Honorably discharged from the service, Albert returned to Massachusetts. Soon, women began complaining to police about a smooth-talking "talent agent" who produced a measuring tape to take the "vital statistics" of those who admitted him to their homes. Convicted of these molestations, he served eleven months of a two-year sentence only to emerge as the "Green Man" because he always wore green work clothes when carrying out a string of sexual assaults all over New England—300 according to police, 2,000 by DeSalvo's count. From Measuring Man to Green Man to Boston Strangler was a short journey. Although it was certain that DeSalvo was the Strangler, prosecutors and famed criminal lawyer F. Lee Bailey struck a bargain that put DeSalvo into prison for the easier-to-prove Green Man cases rather than as the Boston Strangler. Sent to Walpole Prison, he was stabbed to death in 1973, leaving no explanation of why and how he'd become a mass murderer, except madness.

Thirteen years after the Boston Strangler's orgy of death, when I was covering news in New York City, madness appeared to drive David Berkowitz to become the Son of Sam, the terrorizer of twelve million people and the object of the greatest manhunt in the history of the city. Again, the question underlying the police investigation into the "who" was "why?" In a diary note written after an end had been put to his murderous escapades, he wrote, "There is no doubt in my mind that a demon has been living in me since birth. All my life I've been wild, violent, temporal, mean, sadistic, acting with irrational anger and destructiveness."

The scarlet thread of murder, especially multiple murder, is tightly woven into the warp and woof of the United States. We have more repeat murderers than any nation in the world and we account for about three-fourths of the earth's serial killers. Of these, 85 percent are men and 82 percent of them are white. In the first half of the twentieth century, our police recorded an average of 1.2 serial cases per year. Between 1960 and 1980 the average was a dozen a year. In the last decade of the century the rate has escalated to two a month.

The names of some of these killers are more familiar to the American people than those of Presidents, statesmen, generals, educators, businessmen, and philanthropists. Indeed, a few serial killers and mass murderers have transcended history and become folk figures. Even a partial listing is a bloodstained roster: Herman Mudgett, who may have killed as many as 200 in Chicago in 1896; Belle Gunness, murderer of fourteen in LaPorte, Indiana, in 1908; Earle Nelson, killer of twenty-three in a nationwide spree in 1926–27; Howard Unruh, gunning down a baker's dozen on the streets of Camden, New Jersey, in 1949; Nannie Doss, reaping ten lives in Oklahoma in 1954; Charles Starkweather, taking a homicide tour of the Midwest in 1957–58 with his teenage girlfriend Caril Fugate; Richard Speck, savaging the life out of eight sleeping nurses in Chicago in 1966; Charles Whitman, ascending the clock tower on the Austin campus of the University of Texas that same year and calmly sharpshooting sixteen people on the grass and walkways below; the trio of Dean Arnold Corll, Elmer Wayne Henley, and David Owen Brooks, collecting victims in Texas in 1973; mother-hating Edmund Kemper, killing her and going on a death spree in Nebraska that same year; the Zebra murders of the mid-1970s in Los Angeles; the Skid Row Slasher of L.A.; the Zodiac of northern California, who slaughtered in lovers' lanes; John Wayne Gacy, whose specialty was young gay men of the Chicago area in '78; Wayne Williams, slaying black youths in Atlanta in 1981; the Green River Killer, tolling at least forty deaths around Seattle and Tacoma; Theodore Bundy, a suave slayer of young women whose bloody trail stretched from the Northwest to Florida; and the wild-eyed Richard Ramirez, "Night Stalker" of Los Angeles, convicted of thirteen murders and bragging of more. "I've killed twenty people, man," he ranted in court. "I love all that blood."

Are Richard Ramirez, Albert DeSalvo, David Berkowitz, and Ted Bundy as much a part of modern American life as Mom, apple pie, baseball, and the flag? Is there something in us as a nation that encourages serial murder? Or is each case unique? Is every mass murderer or serial killer special? Or is he one of a growing fraternity each of whose brothers is predictably the same as the other?

This book is about a group of men and women who are seeking the answers to those questions and turning their findings to the assistance of law enforcement in identifying and tracking down the mass murderers and serial killers along with the rapists, molesters of children, victimizers of the elderly, arsonists, terrorists, and other violent criminals plaguing America. They are scientist/Special Agents of the Federal Bureau of Investigation's Behavioral Science Unit within the National Center for the Analysis of Violent Crime (NCAVC), which operates as part of the FBI National Training Academy at Quantico, Virginia.

Two of them, Richard L. Ault, Jr., and Robert R. Hazelwood, were the catalyst for this book. Out of a general interest in the disaster that took forty-seven lives aboard the battleship *Iowa* in 1989, I tuned in my TV set to watch Congressional hearings being held on the cause of the explosion. There were two inquiries, one by the House Subcommittee on Investigations and the other by the Senate Armed Services Committee. Hazelwood and Ault testified concerning their controversial personality profile drawn up at the Navy's request on the gun captain in Turret No. 2 at the time of the blast, Gunner's Mate Second Class Clayton M. Hartwig. Because everyone in the gun room had been killed in what the Navy said was not an accident, the incident was, in the words of Ault and Hazelwood, "an equivocal death."

Hearing that phrase for the first time, I asked myself, "What the hell is equivocal about being dead?" Either you were or you·weren't. The agents quickly explained that because the Navy had ruled out an accident, there remained the question of whether the deaths of Hartwig and the other crewmen were a case of suicide, suicide and murder, or mass murder—carried out by whom? What Ault and Hazelwood had been called upon to do was deduce the answer from all available evidence.

Now "deduction" was an area of criminology about which I had some knowledge, primarily from the fictional literature of crime: the supreme reasoner who resided at 221B Baker Street, Sherlock Holmes; the French sleuth Auguste Dupin in Edgar Allan Poe's classic *The Murders in the Rue Morgue*; Agatha Christie's Belgian detective Hercule Poirot using his "little gray cells"; Georges Simenon's Jules Maigret; and a host of others, including Earl Derr Biggers's Charlie Chan. "My experience tell me to think deep about human people," declared Chan in *The House Without a Key*. "Study human people at all times."

That is what Ault and Hazelwood were up to in the *Iowa* case and, I soon found out, in many, many more cases. They and others like them at the FBI were not traditional Special Agents. Rather, they were behavioral scientists taking to heart Chan's admonition by studying humans at all times: *criminally minded*, violent humans who had become the scourge of America in the waning years of the twentieth century.

"Traditionally, law enforcement has not trusted the behavioral sciences," wrote Ault and Hazelwood in an article on the developing "art" of criminal personality assessment. "Nevertheless, investigators can and should make use of advances in the behavioral sciences for the benefit of the law enforcement profession."

In this task the scientist/agents of the FBI have carried out innovative research and brought to bear the latest in technology to write, as you will read, an amazing chapter in the history of criminology.

ONE

Who Killed Precious?

Splayed and looking like a broken doll cast aside onto the grassy knoll, she had on a black-leather-and-suede waist-length jacket with fringe on the sleeve, a turquoise-and-black top, and black Spandex pants that clung to her slight but shapely figure like a second skin. However, the shocked groundskeeper making his early rounds at the modern offices of the Seminary Professional Village on Dawes Avenue in Alexandria, Virginia, on that warm Wednesday morning after 1990's long Memorial Day weekend couldn't see the girl's rouged white cheeks, big blue eyes, and brownish-blond hair because her head was covered by a plastic trash bag tightly knotted around her neck.

Summoned by the shaken caretaker to the hedge-lined lawn where the body lay, police brought all the equipment of modern crime detection at their disposal for answering the timeless questions of the sleuth: who, what, where, when, why, and how?

The last was the easiest, supplied by autopsy. This death definitely was a homicide, ruled the coroner: asphyxiation. A cord was around her neck. A dish towel had been stuffed into her mouth. She'd also been rather badly beaten. And her hands had been bound in front of her.

When had she died? Several days ago, the coroner reported; possibly as far back as Saturday.

Where? Even with a cursory look around the neat, undisturbed ground it was obvious to the police that she'd not been killed where she was found.

Now came the hard part: who was this good-looking girl whom the medical examiner estimated to be about sixteen years old?

Any detective worth his salt recognized that her clothing pointed directly to the answer. From experience and intuition, a cop looking at those tight pants and that clinging top had to recognize the raiment of a street prostitute, and any cop in Alexandria knew the most likely spot to check for clues to a murdered prostitute's identity was across the Potomac River in the capital of the United States of America.

The girls call it "the stroll," but it's nothing as pleasant as that. It's mean work pounding the pavement in high heels and a short skirt in the blocks of L and K streets between 12th and 15th in downtown Washington after government employees and tourists have fled to safe suburban homes and the security and comfort of hotels that cater to out-of-towners, leaving the night to those who go by names as telling as their come-on clothing.

Trixie, a platinum blonde in her twenties, wears a black dress that leaves very little to the imagination of the hot-eyed but shadowy unaccompanied men who study her as they glide past in automobiles with Virginia and Maryland license plates. As ardent an outspoken advocate of the capitalist system as the trendy supply-side politicians in the halls of Congress crosstown, Trixie works the stroll because she's very fond of money. In an average week she earns between $1,500 and $3,000 and doesn't set aside a dime for the IRS.

Not one of the prostitutes on the stroll does less—while it lasts, while she's still got her looks, hasn't been done in by drugs and booze, and hasn't had the bad luck to run into one of those men who go in for rough stuff and leave a girl beaten . . . or dead.

Since the spring of 1989, a lot of women from the stroll had been showing up dead all over the place. Chubby Mary Ellen Sullenberger had fled the taunts and ridicule of slenderer acquaintances in Lancaster, Pennsylvania, and arrived on the stroll, where she discovered men who told her she was beautiful and made her feel wanted, until one of them pumped a slug into her chest on April 19. Cori Louise Jones had also been shot several times in the chest in August of that year. And

Roxanne Lynn Johnson was found with a bullet in her head on October 1 behind a schoolhouse. The slug in her matched the ones that had snuffed out Jones's life.

The killings continued into 1990 with Caroleen Marie Wallace, whose body was found in a storm sewer in Forestville, Virginia, on Valentine's Day—shot in the head. A bullet in the brain also killed Lisa Colleen Grossman in March. Her friends on the stroll remembered Lisa as a vibrant young woman with reddish hair who lived with her common-law husband and two cute sons in a Fairfax County motel and paid for her crack habit by working as a topless dancer and plying the oldest profession around 14th and L.

None of this was lost on Trixie and her colleagues of the stroll. When someone was picking up and killing prostitutes, the word of it spread like wildfire. But what was a girl to do? She had to make a living, and if that meant taking chances, "well, what the hell," said Chauncey—wasn't all of a life just one big risk? Leggy and leery, Chauncey had made it to the stroll from Boston and spoke like one of the Kennedys, turning "car" into "cah" and "yard" into "yahd" despite several years away from her hometown, where she had never had a yard to play in, let alone a car for rides to whisk her away from the decaying black neighborhood of Roxbury.

The murders were also known to a willowy ash-blonde who called herself Irene. She claimed to be a college graduate and to have chosen the street because she couldn't stand the ignorant people she had encountered in the more traditional workplace. It's lots easier to put up with a john in a car for five minutes, she decided, than with the ignoramuses you find in offices for five days a week, fifty-two weeks a year. And the pay was a hell of a lot better.

As a teenager, black-haired, tawny-skinned Maria had tried doling out hamburgers at McDonald's before being discovered by a pimp, turned onto drugs, and put to strolling in fluorescent pants and spike heels and to hell with the fact that prostitutes seemed to be fair game for killers.

With the number of dead hookers accumulating, there'd been plenty of detectives coming around asking questions about them, but nothing had come of it. They'd drifted around again before the

Memorial Day weekend, swarms of police descending on the stroll but not in pursuit of a killer of prostitutes. This time they were there to clean up the area, because Washington had to put its best face forward for the forthcoming visit of Mikhail Gorbachev. It wouldn't do for the head of the Soviet Union, who had ideas about turning Russia into a capitalist country, to look out the window of his long black ZIL limousine on his way to a visit with President George Herbert Walker Bush and find a flock of private-enterprise females in hot pants hustling johns.

Now with that visit history, here came more cops, not to hassle but back to the business of murder, asking "Do you happen to recognize her?" about a girl whose morgue photo they drew from their pockets.

As in the cases of the other dead women, these guarded and wary women would come up with an i.d. eventually. "Oh, that's the one we called Precious," declared Chauncey.

"She was from Detroit," Maria thinks she heard once. "She went by the name Cynthia Baker."

"Her real name was Jodie Phillips," Trixie seemed to recall.

Now with a phone call from a police officer hundreds of miles away, two parents' darkest nightmares about what might have happened to Jodie since she fled their home in Michigan were about to come true.

In Arlington, the Virginia suburb of Washington that is the location of the cemetery for the country's honored war dead and the burial place of John F. and Robert Kennedy, the parents of another frequenter of the stroll already were grappling with the fact that their daughter was dead. The body of twenty-six-year old Sherry K. Larman had been found on Saturday, May 26, on the roof of a four-story parking garage, deserted over the holiday weekend, that served Strayer College and a nearby office building in South Arlington. Nude except for black underpants, the body had been discovered at 9:30 A.M. Suffocation had snuffed out the life of the blond girl, whom her father, a retired District of Columbia police officer, and her mother recalled as a happy child who'd become troubled by the divorce of her parents when she was six. In her teen years she'd gotten into drugs and was enrolled in the Good Shepherd Center, a high school and residential treatment for drug abusers. There she'd excelled in athletics and won trophies for track. She went on from school and worked as a secretary and receptionist, and things were looking good. But then she "fell in with the wrong people," said her grieving mother, and started using drugs again, and within a year she was walking the stroll and using the name Stacy.

A horrifying telephone call from police in Arlington had also been received by the parents of twenty-year-old Sandra Rene Johnson. A prostitute from the stroll, she'd been found dead, fully clothed, with a blow on the head and her hands bound, on the morning of May 27 inside the Country Club Towers apartment house where she lived. This was two blocks from Interstate 395 and less than two miles from the rooftop garage where Sherry Larman's corpse had been discovered.

In addition to the proximity of these discoveries made only hours apart, the police of Arlington had noted that in both cases the head was covered with a plastic bag knotted around the neck.

Now, over the communications system that keeps the law enforcement agencies of Washington and its Virginia and Maryland counterparts up to date on what's going on, Lieutenant Kenneth Madden received a report on the death of Precious, whose head was also wrapped in a plastic bag. In anybody's police academy textbook, it was not likely to be a coincidence when three hookers met death in the same way around the same time. But could these Memorial Day weekend murders be linked to the previous slayings? Might there be other killings of women in the greater Washington area with similarities to the prostitute murders? Was a freewheeling, highly mobile murderer at work? Was this the work of a serial killer?

The only efficient way to answer these questions was to hold a skull session of investigators from all the jurisdictions with murders of women, especially killings of known prostitutes, on their books. It was set for Thursday, May 31, at the Northern Virginia Criminal Justice Academy in Arlington. Taking part would be homicide detectives, forensic specialists, and other representatives of the police departments of Arlington, Alexandria, Falls Church, Washington, D.C., and of the Virginia State Police, U.S. Park Police, and Federal Bureau of Investigation.

Leading the FBI contingent was John E. Douglas. With his fashionable yellow necktie and summer-weight conservative-plaid suit, he represented a new style of FBI Special Agent that bore little resemblance to the G-men who had become legendary in the history of U.S. law enforcement under J. Edgar Hoover—they with their close-clipped haircuts, dark suits, white shirts, and solid-color narrow ties. Famed for dogged pursuit of gangsters, auto thieves, bank robbers, civil rights leaders, antiwar marchers, and communists, those agents held degrees in accounting and law. With a doctorate in education, John Douglas bore responsibilities that reflected something else that was new since Hoover's day. While carrying out a multifaceted role with the weighty title of Program Manager of the Criminal Investigative Analysis Program of the Behavioral Science Investigative Support Unit (BSU) of the National Center for the Analysis of Violent Crime (NCAVC), he also was a member of the adjunct faculty of the University of Virginia, the University of Houston Law Center, and the National College of District Attorneys and a senior research fellow at the University of Pennsylvania. Coauthor with Ann W. Burgess of Penn and Robert K. Ressler of the FBI, he'd also contributed to the literature of law enforcement in a landmark textbook on serial killers, *Sexual Homicide*.

Based at the FBI Training Academy at Quantico, Virginia, as manager of the bureau's Criminal Investigative Analysis Program, Douglas directed a staff of nine analyst-agents who devised psychological profiles of unknown offenders. Constructed through the detailed analyses of forensic evidence of violent crimes and crime scenes and through interviews with known violent sexual criminals, the profiles had been drawn up to provide FBI investigators and other police agencies with advice on investigative approaches and methods, interviewing, search warrant preparation, and strategies for the prosecution of multiple sexual murderers and serial killers and rapists. In 1989, the program had handled 793 cases. In his years with the BSU, Douglas had been called upon to evaluate the evidences of violent crimes and to develop profiles of the unknown perpetrators 450 times.

In order for him and the others at the meeting to decide if a serial killer or killers were responsible for the Washington-area prostitute murders, the cases had to be compared. Besides murder, what was the commonality? All the prostitutes killed since April 1989 had worked the stroll. All were white and fairly tall and, except for sixteen-year-old Jodie (Precious) Phillips, in their twenties. Each had blond or light-colored hair. But for every similarity in the cases before the conferees there was also a glaring difference. Two had been shot in the head and two were shot in the chest. The same gun was used in at least two of the shootings. One died from a blow on the head, one was found in the building where she lived, one had been hidden in a sewer, and others had been dumped in public places. The three most recent were bound, beaten, asphyxiated, and hooded with plastic bags.

Because it appeared to the conferees that these three were the most likely to have been victims of the same killer, concentration on their murders promised the most obvious chance for a breakthrough both through forensic study of fibers, hair, blood, and semen and through sheer detective work—the foot-aching chore of canvassing and recanvassing the stroll to interview prostitutes and others in hope of finding someone who might remember seeing one man in the company of the three victims. Meanwhile, Douglas and his colleagues would come up with a profile of the killer.

While he could not provide the name of the man who had killed Precious, Douglas knew the killer's cousins, starting more than a century ago with Jack the Ripper, whose seven slashed and disembow-eled victims were prostitutes in the squalid streets and alleys of the Whitechapel neighborhood of London's East End. More recently, there'd been a series of prostitute murders in Canada—five killed in British Columbia and one in Alberta between 1985 and 1987, with the case still open. In the American Northwest they were still looking for the Green River Killer after more than a decade of deaths. In Los Angeles, the Southside Slayer had killed an estimated fifteen prosti-tutes between 1983 and 1986 and was also unidentified. Black prosti-tutes had been targeted by a serial killer for two years in New Haven, Connecticut, and that case, too, was still open. Go back in the annals of mankind and you'd find lots of men like Jack the Ripper who were "down on whores."

History also demonstrated to Douglas that the chances favored a serial killer's not being caught. More likely than an arrest would be a complete mental breakdown and quiet private institutionalization. Or he might simply move out of the area, as Ted Bundy had done. He could even be driven by remorse and guilt to commit suicide. The plain truth about serial killers was that they weren't always caught by the police, as the still-most-famous-of-all proved. More than one hundred years after the Ripper's horrendous crimes, Douglas could still find someone ready to debate his identity.

Criminology had come a long way since the days when Saucy Jack stalked Buck's Row and Mitre Square slaughtering whores. These days the police had the advantages of fingerprinting, serology, microscopic matching of fibers, weapons identification, the exciting promise of DNA testing, and countless other wonders of the forensic sciences. But these were of value only when you had a suspect or someone in custody. The wizards of the crime lab could clinch a case, but they couldn't tell the police what sort of person to go out and look for.

It was the task of Douglas and his team to look at the clues left by the killer and deduce from that evidence a personality profile of the killer. Since Jack the Ripper's day, seemingly endless studies and theorizing about men who killed prostitutes offered ready explanations as to why they killed, starting with the oldest but now largely discredited "Madonna-Whore Complex" in which the killer seeks revenge on a promiscuous mother by dividing the world of women into "good and bad" and proceeds to kill the most obvious bad ones—whores. Other experts believed that serial killers chose whores for more practical reasons. They were the easiest women to obtain. They would not be quickly missed. Deaths of prostitutes would probably not have a high priority among overworked police and a public grown used to murder in all ghastly forms, singly or in multiples.

Rather than *why*, Douglas was interested in *how* this fresh manifestation of a whore-killer carried out his crimes.

In the United States in the three decades before the death of Precious the acts of serial killers had been dissected by psychologists, anthropologists, sociologists, neurologists, and behavioral scientists, but Douglas and other agents of the FBI's Behavioral Science Unit had interviewed dozens of multiple and serial killers in their jail cells and on death row looking for data on how they went about murdering. What they'd had to say to their FBI questioners was now in FBI files, having been digested, analyzed, categorized, and computerized.

To begin their analysis of the murderer of Precious and the others, Douglas and his team first turned to the physical evidence—eight-by-ten color photos of the crime scenes, reports typed in the laborious hunt-and-peck style of most cops, summaries of those reports for higher-ups, the autopsy protocols, reports from labs, and the statements of all those who'd been questioned in the three suffocation murders.

Of course, all of this material had been studied already by the police, but Douglas and his team looked at it differently. To them a crime scene was regarded not as evidence of what had been done but as a *symptom* of the aberration of the person who did it. This is a different approach from that taken by the police, who arrive at a crime scene and proceed to work backward in an effort to reconstruct the crime, formulate a hypothesis of what occurred, and then launch an orderly and logical investigation to determine the identity of the criminal. That process is primarily physical: collecting, tagging, logging, packaging, examining. But Douglas had learned that there are some clues left at a crime scene which, by their very nature, do not lend themselves to that process. He was far less interested in items of tangible evidence found on the spot than he was in more subtle clues hinting at the mind of the killer.

How did he select his victim? How did he kill? Did he use a weapon? What did he do about discarding the body? Might there be something telling in the way he disposed of the victim? Did he take anything from the body? Was the body clothed? Did the method of murder reflect rage, or was it coolly carried out? Did the killing take place there or elsewhere? Was there evidence that a car had been used? Was a sexual act involved in the crime? If so, when? Before, during, or after the murder? Did the evidence show whether he took his time or was hurried? What was there at the scene of the crime that might be an insight into what the killer was thinking... before, during, and after the crime?

Once gathered and analyzed and compared with hundreds of other cases, these data could be fashioned into a portrait of that mind—a psychological profile of the personality of the killer. The data could then be compared to patterns of other killers already in the files and permit the profiler to provide police with direction in their manhunt.

In this approach, the psychological investigator studies a crime scene the way one looks at a painting. As Douglas's BSU colleague Robert Ressler put it, to understand the "artist" you have to look at his work.

The picture created by the killer of the three young women as discerned by the FBI profilers was familiar. In Douglas's parlance his profile was that of what the FBI defined as an "organized" killer whose "symptoms" were orderly behavior before, during, and after the crime. In picking up these women in Washington and getting them to Virginia, careful planning had been done. And care had been taken in the choice of the places where the bodies were dumped—secluded areas where being seen or interrupted was unlikely. While the victims could have been picked at random from the women of the stroll, they bore striking similarities in their age and appearance. The bodies had been discarded in relatively close proximity. This indicated that the killer knew the territory and, because none of the murders took place where the bodies were found, had use of a car or other vehicle for transporting the bodies. The method of murder was the same—indicating planning. Here was a man who knew what he was doing and had a structured method of operation.

Because the "symptoms" of this killer indicated that he fell into the "organized" category, Douglas could project with some confidence that the killer, once caught, would fit most aspects of the recognized profile drawn from all that was known about other killers from data sifted from FBI interviews with them. He was likely to be the firstborn son. His father's work would be stable, but parental discipline would have been inconsistent. Although the organized offender has an average or better-than-average intelligence, he often works at occupations below his abilities and has a sporadic work history. He could be a student with an uneven scholastic record. He is socially adept and is usually living with a partner or with both or one of his parents. Stress would be a factor in triggering his violence—a sudden problem with finances, job, marriage, or a romantic relationship. Alcohol or drugs were apt to figure in. A person whose usual demeanor is not suspicious, the organized offender often approaches his victim in an open, friendly manner, preferring to use verbal means to capture his victim rather than physical force—an easy accomplishment when picking up a prostitute. Control over the victim would be vital. Fantasy and ritual would dominate. The murder itself would be an acting out of a long-held fantasy. He was likely to have a car that was in good condition. He'd be likely to take something from his victim to keep as a souvenir. And he would be interested in news coverage of his deeds and could be expected to keep a scrapbook of the clippings.

Reading, hearing, or seeing accounts of his murders was to be easy for the killer of Precious and the two others as the Washington print and broadcast news media picked up the story of the triple murders over the Memorial Day weekend. Accounts appeared in the *Washington Post* and *Washington Times* soon after the discovery of the three bodies, and on June 5, the Cable News Network was on the air nationwide with a report in which its Washington reporter John Holliman interviewed John Douglas. "He's always out there looking for that victim," said Douglas, generalizing about serial killers. "When he sees that victim, he strikes. He takes control of that victim and takes her to where he'll feel comfortable—on his home turf. He then assaults the victim, tortures the victim in some cases, and kills the victim. He's a predatory animal. He's on the hunt nightly looking for his victim of opportunity."

Provided with Douglas's more detailed FBI sketch of the behavior of the man they were looking for, the police were pursuing all the other avenues of investigation in their hunt for a suspect. "I'll tell you this," said Corporal John Avery of the Alexandria police to a reporter on Tuesday, June 5, "there were some red-eyed detectives at roll call this morning." Arlington detectives had crossed the Potomac again to interview the women of the stroll, their pimps, and some of their customers, as well as employees of stores and restaurants in the vicinity of the stroll. Since the weekend they'd put in more than 300 hours of interrogations. State police had a pair of investigators assigned full-time. The D.C. homicide squad was on the case.

While these procedures were underway, the physical evidence recovered from each of the three crime scenes was being examined in laboratories in the hope of finding not only the clues that would prove a killer's guilt beyond a reasonable doubt in a court of law but anything, however tenuous, that might help pinpoint a suspect. It's a painstaking and time-consuming task; even the tiniest bit of possible evidence is gleaned and analyzed for its value.

During that process, one item had provoked curiosity, then attention. Discovered crumpled into the folds of the plastic bag taken from around Jodie Phillips's head, it was a Visa credit card receipt from a drugstore in Arlington for the purchase of garden supplies. The card was in the name of Jagjit S. Matta. A check of Visa records showed Matta's address was South Oakland Street in Arlington, not far from where the bodies of Sherry Larman and Sandra Rene Johnson had been found on May 26 and 27.

It was a modest-looking gray stone house whose residents, the police of Alexandria and the District of Columbia and the FBI soon determined, were Matta, who was retired and spent much of his time gardening, his wife, who was employed at a restaurant, and two sons.

Over the holiday weekend, Mr. and Mrs. Matta and the younger son had been away, leaving twenty-one-year-old Chander at home. Clearly, if the murderer of Phillips, Larman, and Johnson resided in that neat, quiet house, it had to be Chander.

While a twenty-four-hour-a-day surveillance was set up, Chander was checked out, and from all that was quickly learned about him, there was much to ponder about him in the light of Douglas's profile. A 1988 graduate of Arlington's Wakefield High School, Matta, known to his classmates as Bobby, had exhibited two passions in school—the Reserve Officers' Training Corps, in which he became a top officer, and sports, each requiring a fair amount of physical strength. Wearing number 72, he had been a starter several times as a senior on the football team but had an average academic record. After graduation he put in a year at a military academy in Vermont, where he became an expert at martial arts but left with a D average. Back in the Washington area in the summer of 1989, he took courses in business administration at Northern Virginia Community College's Annandale campus.

In April he'd been accepted as a student at Old Dominion University in Norfolk for the fall semester.

He seemed to be driven by a need to prove himself in school and to pay his own way. At the present time he was holding two part-time jobs, as a ticket agent for USAir at National Airport and in the printing office of the Department of Defense at the Pentagon in Arlington, traveling to the jobs in his parents' automobile. Neither of these positions was highly paid, yet in the past few days his bank account had swelled by about $2,000. He had an on-again, off-again relationship with a girl who bore a striking resemblance to the murdered women.

In every police investigation there comes a moment like the split second of critical mass that produces a nuclear reaction. It happened in this case on Sunday, June 10, as the combining weight of the FBI's profile and its remarkable parallels in the life of Chander Matta, the credit card slip, the proximity of the Matta residence to where three bodies had been dumped, and the availability of a car when he was left alone during that deadly Memorial Day weekend fused into a conviction among the team of investigators that Chander Matta was their chief—indeed, their *only*—suspect.

Agreed that the time had come to confront him, Alexandria and Arlington police arrived at the Matta home and took Chander to the Alexandria police department. After a brief, inconclusive interview, they returned him to his home. A short time later, they arrived again at the house, this time with a search warrant, and again, Chander was escorted to headquarters.

Bursting into tears, Chander related to the police and into a tape recorder a statement that would become the basis for his arrest at 9:30 that evening and a triumphant declaration to the news media the next day by Arlington Chief of Police William K. Stover. "We have the physical evidence to link him to all three of the murders," he declared, "and we have confessions to all three of the murders."

Deputy Attorney for the Commonwealth of Virginia Arthur Karp laid out the case for Matta being a systematic killer who had done his deeds with clockwork regularity. He contended that on Friday afternoon, May 25, Chander drove his father's automobile to Washington and picked up Sherry Larman on the stroll. He drove her back to the Matta house and they had sex. As she was putting on her clothes, he attacked her from behind, striking her on the head with an object that left a half-moon cut. As she lay on the bathroom floor, he pulled a gray plastic trash bag over her head and tied it with a cord around her neck. Because his parents and brother were gone for the whole weekend, he was unconcerned about the corpse being discovered and left for his job. Returning from work, he loaded the body into his father's car and drove it to the parking garage on South Highland Street in Arlington, where he dumped it on the rooftop.

It was now Saturday, and that evening, Karp alleged in the courtroom and in his supporting affidavit, "having come to the conclusion that it [murder] was quite pleasurable to do, he went back downtown and picked up Jodie Phillips." The pattern was the same as with Larman. He brought Jodie home, had sex with her, paid her $100, and attacked her from behind. Once again, he left for work, leaving the body in the house until he could discard it later against the shrubbery on the lawn where it was not to be discovered until the following Wednesday.

He then went back to the stroll and picked up Sandra Rene Johnson and drove her to her South Arlington apartment to kill for a third time in thirty-six hours.

In Johnson's apartment, investigators had found a bloody footprint that matched one of Matta's shoes, claimed Karp. And several items had been stolen, he stated, including a telephone answering machine. Alleging that $500 in cash was missing, he pointed out that shortly after the death of Johnson and the other women Matta had deposited $750 in his bank account and bought a $400 money order.

In executing the search warrant at the Matta residence, the investigators had discovered a trove of other evidence to support the charges against Chander. Among items confiscated in the house were a Panasonic telephone answering machine believed to be the one stolen from Johnson, four black umbrellas, women's shoes, women's underwear, house keys, sales receipts, a diary, and a telephone book. Also removed from the Matta home were hair and fiber samples, sweepings from a vacuum cleaner, lint from the family's clothes dryer, fabric samples, and bed linen.

Faced with the weight of the evidence against him, Matta did not deny that he'd killed the three women. Instead, he claimed that he had been insane, driven by an "irresistible impulse" to murder. Admitting that he'd killed them with a choke hold learned at military school, he said he'd covered their heads with plastic bags because he was afraid he might get blood on himself. His state of mind, he said, had been triggered by pressures resulting from failing grades at school and the breaking up of his relationship with his girl friend.

In describing his murder of Precious, Matta told police that he and Jodie Phillips had developed a rapport and that they had played with his pair of pet parakeets. When one of them got loose, he said, she'd helped him catch it. "She really liked me," he said. "She was a nice girl."

"As far as we can tell," prosecutor Karp said of Matta's killing spree, "the only thing that stopped these murders was the return of his parents. We have no reason to believe that if he were on the street, he wouldn't say, 'That was fun, I'll do it again.'"

In making that claim, Karp had the blood-soaked history of modern America to back him up.

TWO

"Something Insidious Has Happened"

On a crisp autumn evening of 1938 in Brooklyn an old woman poisoned a homeless man named Hoskins with a glass of arsenic-laced elderberry wine, placed the body in the storage space beneath a window seat, and blithely awaited the return of her sister in order to bury the body in the cellar. Assisted by their crazed brother, they had already interred the corpses of eleven of the rootless men that were common in the Depression years—all to the riotous laughter and applause of nearly twelve hundred witnesses, the audience for playwright Joseph Kesselring's comedy *Arsenic and Old Lace* in its premiere at Broadway's Fulton Theater. The show ran three years, and in 1944 millions more were entertained by the murderously batty Brewster sisters in Frank Capra's zany screen adaptation, starring Cary Grant.

Why did audiences think multiple murder was funny? Was it simply the dizzy charm of the old ladies and their loony brother, who believed he was President Theodore Roosevelt burying victims of Yellow Fever in Panama Canal "locks," and a second demented brother, who resembled Boris Karloff (played by him on the stage) and who became irate when he discovered his sisters had matched his tally of murders without ever having to leave their house? No, multiple murders were quite rare in America. And those which were recorded were so isolated and bizarre as to appear to have nothing to do with the reality of American life during the first four decades of the twentieth century.

Excluding the violence of gangsters such as Al Capone, Lucky Luciano, John Dillinger, and other gun-toting hoods, and also murders among people who knew one another, from the turn of the century to the opening of *Arsenic and Old Lace*, there'd been but a handful of multiple-corpse homicides in the United States. Distinctive for being the first mass murderer of the era was Belle Gunness, whose wholesale slaughter was unearthed at her farm in Indiana in 1908. Her final tally is estimated at fourteen—estimated because Belle was never located and so wasn't asked the exact figure. For Albert Fish, a string of murders started in Delaware in 1910 and ended with his death in Sing Sing's electric chair in 1936. An admitted molester of more than 400 children in a span of twenty years and a confessed cannibal, old man Fish became notorious nationally when the press named him "the Moon Maniac" and gleefully quoted his words on the way to the chair: "It will be the supreme thrill. The only one I haven't tried." At the age of sixty-six, Fish achieved further distinction as the oldest man to be strapped into the chair, happily helping the executioner fasten the electrodes. Eight years earlier, Earle Leonard Nelson had paid for his nationwide spree of twenty-two known murders carried out between 1926 and 1927 by going to the gallows in New Jersey. Appearing in headlines just before the stage debut of the Brewster sisters and their loony brothers, ax murderer Winnie Ruth Judd of Phoenix, Arizona, caused a real sensation by hacking up the bodies of a pair of female victims and shipping the bodies to Los Angeles in a trunk.

In explanation for these crimes, the American judicial system and the public at large offered the same quick and easy one provided in *Arsenic and Old Lace*: insanity. Except for a few psychiatrists, nobody was much interested in a deeper question: was the insanity of these murderers the result of twisted nature or twisted nurturing? Certainly no one expressed the idea that there might be something amiss in American society as a whole that engendered in individuals a compulsion to kill on a large scale. Legendary defense lawyer Clarence Darrow had tried to use insanity as a defense in the infamous Leopold-Loeb "murder for fun" case in 1924. Using a psychiatrist to explain the actions of Nathan Leopold and Richard Loeb, Darrow hoped to save the young killers of ten-year-old Bobby Frank from the death penalty by showing they had been mentally ill. In introducing insanity as a mitigating circumstance he was decades ahead of today's widespread and controversial use of the "insanity defense" in murder trials. Yet it would be half a century before the FBI began meeting with killers in prison cells to interview them about the why and how of their deeds with the goal of understanding the mind and methods of those who kill again and again.

Despite the horrors of the smattering of multiple murders in the first half of the century, there was not a general feeling that homicide en masse was a major problem for the public to worry about. Statistics showed that the phenomenon was quite rare. In the 1920s, when thirty-nine deaths were attributed to multiple murderers, the average number of killings was 0.325 per month. In the 1930s, the average dropped to 0.06 per month, and the years of World War II added only Salie Lineveldt to the bloody roster when she claimed four victims in New York City in 1940. Because all these people were deemed insane and because their crimes amounted to unimpressive and unthreatening statistics, it is not surprising that multiple murders and the people who carried them out were an acceptable theme for a Broadway comedy and a hit movie.

Then, in 1946, Americans met William Heirens, and suddenly multiple murder wasn't so funny anymore. Born in 1929, Heirens was the only child of well-to-do parents. At the age of eleven he witnessed a couple making love. He told his mother about it and was informed by her that "all sex is dirty" and if he touched anyone he would get a disease. Thereafter, Heirens discovered that breaking into homes gave him a sexual thrill. On June 3, 1945, he was caught in the act by Josephine Ross. Attacking her with a knife, he slit her throat and stabbed her several times and then spent two hours in an orgy of sexual self-gratification. Four months later he was caught again but only punched the woman before fleeing. On December 10, he found thirty-three-year-old Frances Brown coming out of her bathroom, shot her twice, and finished the job with a kitchen knife. This murder shocked the nation, for newspapers reported that the police had found a message from the killer scrawled on a bathroom mirror in his victim's lipstick: "FOR HEAVEN'S SAKE CATCH ME BEFORE I KILL MORE. I CANNOT CONTROL MYSELF." There would be one more victim before he was caught—a six-year-old girl whom Heirens abducted from her home and then butchered in a nearby basement. He wrapped the body parts in paper and dropped them into storm sewers. Arrested as a burglar, the teenager soon startled the police by admitting his homicides but claiming that the crimes were the work of a strange alter ego named George whose last name was Murman, short for Murder Man. "To me, he is very real," said Heirens. "He exists. A couple of times I had talks with him. I wrote lots of notes to him." But clearly, here was another murderer whose deeds could be explained only as the result of madness.

The same had to be true of Howard Unruh. On September 9, 1949, the World War II tank gunner who had distinguished himself on the Italian front went on a twelve-minute shooting rampage on the noontime streets of Camden, New Jersey, killing thirteen innocent Americans as efficiently as he'd mowed down the wartime enemy. "What's the matter with you?" demanded Detective Vince Connelly when Unruh surrendered and was taken into custody. "Are you a psycho?"

Deeply offended, Unruh replied, "I'm no psycho. I have a good mind." His protestations notwithstanding, Unruh did not stand trial for the killings but was declared by a score of psychiatrists to be incurably insane and sent to the New Jersey State Mental Hospital for the rest of his life. There he told a psychiatrist, "I would have killed a thousand if I'd had bullets enough."

Was Unruh insane? Of course. Yet if that were all to be said of him, Unruh might be listed without distinction along with the mass killers who'd preceded him. Instead, Unruh has a significant place in the annals of crime, because the murderous swath he cut through the city of Camden marked the beginning of an era of an escalating incidence of mass murder in the United States that continues until this day. Before Unruh, wholesale homicide had been noted in America, but rarely. After Unruh, there's hardly been a year unstained by it.

The 1950s witnessed a plethora of multiple murderers. Among them was William Cook, one of the most terrifying criminals in modern times, who abducted and killed a husband and wife, their three children, and the family dog in Missouri in 1950. Using their car to flee, he later forced another motorist to drive him to California and then shot the man to death near San Diego. That same year, Ernest Ingenito killed eight people in Minotolo, New Jersey, and in 1952, John Youmans murdered two in Newburgh, New York. Oklahoma's Nannie Doss, in a welter of homicides spanning three decades, killed at least ten, many of them her husbands. In 1957–58 a music-loving sexual sadist named Melvin Rees went out hunting humans and tallied at least eight in Maryland and Virginia. But all of these outrages were soon overshadowed by a roaming killer and his teenage girlfriend who blasted their way across two plains states and into headlines leaving ten corpses in their wake—Charles Starkweather and Caril Ann Fugate.

Virtually unnoticed in this decade of mass death was the murder of a woman in 1958 investigated by Los Angeles homicide detective Pierce Brooks. Studying the crime scene with the keen eyes of a cop with ten years of experience in murder, Brooks felt the cold tug of instinct. This was not the crime of a beginner, a little voice inside him whispered. The killer had traveled, had done this before, would do it again. But the brutal fact of life for Brooks and police across America in the waning years of the decade of the fifties was that there did not exist a system which would allow him to communicate with police departments elsewhere that might have similar unsolved cases on their books. There was no way to show that the murder he had on his hands was but the latest bloody work of a man who had killed before, perhaps often. His only recourse, Brooks decided, was to go to the public library and search newspapers from around the country for reports of similar homicides. In off hours and on weekends he plowed through papers from every major city in the nation. After a year of looking, he read of an arrest in a murder that bore the earmarks of his case. Obtaining the fingerprints of the suspect, he checked them against the prints in his own case and made a match. Over the next few years, he chalked up similar victories in the same manner. But it was a ridiculous way to have to work. How could it be, he asked himself, that in a country that was sending rockets into space there existed no efficient system by which police could exchange information on cases of violent crime? What was needed urgently, Brooks felt, was a nationwide violent criminal apprehension program to deal with the population explosion of multiple killers during a decade of murder the likes of which America had never seen.

Yet worse was to come.

A decade of excesses, the 1960s were to be drenched in the blood of even more victims of mass killers. Leonard Mill killed three people in California in 1960. John Harvey slayed five in Miami, Florida, in 1961. Six were murdered in Arizona in 1964–65 by Charles Schmid. Eight student nurses were strangled and stabbed to death by Richard Speck in Chicago in 1966. Sixteen people were gunned down by the sharpshooting rifleman Charles Whitman from the top of the bell tower on the campus of the University of Texas at Austin in 1966. And the slaughterings of actress Sharon Tate and half a dozen more in two days by the "family" of Charles Manson rounded out the decade in 1969.

As dreadful as these crimes were, they fit the pattern of previous postwar murder sprees in that they were killings carried out within a short period of time. But Pierce Brooks and his colleagues in law enforcement were now realizing they were also dealing with the work of another kind of multiple murderer, one who committed his crimes over an extended period, usually one victim at a time and for twisted personal reasons, mostly sexual—the *serial killer.*

The first of the sixties' bumper crop of this new breed had burst into America's consciousness by throttling and sexually brutalizing thirteen women in Boston between 1962 and 1964, earning the sobriquet "Boston Strangler." Albert DeSalvo's newsy nickname was a precursor of journalistic-shorthand monikers that would use up gallons of printer's ink over the next three decades—the Zodiac, California's most elusive serial killer, who started in 1966 and as of 1990 remained at large; the racially oriented Zebra murders, which terrified San Francisco for 179 days in 1973–74; the Skid Row Slasher, who took eleven victims in Los Angeles in 1976; the Hillside Strangler of Los Angeles in 1978; the Freeway Killers of 1979 and 1980; and Son of Sam in 1977–78.

Serial killers who were not accorded snappy titles but who carried out homicides one by one and nonetheless atrociously included Juan Corona, twenty-five victims; Dean Corll, Elmer Henley, and David Brooks, twenty-seven; Edmund Kemper, ten; John Wayne Gacy, Jr., twenty-seven; and Wayne Williams, killer of young black males in Atlanta, Georgia, in 1981.

Brought into what was called the Atlanta Child Murders case as a consultant by the frustrated investigators, Pierce Brooks found himself working closely with an old acquaintance who had also been invited to Atlanta as a consulting detective, Robert D. Keppel. The chief investigator for the Attorney General's Office in Washington State, he had been a key figure in the efforts to locate the killer of young women in the area who were early victims of one of the suavest serial killers in history—Theodore (Ted) Bundy.

In their frequent encounters during the Atlanta case and in subsequent years, Brooks and Keppel compared their experiences and commiserated over the lack of a national violent criminal apprehension program. The Bundy case proved their point. Had there been a system for police to exchange information on their cases of missing and murdered persons while Bundy was killing pretty, dark-haired women in a cross-country odyssey from Washington to Florida between 1974 and 1978 (when he bludgeoned a pair of University of Florida coeds to death and then kidnapped and murdered a twelve-year-old girl and finally was convicted of his crimes), the handsome, self-assured killer who blended so well into his surroundings might have been caught sooner and lives would have been spared.

By the time the brilliant Bundy was safely in a Florida prison and striving to avert an appointment with the electric chair through ingenious legal maneuvers, the number of victims of multiple or mass murder and serial killings in America had gone from 0.06 a month when *Arsenic and Old Lace* was knocking them dead as a Broadway sensation in 1938 to 9.25 per month at the time Bundy was arrested, a frequency one hundred times that of the murderous 1950s. While there was comfort in knowing that Bundy's rampages were finally stopped, the American people could find nothing comfortable in the fact that between January 1980 and September 1984 they were being introduced to one new killer every 1.8 months.

Since 1962, the overall homicide rate in the United States has more than doubled. In 1980, more than 23,000 people were murdered. The rates for other serious violent crimes, such as rape, aggravated assault, and robbery, were also skyrocketing. Stranger-to-stranger crime was trending sharply upward. But the solving of crimes (in law enforcement jargon, "clearing cases") by arrests was declining. Angered and frightened, the American people demanded that something be done about crime.

Their feelings were voiced vividly and chillingly by the chairperson of the President's Task Force on Victims of Crime. "Something insidious has happened in America," said Lois Haight Herrington. "Crime has made victims of us all. Awareness of its danger affects the way we think, where we live, where we go, what we buy, how we raise our children, and the quality of our lives as we age. The specter of violent crimes and the knowledge that, without warning, any person can be attacked or crippled, robbed, or killed lurks at the fringes of consciousness. Every citizen of this country is more impoverished, less free, more fearful, and less safe, because of the ever present threat of the violent criminal."

Because 1980 was a presidential election year, the "law and order" issue moved to the fore in the contest between Democratic President Jimmy Carter, seeking reelection, and his Republican opponent, Ronald Reagan. Noted for his conservative politics and no-nonsense toughness on criminals in two terms as governor of California, Reagan stumped the country hammering away at the crime issue and pledging that under his administration the law enforcement agencies of the nation would be given the tools and the power to launch a coordinated assault on lawlessness. In speech after speech he painted an unflattering portrait of the Carter term, previous Democratic administrations, and the U.S. Supreme Court as being soft on criminals. The American people were fed up, he charged, with the concerns of "liberals" for the rights of criminals rather than the right of the American people to be free of the scourge of crime. It was a note that resonated in the electorate and helped propel Reagan into the White House.

Appointed Attorney General was an old political ally from California, William French Smith. Following through on Reagan's campaign pledge to tackle the growing menace of crime, stately, gray-haired, and rock-jawed Smith promptly set up the Attorney General's Task Force on Violent Crime. Assembled from experts with a wide range of professional and academic experience in the area of criminology, the task force was mandated to come up with recommendations for curbing the rapid growth of violent crime and reducing its impact on the quality of life. Smith also required each agency of his own Department of Justice to submit a report outlining what it might do to assist in the national effort to combat violent crime. Especially, Smith was interested in the contributions that might be made by the primary entity of law enforcement at the national level—the Federal Bureau of Investigation.

The "Bureau of Investigation" that was founded in 1908 was a badly organized and ineffectual operation hampered by political cronyism and ineptitude until 1924, when Attorney General Harlan Fiske Stone took the advice of President-elect Herbert Hoover and named young bulldog-faced J. Edgar Hoover (no relation) to whip the organization into shape, a chore Hoover carried out so well that he was reappointed FBI Director by every President of the United States until his death in 1972. One of the legacies of the Hoover years was the FBI Training Academy, which opened for business on July 29, 1935, as the National Police Training School, located in Room 5231 in the Department of Justice building on Pennsylvania Avenue in Washington, D.C. It grew over the next fifty years into the FBI National Training Academy, located at Quantico, Virginia. The 23-member experiment of 1935 had become a 1,000-member-a-year training institution in the 1980s, the "West Point" of law enforcement. In that time its curriculum grew from a few vocational skills courses to forty-five upper-level undergraduate and graduate courses ranging from state-of-the-art science to futuristics. The academy composes a city of dormitories, classrooms, library, laboratories, firing ranges, and physical training and recreation areas, and even contains a small "town" called Hogan's Alley constructed for antiterrorist and hostage-situation training.

As the FBI and the Training Academy became more deeply involved with state and local law enforcement agencies and far more closely connected to the battle against crime on a national basis, they soon became a resource for other police agencies through their fingerprint archives and crime laboratories. A major step toward coordinating police activities on a coast-to-coast basis was taken in 1950 with the creation of the FBI's Ten Most Wanted Fugitives program. In previous decades there had been occasional lists of desperately wanted criminals but no sustained program of publicity to keep the names and faces of fugitives before the public. But the Ten Most Wanted program was limited to those criminals sought on federal charges, usually interstate flight to avoid prosecution. There were no means by which the FBI could compile and coordinate a nationwide data file on all crimes and criminals until 1967, when the FBI launched the National Crime Information Center (NCIC). It permitted local and state police both to tap into the FBI's archives and to access a central index where they could post notices regarding wanted and missing persons and information on stolen property. Among categories of records available in the NCIC system were vehicle, license plate, recovered gun, and stolen article. But there still was no data base on unsolved cases and unknown perpetrators of violent crimes of a similar nature in different locations. NCIC was not a system designed to become the violent criminal apprehension program which Pierce Brooks wanted to see.

During the years of the Training Academy's operations, the nature of the courses offered had evolved to reflect the changing nature of crime in the United States. One of these courses was being taught by Howard Teten, a twenty-year veteran of the Bureau and a pioneer in criminal personality profiling. His subject was Applied Criminology, and it was offered to FBI agents and to students from police departments across the country, who soon started bringing Teten their cases. As word spread of Teten's knack for astoundingly accurate deductions, he found himself being consulted on seemingly unsolvable crimes. One of them was a baffler, telephoned from a police officer in California, in which a woman had been stabbed many times. From the briefest description of the particulars of the murder, Teten advised the officer to look for a lonely, skinny, acne-scarred teenager who lived nearby and had killed the woman on an impulse and was now torn with unquenchable guilt. "If you walk around the neighborhood and knock on doors, you'll probably run into him," Teten told the astonished cop, adding, "And when you do, just stand there looking at him and say, 'You know why I'm here,' and the kid will confess." Two days later, the police officer phoned again. "It was just as you said," he exclaimed, "but before I could even open my mouth the kid blurted out: 'You got me!'"

Recognizing that there was a need for a more structured means of providing local law enforcement with the kind of assistance Teten had been offering, the Training Academy created the Behavioral Science Unit. Soon the BSU was assisting federal, state, and local law enforcement agencies by offering training on violent criminal behavior, unsolved cases, innovative investigating techniques, and planning of case strategies. All of this was eventually formalized as the Crime Analysis and Criminal Personality Profiling Program. Its mission was "to develop and provide programs of training, consultation, and information in the behavioral and social sciences for the law enforcement community" which would improve administrative and operational effectiveness. The academic disciplines taught at the BSU were psychology, sociology, criminology, police science, and administration of justice. Its personnel consisted of a unit chief, ten Supervisory Special Agent/behavioral scientists, four Investigative Special Agent/ profiling specialists, and one homicide specialist, who was a former police officer with wide experience. In addition to training and case assistance, the BSU would conduct research into the criminal personality, equivocal death, sexual exploitation of children, the use of deadly force, situational trauma, informant development, and group profiling.

Before the advent of the BSU, drawing up of psychological profiles of unknown criminals as a part of the overall investigative process was a rarity, save for fictional sleuths such as C. Auguste Dupin, Sherlock Holmes, and subsequent imitators. In real life, the first profile of an unknown criminal was offered by crime psychiatrist James Brussel in the hunt for the "Mad Bomber," who had set off devices in 1951 in New York's Radio City Music Hall and other theaters, Grand Central

Terminal, and Penn Station. After studying letters the Mad Bomber had sent to newspapers, Brussel combined an expertise in psychology with a skill in graphology to conclude: "He goes out of his way to seem perfectly proper, a regular man. He may attend church regularly. He wears no ornament, no jewelry, no flashy ties or clothes. He is quiet, polite, methodical, prompt." The Bomber's education, Brussel ventured, was at least two years of high school. He would be an Eastern European man, forty to fifty years old, living with a maiden aunt or sister in Connecticut. From the manner in which the Bomber rounded the sharp points in his W's, Brussel continued, it was possible to deduce the Bomber's deep love for his mother—the W's were heart-shaped. He would be a paranoiac with resentment against his father. When caught, predicted Brussel, the Bomber would be "wearing a double-breasted suit and it will be buttoned." When George Metesky was arrested and charged with the bombings, he was almost precisely the man Brussel described.

Even more impressive than his success with the Mad Bomber was Brussel's portrait of the Boston Strangler. Despite a chorus of other experts insisting that differences in the methods in some of the murders pointed to the work of two or more killers, Brussel psychoanalyzed the Strangler on the basis of the behavior he'd exhibited during each crime. Discerning subtle changes in what the Strangler did over the course of his murders, Brussel quietly suggested that all the killings were the work of one man. The apparent differences in the MO (*modus operandi*, or method of operation), he believed, resulted from changes going on in the Strangler's psyche. "Over the two-year period during which he has been committing these murders," said Dr. Brussel, "he has gone through a series of upheavals—or, to put it another way, a single progressive upheaval. What has happened to him, in two words, is instant maturity. In this two-year period, he has suddenly grown, psychosexually, from infancy to puberty to manhood." In Brussel's estimation, the Strangler was a classic example of the Oedipus Complex—a man whose unconscious sexual desire for his mother left him impotent. To cope with his problem, he destroyed his mother's image by murdering old women. His switch to younger women and evidence of semen at the scenes of their murders indicated the Strangler had been "cured" of his aberrant compulsions, said Brussel. "This came about, of course, in the most horrible way possible. He had to commit these murders to achieve his growth. It was the only way to solve his problems, find himself sexually, and become a grown man among men."

Unlike the police using their traditional investigative methods of studying crime scenes for evidence of the identity of the Strangler and finding conflicting clues that led them to expect more than one killer, Dr. Brussel had examined the crimes in search of the personality that shaped the methods by which the Strangler operated—he had looked at the MO as a symptom.

Like so many of the criminal investigative techniques that have come down through the years, the MO system was developed by Britain's Scotland Yard, specifically, Colonel L. S. Atcherley of the Yorkshire West Riding Constabulary. In assessing the many crimes he'd investigated, Atcherley concluded that an offender followed a consistent pattern in his crimes and that this pattern often included "small, irrelevant acts which had no relationship at all to the actual commission of the crime and which could be accounted for only by the individual." V. A. Leonard in his 1970 book *The Police Detective Function* noted that the system is based upon a conclusion, consistent with knowledge of human behavior, that the criminal "develops individual techniques and methods which he considers conducive to safety and success and, further, that a fairly high degree of persistence of certain factors will be found in the operating pattern of any given individual." By noting these patterns it was possible to link crimes to an individual and to deduce aspects of that criminal's thinking.

While no one would argue about the usefulness of physical clues in identifying an MO, there have been sharp dissents as to the validity of creating a "psychological MO" or criminal personality profile from them. In a scathing denunciation of the profiling procedures adopted by the Los Angeles Police Department in its hunt for the Skid Row Slasher, Colin Campbell, associate editor of *Psychology Today*, writing in the magazine in May 1976, called such profiles "romances of science" that were irrelevant and overtouted. He predicted that psychological profiles would keep appearing both at police departments and in the press because there were more and more specialists available, and the work was exciting. "But to solve a notorious series of murders psychologically from no other clues than the results of demented passion," he said, "would be extraordinary, a victory of intellect over madness worthy of Edgar Allan Poe."

Four years after Campbell's article, demented passion and madness appeared to be the hallmarks of yet another serial killer or killers in Atlanta, Georgia, and its environs. Quite suddenly the officials of the "Capital of the New South" and "the City Too Busy to Hate" were forced by irate mothers to face the fact that a rash of deaths among adolescent and young adult black males that had begun in July 1979 was not simply attributable to the customary violence among the poor. The grieving mothers insisted the murders were the work of a homicidal maniac. Fearing the impact on Atlanta's economy if the city became known as the murder capital of the nation, the city fathers accepted the fact, although seemingly grudgingly, that they were witnessing, in the words of the Atlanta mothers, a "massacre of innocents." A task force was set up, and what became known as the "Atlanta Child Murders" burst into the news coast to coast. The case would remain in headlines for nearly two years. As killings continued and the number of murdered black youths soared into the dozens, Brooks and Keppel were invited to help.

The FBI also became involved at the outset, bringing to the task force all of the forensic specialties for which the Bureau had become world-renowned. But also traveling to Atlanta were John Douglas and Special Agent Robert R. Hazelwood of the BSU. A specialist in the evolving "art" of psychological and personality profiling, Roy Hazelwood had participated in the BSU's analysis of a series of murders of elderly black women in Columbus, Georgia. In the spring of 1978, taunting letters had been received by the police from "the Forces of Evil." Claiming to represent seven people, the "Forces" vowed to continue the killings of blacks until the murderer of two white women was caught. After analyzing the way language was used in the letters, Hazelwood proposed to the Georgia authorities that the Forces of Evil were not a group but one person who was black, was twenty-five to thirty years old, and was serving in the army as a military policeman.

He would possess a schizoid personality and was likely to have murdered the white women as well. Agents of the Georgia Bureau of Investigation began the questioning of soldiers at nearby Fort Benning and two days later arrested twenty-six-year-old William Hance. A nearly perfect match to Hazelwood's profile, he was tried and convicted of the murders of the black women, but the murders of the white women remained unsolved.

When Hazelwood journeyed to Atlanta in association with John Douglas, there were five murders under intensive investigation as probably the work of the Atlanta Child Murderer. Because local authorities believed the killings to be the work of a white man or possibly a group of whites, race hatred was the assumed motive. But in their review of the physical evidence, Hazelwood and Douglas detected that because of differences in the behavior of the killer only three of the five cases could be attributed to the Child Murderer. Then they surprised the task force by stating that the killer would turn out to be a black man who hated his own race.

Because some of the victims' bodies had been dumped in the Chattahoochee River, they forecast that in the next murder the killer would keep to the pattern. Accordingly, on May 22, 1981, a four-man surveillance team from the Atlanta Police Department and the FBI's Atlanta office staked out the area around the James Jackson Parkway Bridge that spanned the river. At 2:00 A.M. they heard a loud splash. Moments later they observed a car coming slowly off the bridge. Stopping it, they took its driver into custody. Two days later, the nude body of 27-year-old ex-felon Nathaniel Cater was pulled from the river about one mile downstream of the bridge. Autopsy showed that Cater had died of asphyxiation. Fibrous debris removed from the body and those of other victims were connected by the FBI to places and objects connected with the young man who'd been apprehended at the bridge.

His name was Wayne Bertram Williams. At the age of 23, he was an only son living with his parents. A high school dropout, he cherished ambitions of fame and fortune as a music promoter. To members of the Child Murders Task Force he appeared to be a homosexual killer with a raging bigotry against his own race.

When he went on trial on December 28, 1981, the prosecution was by no means certain of obtaining a conviction. While there was ample circumstantial evidence, it was scientific and quite technical and could be hard for jurors to follow. Because of this, the outcome of the case was expected to turn on how the jury perceived Williams. To assist the prosecution, John Douglas of the BSU traveled again to Atlanta to advise them on how to cross-examine Williams based on the FBI personality profile of an extremely clever and cunning individual possessing enormous self-confidence and daring.

Drawing on the BSU research into the psychological makeup of serial killers, Douglas warned prosecutors to expect Williams to present himself in court as a sympathetic figure. He might come into the trial considerably thinner in appearance. His attitude would be that of one who felt he was being railroaded. He would appear as a clean-cut individual, Douglas predicted—quite correctly. "The jury was looking for a guy who looks ghoulish or foams at the mouth," Douglas recalled, "but the jurors in Atlanta were looking at the Pillsbury Doughboy."

Tapping prosecutor Jack Mallard on the shoulder, Douglas had another accurate prediction. "One week from today," he whispered, "this guy is going to be 'sick.'"

While there were doubts among the prosecutors as to whether Williams would testify in his own defense, Douglas was confident that he would. "I felt Williams would take the stand," said Douglas, "because he was so egotistical and confident. It was a showcase for him." Douglas advised that the way to handle this type of individual was to speak softly and at some point to physically touch him. "Touch his hands," suggested Douglas. "Violate his body space by moving in real close."

Speaking quietly, Mallard leaned toward Williams and asked, "Wayne, when you killed Jimmy Ray Payne and you wrapped your fingers around his throat, did you panic?"

"No," Williams answered softly. Perceiving an error on his part, he exploded in anger. "I know you've got an FBI profile over there. You're trying to make me fit it. But it won't work," he shouted, pointing at Douglas.

Recalling the moment, Douglas said with satisfaction, "He became extremely violent. The jurors just stared with their mouths open. They'd finally seen him for what he was. And at that moment, Jack Mallard turned around to me and winked. We had him."

On February 26, 1982, Williams was found "guilty as charged" in the deaths of two of the murders and sentenced to a double term of life in prison. Having obtained these convictions, authorities chose not to bring other cases to trial.

"The case was good for our program," says Douglas. "We'd proven that a psychological profile can help convict a killer."

Some doubters insisted that suppressed evidence existed to show the Atlanta Child Murders had been the deeds of a militant member of the Ku Klux Klan. But the task force promptly disbanded and announced that twenty-three of the thirty killings on its list were now considered solved. It also noted that since Williams had been arrested the Atlanta Child Murders had ceased.

The year 1981 saw the FBI profilers involved in a case that had stumped police in a small town in Pennsylvania. A twenty-two-year-old woman who had been baby-sitting was kidnapped, and her body turned up several days later at the local garbage dump. Victim of a fierce, blitz-style attack, she'd been savagely mutilated. The crime bore the marks of a "disorganized" killer who had been frightened and able to carve up the corpse only after the woman was dead. This data pointed John Douglas to a particular type of killer, but he also found evidence that the killer had exhibited elements of the "organized" murderer—the killing had been done elsewhere and the corpse transported by car to the dump. Scrutinizing the conflicting and confusing "symptoms" of the murder, Douglas decided that there must have been *two* persons involved in the crime. Further investigation by the police proved him correct. The woman had been killed during a frenzied attack by her live-in lover, who was assisted in disposing of the body by his brother.

For Robert Keppel back home in the Pacific Northwest, the quick arrest of the serial murderer known as the Green River Killer wasn't in the cards. Brought in as consultant to the King County Police Green River Task Force in Washington State, he was wrestling with a list of more than 2,400 suspects as the death toll mounted. The first victim to be attributed to the killer was sixteen-year-old Wendy Coffield. Her body had been fished from the Green River in July 1982, hence the headline name for her killer. Her name was to be joined by many more—forty confirmed within two years and others suspected.

The FBI profile drawn from the evidence in six of the early victims was that of a white man between twenty and forty years of age (history has proved that older men are not likely to commit such crimes). He harbored a deep hatred of women. (Women were his only victims.) The child of a broken home, he probably had an abusive mother. (A classic cause of woman hatred.) He was fairly intelligent. (No useful clues, not caught.) He was an outdoorsman. (He operated in rugged, rural landscapes.) He'd be a heavy smoker and drinker and possibly would have a criminal record for sexual crimes and assault. (Well-known character traits of this category of criminal.) He'd drive a car and have a thorough knowledge of the area. (A demonstrated ability to travel far and wide in carrying out the crimes.) He may have posed as a police officer. (To commit his crimes, he had to effect quick and unchallenged control of his chosen victim, perhaps by posing as a cop to create a feeling of ease and well-being in his victim.) He would be hungry for publicity about his deeds. (Research had shown this to be a trait of organized killers.)

Notoriety the Green River Killer was to reap in abundance as his killings stretched across the years and he eluded capture to gain the dubious distinction of America's most prolific unidentified serial murderer.

Meanwhile in Denton, Texas, Henry Lee Lucas was charged with the 1982 vicious murder of Frieda Powell, Lucas's fifteen-year-old common-law wife and niece of Ottis Elwood Toole, Lucas's partner during a six-year killing season in which scores had been killed, mostly women.

As the story of this deadly duo unfolded, Americans got a chilling look at the nature of the new breed of multiple killer that had emerged since the 1960s—killers who kill and go on doing so, footloose and free in a country with a magnificent system of interstate highways and no effective means by which law enforcement could track them. Born of alcoholic parents in 1936, Lucas was brutalized by a sadistically cruel mother who twisted his mind against women and became his first murder victim, stabbed, strangled, and raped after death when she was seventy-four and Henry was twenty-three. Committed to an institution for the criminally insane and then imprisoned for eight years, Lucas was released to begin wandering and chalking up some of the most gruesome murders in American history. During the trial for the slaying of Frieda, Lucas admitted killing her and dismembering her body because "it was the only thing I could think of." Speaking freely to police, he confessed that some of his victims were crucified. Unabashedly claiming that he was a cannibal, he said that other victims had been "filleted like fish." By age forty-eight he had killed, by his count, 360 people. "I had nothing but pure hatred," he said. "Killing someone is just like walking outdoors. If I wanted a victim, I'd just go get one."

In 1976 when Lucas met Ottis Elwood Toole in a Jacksonville, Florida, soup kitchen, he found an ideal traveling companion. Like Lucas, Toole stemmed from a family of drinkers, and like Lucas, he had a mother who treated him like the daughter she'd wanted, dressing him in skirts and frilly underwear. Not so doting was Toole's Satanist grandmother, who branded him "the devil's child." Dim-witted and slow, he quit school in the eighth grade and began building a rap sheet. By 1974, when he was twenty-seven, he had started drifting around the country in an old pickup truck and may have killed four people. Two years later he met Lucas, took him home for a night of drinking, sex, and talk about going out hunting together. From that moment on, they were inseparable, save for a stretch of summer in 1981 when Lucas was jailed for auto theft in Maryland and Toole drifted back to his home turf. Released from prison in October, Lucas came back to Florida but lingered there only briefly, running off to Texas with Toole's ill-fated niece Frieda. Feeling betrayed, Toole brooded in the Sunshine State, roamed around setting fires, and murdered at least nine strangers in six states.

When Lucas was charged with the murder of Frieda and began singing to the police about his career as a serial killer and implicating his Florida friend and lover, Toole blithely lent credence to Henry Lee Lucas's confessions. Permitting police to clear 108 murders partnered with Lucas, Toole also owned up to eleven single-handed homicides in eleven states. Listening to these confessions, a Jacksonville detective said, "They tell you about every way in the world to kill people. They say they killed three hundred. I believe them."

But no confession of Toole's to the Florida police riveted their attention as much as the one he made on October 21, 1983. Back in July, he said, he'd grabbed a six-year-old boy from a shopping mall in Hollywood, Florida, abused him, killed him, cut off his head, and tossed it into a canal in Vero Beach. Listening to this, Assistant Police Chief Leroy Hessler was stunned. The murder Toole was describing was that of little Adam Walsh, who'd vanished from the toy department of a store in a Hollywood shopping mall. His murder had been confirmed with the discovery of his head. The remainder of the body hadn't been located. The brutal death had shocked the entire nation and became a motivating force behind the passage of a 1983 federal law to aid parents in their search for missing children. Leading the movement for the law and spearheading a national awakening to what appeared to be an epidemic of vanished children was Adam's father, John Walsh. While news reports detailing his experience focused a sympathetic and outraged nation's attention on the missing-children program, as did a 1983 television film based on the crime, Walsh's son's case remained uncleared. Now here were details "grisly beyond belief" that only the killer of Adam could know. "He did it," Assistant Chief Hessler asserted. "I've got details no one else would know. He's got me convinced." But that certainty evaporated on November first when Toole recanted the confession and the police announced that without an admission, Toole could not be prosecuted for Adam's death.

As dozens of Lucas-Toole cases were being cleared, the FBI had grim news for the nation. In 1982 an estimated 5,000 Americans had been slaughtered by serial killers, the FBI told the news media at the Justice Department on October 26, 1983, and few of those cases had been solved. Roger Depue, chief of the BSU, stated that as many as thirty-five persons who had committed several murders could be at large in the United States at that moment. Each year, he said, 28 percent of U.S. murder cases went unsolved. Serial murderers' killings could be spread over a wide area, he noted. Detection of such killers was more difficult because there was no effective means of connecting them and tracing the killers.

That Depue was making the same point that Pierce Brooks had been stressing since the late 1950s was not a coincidence. During the 1970s, Brooks had conferred frequently with the Justice Department about his ideas and experiences concerning what he termed a Violent Criminal Apprehension Program (VICAP). In 1982, funds were made available from the Law Enforcement Assistance Administration to study the idea. Consisting of homicide investigators, crime analysts, and other criminal justice experts from more than twenty states and local law enforcement agencies taking part, the group became known as the VICAP Task Force. Coincidentally, the members of Depue's BSU and officials of the Training Academy at Quantico and the top echelons of the FBI and the Justice Department on Pennsylvania Avenue had been exploring ideas for a national center for the analysis of violent crime that would incorporate the work of the BSU and expand it into an integral part of an apprehension program like that being explored by the VICAP Task Force, whose members included a representative of the BSU.

Pierce Brooks saw all of this as a major step toward the realization of his dream of a quarter of a century, but he was an experienced and savvy lawman and knew that there was still a long way to go. "We're caught up in an epidemic of homicidal mania," he warned, "and it's going to get worse before it gets better."

THREE

Mr. Brooks Goes to Washington

On a sizzling Tuesday morning, July 12, 1983, Pierce Brooks hurried past colorfully clothed tourists making their way to explore the Capitol Building with its majestic dome gleaming in the sunlight. His destination was the Dirksen Senate Office Building on the north side of the Hill, named for the late Senator Everett McKinley Dirksen of Illinois, a Republican who'd never gotten the chance during his two decades in the U.S. Senate to preside over it as the Majority Leader. But in 1980, Republicans won control of what senators boasted was "the world's greatest deliberative body," swept into the majority by the Ronald Reagan landslide with a mandate from voters to do something about crime. Pursuing that goal in the air-conditioned comfort of Room SD-236 on this hot morning, the Subcommittee on Juvenile Justice of the Senate Judiciary Committee was convening hearings on the dilemma which had occupied Brooks for a quarter of a century—how to track and catch serial murderers.

Chairman of the subcommittee was Arlen Specter, a pugnacious former district attorney from Philadelphia. Distressed by what he termed "a unique phenomenon on the rise on the American criminal scene, a pattern of murders committed by one person, in large numbers with no apparent rhyme, reason, or motivation," he'd sent a letter in April to William H. Webster, Director of the FBI, concerning the subcommittee's interest in examining the concept of a federal tracking system which would collect and disseminate information on serial murders. "Such a system would solicit and analyze information concerning random and senseless murders, attempted murders, and the kidnapping of children," he wrote. "The information would be systematized by state and local police agencies based upon the evidence of one of the specified crimes. This data would be analyzed at a central location and compared with similar assaults. Where a possible connection is identified, two or more agencies would be linked up in their investigations." Suggesting to Webster that the concept appeared to have merit, he asked the FBI to provide its assessment of (1) the need for such a system to track and analyze serial murders; (2) whether such a system should be a separate organization or be integrated with the Behavioral Science Unit at the FBI Academy, and why; (3) the cost of such a program under FBI auspices; (4) how soon the system could be implemented; and (5) whether such a system should include data concerning convicted murderers.

Joining Specter as a witness and questioner at the hearings would be Senator Paula Hawkins, Republican of Florida. Having become deeply interested in the apparent epidemic of kidnapped and missing children since the abduction and murder of Adam Walsh in her state in 1981, she'd discovered that for every celebrated case such as Walsh's there were "many cases known only to the citizens who followed the tragedies in their communities." The whole country had heard of the Atlanta Child Murders case, she noted, but scant attention had been given to seven young children between ten and sixteen years of age who had been brutally murdered in a fourteen-month period in 1976 and 1977 in Birmingham, Michigan, by a killer who was yet to be caught. "For every Ted Bundy," Hawkins asserted, "there are dozens of unknown killers who have been responsible for untold deaths."

Appearing as a subcommittee witness, Hawkins noted that for some reason, Florida had been particularly hard hit by these multiple or pattern murderers. Ted Bundy was finally apprehended and given three separate death sentences for the murders he committed in Florida, she noted, but not everyone in her state was aware that Gerald Eugene Stano had also cut a path of murder and bloodshed across the state from 1973 until 1982. "Since his apprehension and arrest by a dedicated homicide investigator, Sergeant Paul Crow, of the Daytona Beach Police," she said, "Stano had reportedly admitted to the murder of thirty women." Almost all of these were committed in her state of Florida, she added. "During our investigation we also learned that no one truly knows the extent of the multiple-murder problem," she went on. "Many of the individual homicide investigators are unaware that they are tracking the same killer who committed similar crimes in other communities around their state and, in some cases, in other parts of the United States." In her probe of serial killings, she declared, she'd learned of the VICAP system to track this epidemic that had been envisioned by Pierce Brooks. But there existed nothing like it within the federal government, she said. She stressed the need for adoption of a VICAP program, adequately funded, as part of the FBI's Behavioral Science Unit.

The second witness was Ann Rule, a former police officer and now a full-time author of true-crime books, including two on Ted Bundy, whom she had known as her partner at the Crisis Clinic in Seattle. Out of that experience she'd published *The Stranger Beside Me* in 1980. As an example of a case in which a VICAP program might have saved some lives, she pointed out that Ted Bundy had driven far and wide in a Volkswagen "bug" looking for slim, pretty young women with long dark hair parted in the middle. Had the police of the nation been aware of these hallmarks of crimes, she stressed, Bundy might have been caught sooner. "The thing that I have found about the serial murders that I have researched," she explained, "is that they travel constantly, they are trollers. While most of us might put 15,000 to 20,000 miles a year on our cars, several of the serial killers I have researched have put 200,000 miles a year on their cars. They move constantly. They might drive all night long. They are always looking for the random victim who may cross their path." When Bundy was finally caught in Florida, he was in a VW, trolling.

Another typical example of the wandering serial killer, Rule testified, was Gary Addison Taylor, who'd started attacking women in Florida when he was about thirteen years old, beating the girls when they got off buses. He moved to Michigan and became known as the

Birmingham Sniper. Eventually he moved to Seattle, Washington, where he soon kidnapped and killed a young bride. Inconclusively questioned in that incident, he was released because police could find no warrants for him. He moved to Texas, where he killed two more women. When he was at last arrested it was discovered that he had murdered three women in Michigan. He had been a sadistic woman-hater since childhood.

Noting that the problem of serial murder was a relatively new phenomenon dating from the 1960s and 1970s, Rule provided the hearing with ghastly examples: Kenneth Bianchi, the alleged Hillside Strangler, who was believed to have killed twenty-one women in Los Angeles before moving in 1978 to Bellingham, Washington, where he killed two more and was caught only because a former L.A. cop living in Washington noted similarities between the Hillside Strangler's Los Angeles victims and the ones in Bellingham; Harvey Louis Carignan, killer of women in Alaska, Minnesota, Washington, North Dakota, Kansas, and California, who, when caught, had maps in his possession with 180 red circles drawn on them, presumably places where he'd killed because he considered it his God-given assignment to humiliate and destroy women; Jerome Henry Brudos, who murdered at least four women in Oregon; Randall Brent Woodfield, a handsome star athlete from a good family in Newport, Oregon, who'd been a member of the Campus Crusade for Christ and a draft choice of the Green Bay Packers but was also a roving rapist and killer, caught because police in Washington, Oregon, and California picked up on his pattern and joined forces; and her onetime colleague Theodore Bundy, who was discovered only because he was stopped by a cop who suspected that the car Bundy was driving was stolen, as indeed it was.

"Would assistance such as VICAP have affected the course of Ted Bundy?" asked Senator Hawkins.

"I think VICAP would have saved fourteen to fifteen young women's lives at the very least," answered Rule grimly.

"How?" asked Senator Specter.

The Utah police, when they found bodies that had the same types of injuries as bodies of women found in Robert Keppel's state,

Washington, would have gotten together with police of Seattle, Rule said. "I think between them they would have had enough evidence to have identified Ted Bundy and arrested him instead of his being given a chance to continue his roving. I think they would have had him."

How ironic it was, Rule said in her prepared statement, that in an era of advanced technology, America's homicide detectives were working with a horse-and-buggy system. "They are invariably overworked; they cannot possibly keep in touch with what is happening in other police jurisdictions halfway across the country. So many of the serial murder cases that *are* solved are solved accidentally. With a computer to allow detectives to pool their information, lawmen would no longer have to rely on such flukes to solve their crimes. Indeed, many, many homicides are *never* solved. The idea that 'murder will out' only works in fiction."

During her chilling testimony, Rule described what she'd learned, covering more than 1,400 murder investigations in fifteen years as a writer, of the effects of serial murders beyond the immediate victims: "I have seen the agony of parents, children, spouses, and friends of murder victims. For each of these violent deaths, there is a ripple effect and scores of lives are forever blighted. It is not just the victim who is lost; it becomes a kind of death for their families, and, indeed, the death of a small part of our entire society."

Then she talked about the choice of victims: "The serial killer seldom knows his victims before he seizes them. They are strangers, targets for his tremendous inner rage. He is ruthless, conscienceless, and invariably cunning."

Just such a man had murdered the son of the next witness. By now a familiar figure in raising the nation's consciousness of vanished children, John Walsh cited his own frustrations at the lack of a violent criminal apprehension system as he desperately sought to recover his son. "I spent days in our police station asking our police if they knew that two little boys were murdered in southern California prior to Adam's murder. 'Do you realize that two little boys were murdered, one in Lakeland, Florida, and one in south Florida, right after Adam?' 'No.' The police agencies in Los Angeles, in St. Louis, in Florida, had no idea that there were similar murders to Adam's. No one links these up. I asked, as I sat at the police station for the nine days during Adam's investigation, about the ticker tape, the wire, the all-points bulletin, and I said, 'Who is reading this wire?' I saw it piling up. They said, 'Well, we are busy researching your son's case. We do not have time to do this.' I said, 'Okay, give it to me. I have an office staff.' It took my office staff twenty-four hours a day, three days, to complete the calls. Seventy-two percent of the sheriffs and police chiefs in the state of Florida did not even know that Adam was missing." In utter frustration, Walsh said, he hired a private plane and went all over Florida holding news conferences, pleading for the return of his son. "I realized that no system existed," he testified. "The Hollywood, Florida, police looked long and hard for Adam but he was found dead 125 miles away and no one knew he was missing. There is no system." The solution to this glaring inadequacy in the criminal justice system, said Walsh, turning to look at Pierce Brooks, was VICAP.

Now it was Brooks's turn to formally present his twenty-five-year dream to the United States Senate, a circumstance he could hardly have expected in 1948, when he became a police officer in the City of Angels, nor during those long hours he'd spent leafing through the pages of out-of-town newspapers in the library in hopes of finding clues to serial killers. "Over the years, that primitive system worked for me two or three times," he said as Senators Specter and Hawkins leaned forward, listening intently. "The real tragedy is that we, the police, are still doing it the same way today."

After twenty-one years, Brooks had left the LAPD with the rank of captain to become chief of police in Springfield, Oregon, for two years, after which he served as chief of Lakewood, Colorado, for five years. Returning to Oregon in 1977, he headed the police department at Eugene. Now he was on his own as an investigative and management consultant who'd been called in during the Atlanta Child Murders and in the 1981 Tylenol-cyanide murders in Chicago. All of that added up to thirty-five years of police work, much of it in the role of homicide investigator. Lately he had been doing all he could to bring about the creation of a federally run VICAP, including numerous conferences with the top brass of the FBI and the members of the

Behavioral Science Unit. The agents of the BSU had made outstanding progress in developing personality profiles of these types of killers, he told Specter and Hawkins, "but what is missing is our ability to analyze crime information and communicate amongst ourselves, and that is what VICAP is all about." The obvious place to establish it, he concluded, was in the BSU facilities at the FBI Training Academy in Quantico.

From there to testify had come the unit chief of the BSU, Roger L. Depue. He'd joined the FBI in 1968 after having served as a city police officer, county juvenile officer, and chief of police in Clare, Michigan. One of the new breed of FBI Special Agents, he'd earned a bachelor's degree in psychology with a minor in sociology from Central Michigan University and a master's degree in the administration of justice from American University and had just completed course work on a Ph.D. in counseling.

Senator Specter moved quickly to the point. "Does the FBI have anything in existence which would deal with these serial murders?"

The FBI had two programs already functioning within the Training Academy at Quantico, answered Depue. One was the ongoing Behavioral Science Unit, providing crime analysis and criminal personality profiling that had evolved out of Howard Teten's criminology course in the 1970s. The other was a relatively new criminal personality research project in which, thus far, thirty-five serial murderers had been interviewed at great length by the men and women of the BSU in an effort to gather as much information as possible on them and their crimes, in search of any common denominators that might lead to a better understanding of the mind of those who killed one at a time over a long period of time. "We have worked with Pierce Brooks in that project," said Depue, "and he is a member of our advisory board for that research project and we are very supportive of him because we are all trying to accomplish the same thing."

Having derived from its witnesses at the hearing a consensus that there was a dire need for a national apprehension program and that the logical place to set it up would be within the existing FBI Behavioral Science Unit, Senators Specter and Hawkins joined in sending a letter to Attorney General William French Smith endorsing

VICAP, urging "careful consideration of this potentially invaluable program," and noting that it was especially attractive "in view of the very reasonable cost estimates associated with it . . . as low as one-half million dollars."

As soon as the hearings had ended in the Dirksen Senate Office Building, Pierce Brooks and Roger Depue rushed halfway across the country to Houston, Texas, where a conference was just getting underway at the Criminal Justice Center of Sam Houston State University. Made up of representatives from the Justice Department and other federal, state, and local law enforcement agencies and other interested parties, the three-day conference had on its agenda the establishment of a federal law-enforcement-oriented behavioral science resource center designed to assist all law enforcement agencies dealing with serious, unsolved violent crimes of a psychopathological nature. It not only would provide the services envisioned in VICAP but would include criminal personality profiling of the kind being done by the BSU; training in these areas for federal, state, and local law officers; and research and development, including the integration of all these functions into a computerized data storage and retrieval system.

In September, on behalf of Attorney General Smith, FBI Director Webster responded to the July letter from Senators Specter and Hawkins with six pages, single-spaced, of the FBI assessment of the need for a system to track and analyze serial killers. Briefly put, Webster replied that the FBI believed there was a need for VICAP, that the obvious people to create it were the BSU experts at Quantico, and that the new program and all existing BSU functions should be separate from the existing National Crime Information Center (NCIC) and be put under the umbrella of the new entity that had been proposed at Houston. As estimated by Pierce Brooks and Roger Depue, the cost to America's crime-weary taxpayers of the first two years of this organization would come to slightly less than three million dollars.

Nine months later, in June 1984, the birth of this new entity was announced by President Ronald Reagan.

Details were provided by a Justice Department press release bearing the names of Attorney General Smith, FBI Director Webster, and

James Stewart, Director of the National Institute of Justice, which would be funding the operations along with the Office of Justice Assistance, Research and Statistics, until 1985, when the FBI would assume all costs.

It would be called the National Center for the Analysis of Violent Crime (NCAVC).

■ FOUR ■

Dialogues in Hell

Behind the bleak stone walls of Attica Correctional Facility in the seclusion of upstate New York waited prisoner 78-A-1976, known as Son of Sam.

How to explain him? In the words of poet William Wordsworth?

> *Heaven lies about us in our infancy!*
> *Shades of the prison-house begin to close*
> *Upon the growing boy.*

Born out of wedlock on June 1, 1953, he was the son of a Long Island businessman named Joseph Kleinman and a waitress named Betty Broder Falco. Himself named Richard David Falco, he was put up for adoption because his mother could not keep him. Taken in by Nat and Pearl Berkowitz and renamed David Richard, he grew up painfully aware that he'd been adopted and showed evidence of being phobic and feeling rejected. Never very good in school or at making friends, he created for himself a concealing veneer made up of braggadocio, boastings of sexual conquests that had never happened, and a bullying toughness. In his youth he set many fires in empty lots. Bizarre fantasies entertained him. He began to think about being possessed of demons. Shrieking, they beckoned him to the conquest of women by killing them.

His first weapon had been a knife, slashed and stabbed into a woman he'd encountered on Christmas Eve 1975 where he lived in a sprawl of urban anonymity called Co-op City in the Bronx. Half a year later he drove to Houston, Texas, where with the help of an old Army buddy he purchased a Charter Arms Bulldog pistol. Its big bullets dug out of the flesh of the ten women and men he shot over the next thirteen months would give him one of the catchiest of the colorful names so fancied by headline writers of the New York tabloid papers: the .44-Caliber Killer.

In a very short time, this drab, soft-faced, overweight nonentity had transformed himself into a feared figure that struck in the darkness and terrorized the world's greatest metropolis. He made up names from himself: Wicked King Maker, the Chubby Monster, the Duke of Death. Then an even better name came to him, scribbled down on a piece of paper in his crude, unlearned hand and sent off to New York Police Captain Joseph Borrelli, who'd been on TV calling the unknown killer a hater of women:

> I am deeply hurt by your calling me
> a wemon [sic] hater. I am not. But
> I am a monster. I am the "Son of Sam."

Later he would claim that orders to kill came from a dog owned by a neighbor of his in Yonkers, Sam Carr. Its barking, Berkowitz maintained, was the way a demon communicated with him, urging him to prowl the streets looking for fair game. "The wemon of Queens are prettyist of all," he wrote to Borrelli.

In 1981 the Son of Sam was prisoner number 78-A-1976 and about to be interviewed by Special Agent Robert Ressler of the Federal Bureau of Investigation.

The journey which brought Special Agent Robert Ressler to Attica began around the time Son of Sam was plaguing New York City—1977. The director of the Training Division of the FBI had issued a mandate to the Training Academy's BSU staff to conduct original, in-depth research that would advance the state of knowledge in areas relevant to the law enforcement community. Ressler had come to the FBI in 1974, serving as an instructor and criminologist at the academy.

Before that he'd served ten years in the army as a military policeman and criminal investigation officer and still kept up his military connection through the reserves. Mulling over the order concerning innovative research, he turned his attention to the ongoing work of the Behavioral Science Unit in the profiling of criminal personalities of *unknown* offenders that had its genesis in the Teten criminology course. A logical extension of that activity, Ressler figured, ought to be development of profiles of *known* violent criminal offenders (serial killers, sexual murderers, and assassins) who were in prison. Interviewing them, he reasoned, would provide a wealth of new data that could provide insights into the workings of the minds of the most violent criminals in America.

Formalizing the concept, Ressler proposed a systematic study of incarcerated offenders whose appeals had been exhausted, thus permitting them to talk freely about their crimes without fear of undercutting their constitutional rights. The project also would include a review of all the relevant documents and pertinent case records. He proposed beginning with a pilot study.

A list of possible participants was drawn up that included Charles Manson and the rest of his "family," who were doing time in California for killing Sharon Tate and others in 1969; a serial murderer of ten, Edmund Kemper III; Hebert Mullin, killer of fourteen; and three assassins: Sirhan B. Sirhan, who had killed presidential candidate and Senator Robert F. Kennedy on the night of Kennedy's primary election victory in California in 1968; Arthur Bremer, who had tried to kill but only wounded and paralyzed Alabama Governor George Wallace in a shopping center parking lot in Maryland where Wallace had been campaigning for President in 1972; Lynette (Squeaky) Fromme, who'd been a Manson follower before being grabbed by a Secret Service agent as she was about to shoot at President Gerald R. Ford in Sacramento on September 5, 1975; and Sarah Jane Moore, who opened fire on President Ford in San Francisco without effect seventeen days later.

Having selected a roster as a starting point, Ressler and the team that would conduct the interviews began planning the means for carrying them out. How to structure the questions? At the outset it was agreed that they must differ from the kind of psychiatric examination all of the participants had undergone in connection with their trials. These FBI "chats" would be conducted strictly from a law enforcement perspective. The object was not to psychoanalyze the killers but to build a body of knowledge based on a study of their behavior to be used by law enforcement agencies to detect, identify, locate, and apprehend other homicidal offenders and then successfully prosecute them.

The interview protocol they developed eventually became a fifty-seven-page instrument crafted to determine any commonalities of background, developmental history, behavior, and methods of operation associated with various kinds of homicidal personalities. Behind this document was an acknowledgment that crime is a human behavior and that violent crime is *significant* human behavior. To fully understand the mind of a serial killer, one would have to scrutinize the most significant behavior the offender ever exhibited. The thrust of the questionnaire was centered not on why but on *how.*

Although it began in 1978 with a mixture of assassins, mass murderers, and serial killers, the Criminal Personality Interview Program soon shifted its emphasis exclusively to serial murderers, with a goal of interviewing one hundred. They would be divided into three categories: sex murderers, rapists, and child molesters. During 1979, twenty-six men who had been convicted of sex-related homicides, many of them serial killers, were interviewed.

In 1980, the interviewing team included Special Agents Ressler and John Douglas and two internationally recognized authorities in the field of sexual assault. Dr. Ann Wolbert Burgess was professor and director of nursing research at Boston University School of Nursing and a specialist in psychiatric mental health nursing who had worked with victims of sexual assault. Dr. A. Nicholas Groth was the director of the Sex Offender Program of Connecticut's Department of Correction. In October 1982, the study led by Dr. Burgess received a grant of $128,000 from the National Institute of Justice to carry on the work.

By 1983, thirty-five interviews had been completed and the material was being analyzed by a BSU team consisting of Agents Ressler,

Douglas, Depue, Hazelwood, Richard Ault, James Reese, Swanson Carter, Robert Schaeffer, and Kenneth Lanning. Because of the sheer volume of material, computers had been programmed by a group led by the FBI's Dr. David Icove. Dr. Murray Miron of Syracuse University was developing a computer-supported psycholinguistic analysis process for threat analysis. Kenneth Wooden, founder and director of the National Coalition for Children's Justice, was working up a plan to use computers to find child victims and the procurers who sexually exploited them—exactly the system John Walsh longed to see.

In the interviewing process, the subjects had to agree to participate. How might that be accomplished? The answer lay in a subtle appeal to the ego. By cooperating with the FBI, they were told, they would be making a positive contribution. They would be shedding important insights into how they were so successful in carrying out their crimes. They were assured that the information obtained would be used to improve law enforcement investigative techniques and in training programs for persons professionally involved in the criminal justice system. Because they would be talking only about themselves, they'd be violating no jailhouse "code of behavior" and incriminating no one. For those who were troubled by what they'd done, cooperation could be a way to gain perspective and understanding of their behavior or an effort to compensate and make some type of restitution. Others who felt forgotten and ignored simply responded to the fact that someone was paying attention to them. A few were fascinated with law enforcement—had even posed as cops during their crimes. Some seemed to expect favors and benefits. There were those who felt they had nothing to lose. For others, there may have been the thrill of reliving their dark deeds and experiencing again some of the excitement they'd felt when they carried out their crimes. And there were those who just welcomed the chance to get out of their cells and into fresh surroundings, however briefly.

The site of the interviews was a matter of careful planning and often depended upon the "status" of the person being talked to. For instance, the inmate whose talents made him the chief plumber of the prison where he was incarcerated was questioned in his own office. Wherever it was conducted, the process was intended to evoke rapport. "From the investigator's perspective," said Ressler after years of talking to the participants in his research, "establishing rapport during an interview requires ignoring one's personal feelings about the nature of the crimes in order to be open to the subject's answers to questions. One way to obtain this objectivity is to focus on the value of the information for law enforcement and protection purposes. Understanding why a subject thinks and acts in a certain manner will help the subject recall the events and motivation of a crime."

It was with these precepts in mind that Ressler arrived at Attica prison to interview David Berkowitz. In the file on him was a psychological profile that had been worked up at the height of his shooting sprees by New York police, doctors, and social workers. It described Son of Sam as white, male, quiet, a loner, and ordinary-looking, someone who worked in a regular job but harbored a seething resentment and animosity toward the world and himself. In psychiatric examinations after his arrest, he'd proved the latter point—page upon page of the psychiatrist's report was filled with hatred.

He resembled the photos taken of him while he was being processed after his arrest—a dumpy figure with a silly smile on his face. That grin, Berkowitz had said later, was just amusement at the sight of hundreds of cameramen scrambling and fighting and falling all over themselves to get pictures of him. "I never expected anything like it," he said. "I guess I smiled. So right away they began saying, 'Ah, you see, he's smiling. He's happy he did it.' I guess that's what everyone thought."

One writer looking at that smile thought the smirk was not that of one who despised his audience, as many journalists had charged, but was the smug and self-satisfied response of someone who was very shy but was suddenly discovered to have done something amazing.

Was he happy about what he did?

"After the shootings," Berkowitz said, "I thought I might weep for some of the people I killed. But I couldn't. It was all puzzling, you know. You hear so much news about victims, all those sob stories. Women in tears. After a while you don't feel anything at all." In a talk with his court-appointed psychiatrist, Dr. David Abrahamsen, he had shrieked, "I don't want forgiveness. Who needs that?"

How did he carry out all those shootings?

They took from several minutes to an hour. The first had taken twenty minutes. This time was spent stalking and watching. He'd walked around the block several times. Checked alleyways. Looked up to windows of all the apartment buildings to see if anyone was looking out. As for the couple in the car whom he'd decided to shoot, he hoped they would drive away. The second murder was quicker, about ten minutes. "I could have waited longer, but I was anxious. I wanted to get it over and then head home," he said. Shootings of Valentina Surani and Alexander Esau in the Bronx on April 17, 1977, took much, much longer. He had been cruising about six hours and was headed toward Yonkers on the Hutchinson River Parkway service road when he saw two heads over the seat of the car. He drove around a corner and parked, then walked to the couple's car, dropped a note at the scene, and opened fire. On June 26, his seventh shooting, he'd stalked out an area of Queens for hours before he saw Judy Placido and Salvatore Lupo. "I saw them and just finally decided that I must do it and get it over with," he said. His final attack was on July 31 in Brooklyn. He'd come from work, had a snack at a diner, checked out Queens, where he found no one to interest him, and moved over to Brooklyn. The lovers he watched late that night were Stacy Moskowitz and Robert Violante. Seeing their passionate kissing, he had an erection. Minutes later, when they were back in their Buick, he recalled, he "just walked up to it, pulled out the gun, and fired into the car on the passenger's side. I fired four bullets. I really wanted the girl more than anything. I don't know why I shot the guy. But they were so close together."

Highly organized, plodding, patient, and methodical, he had in the course of a year and a half stabbed or shot seventeen people, killing six, paralyzing one woman, and blinding a man. "You just felt very good after you did it," he said. "It just happens to be satisfying, to get the source of the blood. I had a job to do and I did it. I came through. I know that 'Sam' was relieved."

Berkowitz talked about how he'd been influenced by demons. "I used to watch horror movies on TV. Everything from *Dracula* to *Godzilla*. The monsters haunted me. I couldn't sleep. I'd have to have the light on. The monsters planned to take me over even when I was a kid. I'm almost certain that they're the same ones who got me later. I think I was born so they could take me over."

The worst of these demons took the form of Sam's dog.

To Ressler, the dog was nothing but Berkowitz's way of denying responsibility for his acts. Impatient, he cut Berkowitz off. "Don't hand me that bullshit about the dog, David," he said. "I'm not buying it."

Through the infamous smirk, Berkowitz said, "You're right."

The demons were a lie. He'd invented all of it and had been amazed at the attention his story got.

Having swept the monsters, demons, and "Sam" aside, Ressler turned to genuine fantasies. Berkowitz said he envisioned himself sexually as a superb lover who was passionate and well endowed, with abundant stamina, able to please a partner by giving her multiple orgasms. Most often his sexual fantasies involved oral sex.

What did he imagine when he was a child? As a kid when he played soldier he always took the part of the German. "I always wanted to be the guy who got shot down. When you play war, you know, the Germans always lose."

In the real world of winners and losers, of punishment to fit the crime, Berkowitz did not stand trial. He pleaded guilty. But he turned his appearance in court for sentencing into a show. Handcuffed and guarded by five burly officers, he peered into the spectators' section and saw the mother of Stacy Moskowitz, his last victim. He broke into a singsong chant: "Stacy is a whore, Stacy is a whore. I'll shoot them all." As court officers struggled to restrain him, he bit one and twisted the head of another. In this furious final outburst Dr. Abrahamsen saw Berkowitz attempting to "maintain his status as the star of the show."

Son of Sam's sentence for his crimes added up to 547 years.

On July 11, 1979, Berkowitz was attacked by another inmate at Attica and badly slashed. Refusing to name his assailant, he instead looked on the incident as justice for all his own crimes. In a letter to

Dr. Abrahamsen, he explained, "I've always wanted punishment, the punishment I deserve—I love being punished. So, this was it. I've been trying to expiate my sins for so long."

Like Berkowitz, all the killers being interviewed in the Ressler study evidenced a powerful attachment to fantasies about murder that inevitably exploded in reality. "The preference for fantasy and its centrality in the life of these men marks it as a private and powerful reality," says Ressler. "Murder is compensatory in the fantasy world of the murderer. Because offenders believe they are entitled to whatever they want and that they are living in an unjust world, fantasy emerges as an important escape and a place in which to express emotion and control regarding other human beings."

The fantasizing starts early and may be mistaken by those who notice it as simple daydreaming, but, as one of the offenders told the FBI, "I was dreaming about wiping out the whole school." Understanding that childhood fantasies are usually positive and aimed at promoting the child's learning, Ressler noted that in the interviews of offenders there was an absence of recounting positive childhood fantasies.

What burrows into the young mind is likely to emerge in the life of the adult. The interviews showed that adult killers will incorporate their early remembered acts of play into their acts of murder as adults. A killer who beheaded his victims had pulled heads off Barbie dolls as a child. Another who once chased a playmate with a hatchet used a hatchet in his adult murders.

"I knew long before I started killing that I was going to be killing," said one of the interviewees. "The fantasies were too strong. They were going on far too long and were too elaborate."

For more than half of the initial group of participants who were interviewed about the age at which they began to fantasize about rape, the answers ranged from five to twenty-five years old. Seven of these men acted out their fantasies within a year of becoming consciously aware of them.

Summing up the role that fantasy plays in sexual murders, Ressler and his coauthors wrote in their book *Sexual Homicide* that the murderers identified fantasy as being very important. Do men murder because of the way they think? And is the way they think directly related to early experiences such as abuse? Did their play as children turn into rehearsals for violent crimes they would commit as adults? Interviews pointed to that conclusion.

In quizzing Berkowitz concerning fantasies, Ressler had been surprised to learn that on nights when Son of Sam couldn't find a victim to kill he returned to the scene of a previous shooting to relive the crime and fantasize about it. "Now that's a heck of a piece of information to store somewhere to see whether others do the same thing," said Ressler. If it could be shown that the criminal *does* return to the scene of the crime, it would be of help to investigators—take notice of the faces in the crowd!

As the project proceeded, agents fanned across the country. One journeyed to the insane ward of the Mendota Mental Health Institute in Madison, Wisconsin, for a chat with the oldest of the killers to be interviewed, seventy-seven-year-old Ed Gein. Known as the Ghoul of Plainfield because of his nighttime diggings in the graveyard of the small Wisconsin town, Gein is believed to have come to the attention of movie director Alfred Hitchcock, who embellished on the idea of fascination with corpses for his movie *Psycho*.

However, method, not madness, was what the BSU project was interested in during the long conversations with America's bewildering array of killers, including Gerald Eugene Stano, mentioned by Senator Paula Hawkins at the hearings on serial killers. Besides his thirty-three murders in Florida, he'd killed four in Pennsylvania and a pair in New Jersey. His victims were mostly hitchhikers and prostitutes between 1969 and 1980. Many of them when killed were wearing blue, a color favored by Stano's brother and childhood rival.

Among those interviewed was John Wayne Gacy, Jr. On the outside in the years between 1972 and 1978, the burly Chicago building contractor appeared to be a jolly, civic-spirited citizen active in Democratic politics and an entertainer of kids as Pogo the Clown at parties and charitable events. But Gacy had a growing number of secrets buried under his house—the bodies of dozens of boys and young men whom he had taken home, attacked, shackled, tortured, and killed. The method was what he called "the rope trick." Sometimes while he was strangling his victim he would recite the Twenty-third Psalm.

How killers like Gacy disposed of bodies was of considerable interest to the FBI. For one thing, the realization that there was a corpse to be disposed of often was a jolt of reality into what previously had been the acting out of fantasy. The questions put to the murderers on this phase of their crimes dealt with what was done with the body, how the killer left the scene, what was taken from the body or crime scene (if anything), and what the killer was thinking about and feeling. In Gacy's case, five of the bodies had been dumped into rivers but twenty-eight had been buried beneath his house, although not very well, because the smell of rotting flesh could not pass unnoticed when police came by to question Gacy about the disappearance of a young man last seen on his way to talk to Gacy about a job.

The task of probing the methods and means of the murderous, matricidal, necrophilic Edmund Emil Kemper III, who weighed 300 pounds and stood six feet nine, fell to John Douglas.

When he was convicted on eight counts of murder, Kemper was asked by the judge what punishment fit his crimes. "Death by torture," he replied. He got life instead.

Born in 1949, Kemper had a shrewish, domineering mother who'd belittled him, locked him up in a cellar, and berated him for his failures. She held the position of administrator at a college and was embarrassed that her son grew up to become a mere flagman for the California Department of Highways. Desperately, he wanted her to be "a nice motherly type and quit being a damned manipulating, controlling, vicious beast." Feeling inadequate and unworthy, he developed a fixation on the need to be punished that exhibited itself in a bizarre game with his sister in which the ten-year-old boy staged his own execution. In the rules of the game, she had to lead him by the hand to a chair, blindfold him, and pull an imaginary lever. Gleefully, Edmund then writhed in mock death throes. When his sister was presented with a doll for Christmas, Kemper stole it and cut off its head and hands in a rehearsal of what he would do with living women later. Next, he was suspected of shooting a neighbor's dog. But cats became his main fancy. Then he started considering human victims.

One plan called for him to bash his stepfather over the head with an iron bar, but his will failed him. Shrinking from her son's constant morose and empty stares, his mother called him a "real weirdo."

Just how weird Edmund was became apparent when he turned fourteen and was living with his grandmother. Sitting at her kitchen table, he pointed a .22 rifle at her graying head and "just wondered how it would feel to shoot Grandma." To find out, he pulled the trigger. When Grandpa ran in to find out what had happened, Edmund gunned him down, too.

After seven years in the Atascadero maximum-security mental hospital, Kemper was set free, against advice of psychiatrists, by the California Youth Authority. Between 1970 and 1971 he drove around the area of Santa Cruz picking up female hitchhikers but not molesting them. He was rehearsing and perfecting the "gentle giant" approach to women that he used two years later toward two eighteen-year-old Stanford University students whom he picked up on a freeway ramp. Charmed by him, the girls had not an inkling that he was driving them to a death by strangulation and stabbing and an orgy of butchering. He kept the heads as souvenirs for a time and then discarded them in a ravine.

Heads of his victims were his trophies. "You know," he said, "the head is where everything is at, the brain, eyes, the mouth. That's the person. I remember being told as a kid that if you cut off the head, the body dies. The body is nothing after the head is cut off. The personality is gone."

He spoke of the need to possess, but the possession could only be achieved through death. "Alive, they were distant, not sharing with me. I was trying to establish a relationship. When they were being killed, there wasn't anything going on in my mind except that they were going to be mine." The obsession to possess drove him to cannibalism. "I wanted them to be part of me," he said, "and now they are."

In February 1973 he picked up twenty-three-year-old Rosalind Thorpe hitchhiking on the campus of Santa Cruz's Merrill College and then offered a ride to Alice Liu. Thorpe was first to die. "She had a rather large forehead," he explained, "and I was imagining what her brain looked like inside and I just wanted to put it [a bullet] right in the middle of that." Liu was shot in the temple. With the bodies stuffed in the trunk of the car he drove to his mother's house. There he waited until she left for work, then decapitated the corpses. After making love to Liu's headless body in the house, he carried Thorpe's head inside and dug out the bullet. The remains were then dumped some distance from Santa Cruz.

At Easter, he made up his mind to give his mother "a nice, quiet, easy death." Using a hammer, he bludgeoned the life out of her in her bed. "What's good for my victims," he said, "was good for my mother." So he cut off her head and hands, and also removed her larynx and threw it into the garbage disposal. He left a note for police.

Appx. 5:15 A.M. Saturday. No need for her to suffer any more at the hands of this horrible "murderous butcher." It was quick—asleep—the way I wanted it. Not sloppy and incomplete, gents. Just a "lack of time." I got things to do!!

From Santa Cruz, he drove to Colorado, where he was stopped by police and was amazed to discover that he was being halted for a traffic infraction. Eighteen hours after he'd killed his mother and left a note for the police, he was astounded to find out that there was no all-points bulletin out for him. But this was 1973; a violent criminal apprehension program was little more than a gleam in Pierce Brooks's eye, and the Senate hearings on VICAP were a decade in the future. Even when Kemper telephoned police in Santa Cruz to confess, members of the force who were unaware of his past would not believe him. But after persistent, pleading calls to them from Kemper, they asked the cops in Colorado to pick him up. They found him waiting at the phone booth.

Why did he turn himself in? "The original purpose was gone," he said. "It was starting to weigh kind of heavy. The need that I had for continuing death was needless and ridiculous. It wasn't serving any physical or real emotional purpose. It was just a pure waste of time. I wore out of it."

More significantly, Kemper said he realized that he was losing control. "I had never been out of control in my life."

Control, the FBI's interviews with serial killers were showing, was a significant factor—the need to control and to demonstrate that control by dominating another human being; and there is no greater control than that of deciding between life and death. Kemper spoke of "admiring my catch like a fisherman." If he was not in control of himself, how could he control the women he chose to kill?

Perhaps it was having finally rid himself of his mother that led him to surrender. Surely there was significance in his having torn out the voice box of the woman who'd constantly harangued and berated him.

Why did it take him so long to get around to killing her? "I never had the nerve," he said. "I had always considered my mother very formidable, very fierce and very foreboding. She would get madder than cat shit. I felt quite relieved after her death."

What would he think about if he saw a pretty girl walking along a street? "One side of me says, 'Wow, what an attractive chick, I'd like to talk to her, to date her.' The other side of me says, 'I wonder how her head would look on a stick?'"

Kemper spoke freely but with seeming embarrassment. Murders were not spontaneous urges, he insisted, but had deep meaning to him. "It's not a kicks thing, or I would have ceased doing it. If I had kept my mouth shut, I would have gotten away with it, I think, forever." But, he added, smiling, "I didn't want to kill *all* the coeds in the world."

Douglas's interview with Kemper was spread over several days, and the final one took four hours. Finished at last, Douglas pressed a buzzer to summon a guard to let him out of the room. No guard appeared. Douglas buzzed again; still no guard. Concerned, he buzzed one more time, impatiently.

"Relax," said Kemper. It was time for a shift change, he said. It was also feeding time for some inmates. It might be fifteen or even twenty minutes before a guard would come, he said, grinning broadly. Then the smile vanished and his face darkened. "If I went apeshit in here," he said, "you'd be in a lot of trouble, wouldn't you?" What would another killing amount to for somebody already doing time on seven counts of murder? Killing an FBI Special Agent would give him more than enough jailyard status to offset any time that might be added to his term! "I could screw your head off," he chuckled, "and place it on the table to greet the guard."

Not lost on Douglas was the fact that beheading was Kemper's specialty.

"Surely you don't think we come in here without some method of defending ourselves," Douglas scoffed.

Kemper's grin widened at Douglas's bravado. "You know as well as I that weapons are not authorized in here."

True. Douglas had been required to leave his gun outside.

At that moment, the guard arrived.

Gently draping his powerful arm over Douglas's shoulder, Kemper winked at Douglas and said, "You know I was just kidding, don't you?"

"Sure," said Douglas as he left the room.

Thereafter, single-agent interviews were ruled out as part of the standard operating procedure.

Kemper butchered his victims after killing them. The FBI was interested in what each killer did immediately after his crime. Did he wash his clothes? Go out with friends? Go to sleep? Eat? How had he thought and felt about what he'd done? Did he think about it? Did he dream of the killing? Did he go back to the scene? Return to observe the police investigation? Attend the funeral? Read about the crime in the newspapers? Watch and listen for coverage of it on TV and radio? Also carefully included in the questionnaire was whether, after being apprehended, a killer assisted the police in locating the bodies of his victims. Was he present when they were recovered? Was his confession necessary for police to find the body?

None of the killers questioned during the survey could be quite as voluble concerning his deeds as Charlie Manson. Since the 1969 slayings of actress Sharon Tate and four others in the hills overlooking Hollywood, Manson had hardly kept his mouth shut. After being booked by police and giving his name as "Manson, Charles M., a.k.a. Jesus Christ, God," he'd been a figure of enduring fascination—the walking, breathing, *talking* definition of madness who still mesmerized the country two decades later and got a page to himself in

Newsweek in an edition devoted to the 1960s: ". . . this scrawny thirty-four-year-old ex-con, illegitimate son of a teenage prostitute; this raving, guitar-strumming megalomaniac who lived in desert shacks with his harem of lost girls, mesmerizing them with sex and music until they would do anything for him, even kill."

No compendium of death could be complete without Manson. As an example of a cunning, conning, manipulator, Manson had no par. Nor conscience about the gruesome murders that took place on the night of August 9, 1969, at 10050 Cielo Drive in fashionable Bel Air. Learning that the people he'd sent to do the killings had brought back only $100 from a house reportedly full of expensive items and stashes of narcotics, he felt cheated. "Whatever else went on in my mind regarding the previous night," he said, "remorse or compassion did not affect me." In fact, he planned a follow-up to the massacre, sending his minions out one more time in the hope that it would appear that a full-scale war was being waged against whites.

When he first arrived on death row, Manson would have his interviewers and the public believe, he'd wanted only to be a forgotten person with a normal prison number. He wasn't buying into the propositions that he had charisma and power over people. The load of being the most notorious convict of all time, he stated, was too heavy to bear. "I ain't never been anything but a half-assed thief who didn't know how to steal without getting caught," he declared.

The murders carried out by Manson's "family" were supposedly conceived by Manson to be a means of causing a race war. Motives for the murders committed by most of those interviewed were not as grandiose. Questions in this area were organized in what the question-naire listed as "the precrime phase" and were intended to establish what it was that triggered the murder. Those killers who'd acted out of conscious intent were able to answer forthrightly while those who had been impelled without a conscious motive usually answered that they couldn't remember why they killed.

Phase two of the questioning dealt with the murder event. In cases where the killer had deliberately planned it, he remembered in considerable detail. In this area, questioners ran up against offenders who, although they were in prison for their crimes, did not admit their guilt. One explanation for this appeared to be that the man being interviewed was attempting to exert control over the interviewer— which often is what he'd been seeking in the act of murder: control of another person. In the Berkowitz interview, this denial took the form of Berkowitz's claim that the murders were really the work of a centuries-old dog. But when Robert Ressler teasingly said that it was too much to expect that these "carefully planned and executed" murders originated with a dog, Berkowitz took "credit" and abandoned all further mention of a demon-driven canine as the mastermind.

Another offender steadfastly clung to a claim of innocence and offered explanations for all the evidence that had been shown to prove his guilt, including a confession. Coercion or drugs secretly given to him had been behind that, he stated. Friends had given him the one hundred pairs of women's shoes found in his closet by investigators. Incriminating photos in his possession hadn't been taken by him because he could not have been that sloppy a cameraman!

To deal with denial, the interviewing Special Agent often had to be creative in the questioning. "Suppose we do it this way," said one confronted by a murderer who could not face up to what he was. "Let's just divorce you from that situation. Suppose it wasn't you involved and it was someone else. What, in your mind, would be the reasons for someone doing something like that?"

The subject answered: "I'd say she either said something or did something extremely wrong."

"Like what, for instance?"

"It could have been his sexual performance was inadequate. She might have thought it was. Or he might have thought it was and she said something about it."

Interviewers found that when someone denied that he had murdered or had had anything to do with a crime, the use of an imaginary third person was helpful. Berkowitz had "Sam." Ted Bundy couched his discussion of his multiple murders in the third person singular. When Bundy spoke of murder it was never "I" but "he" that did it.

In the long and unending history of murder, Theodore Robert Bundy is likely to find the same immortality that's been afforded Jack the Ripper, although, compared to Bundy, London's Ripper was a piker credited with only five murders (perhaps a few others, depending on who is counting), while Bundy was responsible for at least twenty-five. Though the never-apprehended Ripper will be forever cloaked in anonymity and mystery, Ted Bundy had been examined thoroughly by the police, courts, psychiatrists, authors, and millions of fascinated TV viewers, who caused enormous ratings for a miniseries devoted to Bundy's crimes. Like Manson, Bundy was never at a loss for words.

He offered plenty to veteran journalist Stephen G. Michaud, formerly of *Newsweek* and *Business Week,* and four-time Pulitzer Prize nominee Hugh Aynesworth in their compelling book about Bundy, done with Bundy's cooperation, *The Only Living Witness,* published in 1983. Note Bundy's use of the third person singular:

> Mobility is very important here. As we've seen . . . the individual's modus operandi was moving large distances in an attempt to camouflage what he was doing. Moving these distances, he was also able to take advantage of the anonymity factor. . . .
>
> In his readings and his observations and what-have-you—in his fantasy world—he'd imagined for some reason people disappearing all the time. He was aware of how people dropped out and became runaways and whatnot. In devising his scheme, he'd taken this somewhat unrealistic conclusion that under the correct circumstances he could select any person as a victim and that there'd be virtually no attention paid. . . . He was always amazed and chagrined by the publicity generated by disappearances he thought would go almost totally unnoticed.

For the sheer horror of the mind of a serial killer the FBI did not have to look further than the words of Ted Bundy:

"What's one less person on the face of the earth anyway?"

"I don't feel guilty for anything."

"I feel sorry for people who feel guilt."

"I'm the most cold-hearted son of a bitch you'll ever meet."

"I've always felt somehow lost in my life."

"I want to master life and death."

Concerning his killings: "The next time, it took him only three months to get over it."

The bodies he carried in the space vacated by seats he'd removed from his Volkswagen he referred to as "cargo."

Acutely aware that he was an illegitimate child, he said, "Without a past it was impossible to have a meaningful relationship [with a woman]." And "One thing I had to come to terms with long ago was the circumstances of my birth."

In prison he said, "Anybody matures, I'm sure, no matter where they are. But so many times in these past couple of years I felt like I was looking down from a mountain and seeing so many things I never saw before. I feel much more confident about myself. It's really marvelous. I feel not powerful, but in control of things."

Bundy was still exerting that control long after he talked to the FBI. On the eve of his death in Florida's electric chair he began spouting confessions to murders, naming at least sixteen in Western states, but in doing so he was in effect bargaining for his life—"let me live and I'll tell you more!" But Florida Governor Bob Martinez, outraged, immediately rejected the bid as "despicable" and refused to negotiate with the killer.

Undaunted in his need to be in control, just before he paid the price for being one of the worst serial killers in history, Bundy granted an interview to the host of a California religious radio broadcast in which he lectured in a righteous voice on the evils of pornography...and got national coverage of his views by the news media.

When prison officials pronounced him dead at 7:16 A.M. on January 24, 1989, hundreds of spectators who had gathered outside the prison cheered. Many wore T-shirts bearing the slogans "Burn, Bundy, Burn" and, referring to the Chi Omega sorority where he'd murdered, "Chi-O, Chi-O, It's Off to Hell I Go."

Oregon police detective James Dobson, who'd spent years in pursuit of Bundy, said that Bundy had been totally obsessed with murder twenty-four hours a day. "He was constantly searching for victims, planning his next murder, visiting the sites where he'd dumped the bodies."

Who was Ted Bundy? "There is no true answer," Bundy had said at his final trial, "only controversy."

Yet in the files on Bundy at the FBI's National Center for the Analysis of Violent Crime there *are* answers to the who, what, and why of Ted Bundy, for he was, after all, very much like the scores of other killers they'd interviewed. As a direct result of this unprecedented series of interviews with men who murdered, the FBI was ready to begin sifting the data with the aim of devising a system of psychological profiling for use by those who would have the task of tracking them down.

FIVE

Supersleuths at Work

She'd dressed up for a Saturday-night party in a yellow blouse, brown skirt, and tan low-heel shoes. Because the forecast was for cooler weather and the possibility of rain, she threw on a brown sweater. The next morning, it lay muddied and crumpled next to her twisted, lifeless body as police waited in a grim, silent circle around the coroner examining her in the glare of floodlamps. Like lightning, bursts of the strobe lights atop patrol cars and an ambulance illuminated the facades of the complex of high-rise apartments where she'd lived.

The coroner took note that the clothing she had on was slightly disarrayed and that her smooth pale skin was bruiseless except for a livid ring around the neck, which pointed to strangulation as the likely cause of death. The definitive explanation would come from an autopsy, along with the official verdict on whether she'd been raped, though everyone present already knew the answer. Of course she'd been raped—like all the others.

The first victim, a woman in her late twenties, had been found not four months ago about 150 yards away. Stuffed into the shallow stream of a culvert. Sexually assaulted. Strangled. Drowned. She'd put up a struggle, judging by scratches on her arms and face. There'd been no mutilation. Shoes discovered a short distance away suggested where the fight and rape had taken place. At the site, smudged and useless footprints of a man had been located. There were no tire tracks. The victim's car was in a nearby parking lot in the spot where she usually left it when coming home late at night from her job. The only item taken from her was a ring of little value, so robbery had not been the rape/murderer's motive.

A few days later, a woman in her mid-twenties became the second victim. Found fully clothed in another woody patch less than a quarter of a mile from the place of the first killing, she'd been stabbed repeatedly late at night.

Circumstances of a third case were similar, although it appeared that this young woman had been hurriedly re-dressed by her attacker after being manually choked to death at the edge of the woods.

Several months of fruitless investigation passed before the fourth body turned up in the same vicinity. A black woman in her early thirties, she'd been sexually assaulted, strangled, and drowned while returning home late after working as a waitress.

Now, here was this girl, her life snuffed out in its prime.

In the cool, misty morning, Chief of Police Walter Tinney mopped his damp, usually cheery Irish face on a coat sleeve as the first of his officers to have arrived on the scene summed up what they knew. The name of the dead girl had been discerned from the contents of her purse. She lived in one of the nearby apartments. A student, she'd been to a party at a friend's home; her car was in the lot close by, its engine still warm. The report was efficient police work, as had been all the investigating by the men and women of Tinney's small city force since it became sickeningly apparent that all these women had been killed by the same person—a serial rapist and murderer.

Suspects? There'd been plenty. Dozens of men picked up and brought in for questioning. Known sex offenders, mostly. Standard operating procedure. As the fellow said in the movie: "Round up the usual suspects!" Only in this case, the usuals were cleared.

Witnesses? The accosting, raping, and killing had been done late at night or early in the morning when the hardworking folks in the nearby apartments were asleep or watching TV or making love or whatever it was that law-abiding people did late at night. Had anyone heard anything unusual? Maybe a scream? A shout? A struggle? The roar of a car speeding away? No, nothing had been heard.

Was there anything in the lives and backgrounds of the dead women that might connect them? Had there been one man who might have known them all? Did some Don Juan who'd courted them all go off the deep end? Nope. The only link between the women was that they were night owls, lived in the same area, and shared the same fate.

Clues to the criminal? No fingerprints, no footprints. Only a few fibers from a man's blue jacket that, the laboratory boys could make clear to a jury, placed its owner at the scene of all the killings—if the owner could be found. The problem was, no one had a hint of whom they should be searching for. They were against a stone wall—at a dead end.

As a kid, Tinney never had a doubt he'd grow up to be a cop. Policeman's blue was as much a part of his family as the wearin' o' the green on St. Patty's Day and his policeman father's red hair as he bent over his son and shook his head in dismay at the comic books Walter Jr. was reading. Batman, urgently summoned to assist stymied police by a "bat signal" flashed into the sky over Gotham City. Superman leaping into a telephone booth to change into his uniform and then flying off to battle the bad guys. Captain Marvel, the Green Hornet, and Dick Tracy with his two-way wrist radio to call for immediate assistance. "In real life," said Walter's father with a chuckle, "it ain't that easy, son."

In his own years in police work and working up through the ranks, Tinney found out his father had been right. But in getting to be a chief of police, he'd made it his business to keep up to date as law enforcement techniques evolved almost to the match of Dick Tracy's gadgets and the wonders of the Bat Cave. In his father's and his own years wearing a badge, policing had leaped from the lone cop on the beat to patrol cars equipped with the latest that high-tech late-twentieth century America could provide.

Like a doctor who kept in step by reading medical journals, Tinney made sure he read the issues of the FBI *Law Enforcement Bulletin* that came to his office every month. In the March 1983 issue he'd devoured what Special Agents George Lyford and Udy Wood, Jr., had to say about the National Crime Information Center, updating readers on the work of the NCIC and reminding them that available for their use was one of the most sophisticated law enforcement telecommunications systems in the world. But NCIC wasn't a tracker of killers of women in the dark of night when all they had on their minds was getting some sleep after a hard night's work or play. In December 1986 he'd read in the *Bulletin* a report about the new Violent Criminal Apprehension Program by crime analysts James B. Howlett and Kenneth A. Hanfland and the boss of VICAP, Special Agent Robert K. Ressler. The Ressler name was a familiar one—the fellow who'd carried out research into sexual killers and a top man in the new Center for the Analysis of Violent Crime. It had been damned interesting stuff to read about, Tinney had thought, never dreaming that the day would come when he'd have a serial killer on his hands.

"Well, Pop, things have changed since your day," he said as he searched his files for FBI VICAP forms that had been sent out by the NCAVC and its staff of psychological sleuths. "They may not be Batman or Superman," he muttered as he found the fifteen-page document and took it his desk, "but they're worth a try!"

For the FBI to assist Chief Tinney in the five rape/murders that remained uncleared on his books, the crimes had to meet one of three criteria:

1. They had to be unsolved homicides or attempts, especially those that involved an abduction; were apparently random, motiveless, or sexually oriented; or were known or suspected to be part of a series.
2. There had to be a missing person, where the circumstances indicated a strong possibility of foul play and the victim was still missing.
3. There had to be unidentified dead bodies, where the manner of death was known or suspected to be homicide.

Tinney's cases clearly fit the first criterion. What he needed to know now was if the FBI would get involved. The first step in finding out was to contact the local FBI Office and file a request through the criminal profile coordinator, who would then advise on preparation of the request and submit the package to the offices of the NCAVC at Quantico. A self-avowed place of last resort with limits on time and personnel, NCAVC did not take on every case. But if its sleuths did accept a case, Tinney had heard, the chances of clearing the case brightened considerably.

Receiving Chief Tinney's material, the NCAVC Special Agent who would review it in hope of developing a profile of the killer of the five women would face the challenge of looking at the evidence of crimes and discerning from it the rage, hatred, fear, misplaced and twisted love, irrationality, and other intangibles that went into the crime. Could a Special Agent of the FBI be like Sherlock Holmes and find in the evidence sent by Chief Tinney "some slight indication of other similar cases"?

Likening the work of the profilers at NCAVC to the sleuth of Baker Street was not so farfetched. Like Holmes, they were not detectives themselves. "We don't pretend to be," said Special Agent Richard Ault, a seasoned veteran of the BSU and police work in the West before that. "We are behavioral scientists. When detectives begin to run out of things to do in an investigation, then we begin to find that they turn to us. When they have some questions about people that have to be answered, they come to us. Looking at how to apply behavioral science to homicide investigations, we begin looking at crime scenes as a symptom of the criminal and, like Sherlock Holmes, go back and try to describe the kind of individual who might have done this sort of thing."

It is a seven-step process:

1. Evaluation of the criminal acts
2. Comprehensive evaluation of the crime scenes
3. Comprehensive analysis of the victims
4. Evaluation of the police reports
5. Evaluation of medical examiner autopsy protocols
6. Development of a profile with critical offender characteristics
7. Investigate suggestions predicated on the profile

The method is quite similar to that used by a physician to make a diagnosis. Data are gathered and assessed, the situation is reconstructed, a hypothesis is formulated, a profile is developed and tested, and the results are reported.

Since beginning its research into the methods of sexual and serial killers, the FBI had accumulated, sifted, analyzed, and programmed into computers the largest data bank on violent criminals ever assembled—a chilling collection of collated facts about crimes and criminals that for the first time in history permitted a systematic understanding of those who commit serial crimes of violence and the telltale signs they unwittingly leave behind to mark them and guide those who seek them.

The first results of this undertaking were presented by Robert Ressler, John Douglas, Ann Burgess, and Ralph B. D'Agostino (professor of mathematics and statistics, Boston University) at the tenth triennial meeting of the International Association of Forensic Sciences held at Oxford, England, in September 1984. They began by differentiating between sexual and nonsexual homicides on the basis of the number of victims in relation to the period of time in which the killings occurred. The categories were homicides involving one victim, double homicides, and triple homicides; mass murder involving four or more victims killed in a short period of time; spree killings in which the deaths are sequential over hours or days without a "cooling-off" period; and serial homicides in which there are time breaks between victims in which the killer "cools off" for as little as two days to as long as months, perhaps years.

Sexual homicide was described as resulting from one person killing another in a "context of power, sexuality, and brutality." The telltale signs of this crime, the report stated, may be "the attire or lack of it found on the body; sexualized position of the body; sexual injury; evidence of sexual activity on, in, or near the body and evidence of substitute sexual activity or sadistic fantasy."

These data had been construed from the interviews which the BSU had conducted with thirty-six sexual murderers. An analysis of the background of these men indicated outstanding features:

32% were white.
43% had at least one parent missing in the family.
47% had no father present by age twelve.
72% reported a cold relationship with a father or father figure.
66% had a domineering mother.
41% had a pre-adult history of institutionalization.
86% had a psychiatric history.
36% had attempted suicide.

80% had a history of unsteady employment.

68% were unskilled workers but had good intelligence with mean IQ around bright normal.

50% or more came from families that had criminal psychiatric and alcoholic histories.

42% had been physically abused as children and 74% were psychologically abused.

70% had sexual interest in voyeurism, fetishism, and pornography.

Although their birth years ranged from 1904 to 1958, most of the thirty-six grew up in the 1940s and 1950s.

In addition to these classifications, the study provided the FBI with a revolutionary way of looking at this type of murder that demonstrated common characteristics that could be detected by trained experts analyzing crime scenes as readily as a set of fingerprints. In fact, the clues *are* psychological/personality prints. The symptoms of the aberration of the perpetrator of the crime, they are described by the FBI profilers as "organized" and "disorganized."

CRIME SCENE DIFFERENCES

ORGANIZED	DISORGANIZED
Planned offense	Spontaneous offense
Victim: targeted stranger	Victim/location known
Personalizes victim	Depersonalizes victim
Controlled conversation	Minimal conversation
Demands submissive victim	Sudden violence to victim
Restraints used	Minimal restraints used
Crime scene reflects control	Crime scene random and sloppy
Aggression prior to death	Sexual acts after death
Body hidden	Body left in view
Weapon: absent	Weapon: left in view
Transports victim or body	Body left at scene

PERSONALITY CHARACTERISTICS

ORGANIZED	DISORGANIZED
Average intelligence or above	Below average intelligence
Socially competent	Socially inadequate
Skilled work preferred	Unskilled work
Sexually competent	Sexually incompetent
High birth order status	Low birth order status
(first or second son)	(older siblings)
Father's work unstable	Father's work unstable
Inconsistent child discipline	Harsh discipline as child
Controlled mood during crime	Anxious mood during crime
Use of alcohol with crime	Minimal use of alcohol
Precipitating stress	Minimal stress
Living with partner	Living alone
Mobile: car in good condition	Lives/works near crime scene
Follows crime in news media	Minimal interest in news
May change jobs, leave town	Significant behavior change

An immediate signal of which of these categories applies to the murderer is the manner in which the victim was attacked. A telltale sign of the disorganized killer is the use of a "blitz" attack. In this instance the victim is completely off guard. The killer either approaches her from behind to overpower her or he kills suddenly, as with a gun. The attack is a violent surprise, occurring spontaneously and in a location where the victim is going about her (in some cases his) usual activities.

In the August 1985 issue of *FBI Law Enforcement Bulletin*, devoted entirely to the results of the interviews with the thirty-six convicted sexual killers, murder was described as the ultimate expression of dominance in which the offender's aggression was self-generated from his fantasies, "not from any societal model of strength or power." The idea of mastering other people emerges through his violence and aggression. Sexual interest is linked to violence and exploitation rather than gentleness or pleasure. "Acting out the fantasy links the fantasy to reality," the FBI interviewers concluded, "and the fantasy *becomes* reality. The offender believes he can now control reality."

Did Chief Tinney's killer fit into all of this?

Almost everything about the crimes indicated the killer belonged in the "organized" category. The murders occurred at night when the victims were returning home but were not sudden, ferocious blitz attacks. The assaults generally began as the woman was walking from her car with the killer lurking nearby and carefully calculating when and where to strike. He'd used the same method of carrying out all the crimes; he was a planner. He knew the territory and was likely to be a resident of the area; that he'd not used a car was further indication of this important fact—all of this being characteristic of the organizer. Because no scream or resistance had been evident, it could be deduced that he'd carried a weapon (further evidence of his planning) and forced the victim by threat of harm to accompany him to the secluded area where the attacks took place. This pointed to a persuasive and articulate individual who convinced victims that no harm would come to them if they did what he wanted—a sure sign of the organized killer. These were signs of a manipulative personality who possessed a history of antisocial behavior—common traits of the organized killer. He may have raped before. In keeping with the organized-offender profile, he would be young and aggressive and white and likely to be the firstborn of his family and living at home. Something had happened recently to trigger the first attack. It was likely that he'd had a falling-out with a girlfriend. Because he knew the area of the crimes it was probable that he was known in the area, hence he felt he had to kill to avoid being recognized and identified. In keeping with the general profile of an organized killer, he'd follow the reports of his crimes in the news media and may have been hanging around with other onlookers who'd been drawn to the scenes of the crimes as the police carried out their investigations.

As thorough as this profile was, it could not, of course, provide the name, address, and phone number of the killer. The gleaning of that information still belonged to Chief Tinney and his investigators. For them, more legwork, door-to-door in the neighborhood, asking questions. But this time they wouldn't be on the lookout for the usual suspects. It was the *unusual* one they sought with their queries—the one who matched the FBI profile.

"Have you ever known someone who . . . ?"
"Did you ever see a young man that . . . ?"
"Is there some fellow you know . . . ?"
"Can you recall . . . ?"
Answers trickled in. Bits. Snippets.
"Yes, there was a boy like that."
"Some months ago I knew somebody living here that . . . ."
"A kid used to live around here but he moved."
Far away?
"I still see him around the apartments sometimes."
"He often wore a blue jacket."
Within a week of receiving the FBI profile, Chief Tinney had a
suspect seated before him—wearing a blue jacket. When crime-lab
comparisons of fibers from it and those found at the crime scenes
linked him to the murders, he signed a confession. A white seventeen-
year-old male, he'd lived around the scene of the crimes until
recently. He had a lengthy juvenile record that included sexual assault
and rape, but because he'd moved away, he'd not been on a suspect
list. He was bright but had been a marginal student. An only child, he
resided with his mother. He did not own a car. By his friends, he was
viewed as a "macho ladies' man" and "con artist." His girlfriend had
jilted him shortly before the time of the first murder. He had followed
the investigations of the murders, he told Tinney, and had even been
present to observe the police at one of the scenes.

"Criminal profiling will never take the place of a thorough and
well-planned investigation, nor will it ever eliminate the seasoned,
highly trained and skilled detective," said Richard Ault of the NCAVC,
"but it has provided another weapon in the arsenal of those who must
deal with violent crime. The offender, on the other hand, has the
added worry that in time he will be identified, indicted, successfully
prosecuted, and sentenced for his crime."

That is what happened in the case of the murders of a pair of
teenagers whose sexually mutilated bodies were found floating in a
Midwestern river in April 1983. Consulted by the baffled local police,
profilers at Quantico studied the data and soon reported that the
killings appeared to be the deeds of a male in his forties who knew the

children. He was likely to be self-employed, to lead a macho life-style, to wear Western boots, to be a hunter and fisherman, and to have a four-wheel-drive vehicle. He'd have been divorced, probably several times, and he'd have a minor criminal record.

In the eyes of the police, this description fit the dead girls' stepfather. Their subsequent investigation led to his arrest and conviction.

The analysis of the details of a murder in accordance with the generalities of personality and behavioral characteristics of killers, a process known as "criminal profiling," became widely available to American law enforcement agencies in the mid-1980s through the Criminal Profiling and Consultation Program within the BSU and under the organizational umbrella of the NCAVC as part of the Training Division. In 1985 more than 600 requests were received. Handling the work in 1986 was a staff consisting of one program manager and seven criminal profilers and crime-scene analysts. As VICAP came into being, more applications for the FBI's assistance were expected to be forwarded through fifty-nine field offices. Clearly, not all of this burgeoning caseload could be taken on. Therefore, only the toughest could be accepted. "These are the cases usually considered unsolvable," said Roger Depue.

Bizarre crimes were significantly on the increase. Whereas two decades earlier the rule of thumb was that in more than 80 percent of murder cases the killer had some kind of previous relationship with a victim, in the mid-1980s, out of more than 22,000 killings in the nation some 45 percent were either "stranger murders," in which killer and victim had never seen each other before, or murders in which the killer was "unknown." The FBI estimated that as many as one-fourth of "stranger" homicides fell into the category of murders committed for which there appeared to be no reason. By another estimate, some 5,000 people were being killed each year in bizarre ways by strangers.

Why the upsurge? "I think it is a little of everything," Robert Ressler told an interviewer from the *Fairfax Sentinel*, a publication of the Fairfax, Virginia, Police Association. "It definitely is social, psychological, environmental, cultural, economic, as well as strains in the American society. You can make broad statements, but personally, I think the mass media and their approach toward homicidal behavior goes a long way to perpetuate this type behavior. A substantial number of psychopaths have gotten into mass murder mainly due to the desire to have their name and picture in the paper." Citing David (Son of Sam) Berkowitz's obsession with writing letters to the newspapers, Ressler pointed out that Montie Rissel, who raped and murdered five women in Alexandria, Virginia, during the spring and summer of 1978, told investigators that he got his start from reading about Berkowitz. "There is no question that the media are a catalyst to the mass murderer," Ressler continued. "You have to understand that many types of inadequate people who have a warped sense of satisfaction enjoy and seek to have their picture and name in the paper."

But the purpose of the profiling program was not to explain why there was an apparent increase in multiple homicides in the United States. "This program is not intended to turn law enforcement agents into psychiatrists," explained FBI Director William Webster. "It is intended to take advantage of what we know about repetitive criminals, to apply that to increase our investigative capacity and to have some sense of where we ought to be looking for a person who has not yet been identified."

"We don't get hung up on why the killer does the things he does," Special Agent Roy Hazelwood told *Psychology Today*. "What we're interested in is that he *does* it in a way that leads us to him."

In probing the method of the madness, BSU researchers had shone a new light on a particular kind of killer who was driven not by simple greed, hatred, envy, revenge, or spur-of-the-moment violence but by deeper, long-harbored compulsions. Through their interviews with this breed of murderer and subsequent analysis of the data, the men and women of the FBI showed that a dangerous pattern of behavior exhibited very early in life was a rehearsal for crimes to come. The research showed clear evidence that most had been victims of horrendous abuse as children at the hands of their mothers and in the virtual absence of a strong father or father figure.

Regarding the sadism and cruelty shared by serial killers, the BSU researchers showed that the men became murderers because they couldn't achieve a satisfactory sexual relationship with a living woman;

they were lust murderers, but the lust was driven by a need for power and control, not by sex in itself. The choice of a victim was based on what the woman represented, not who she was; she was a symbol, not a human being; e.g., long hair in the case of Ted Bundy, heads in the case of Edmund Kemper.

But the most important discovery through the FBI interviews with the men who kill again and again was that a serial killer is a compulsive troller who travels relentlessly, near and far, in the search for victims—a stranger on a horrible odyssey.

SIX

Murder by Person Unknown

*T*he horsing around ended when the boys saw the naked woman. This was a rather remote area of southern Hillsborough County, Florida. Maybe she was a sunbather, they thought as they drew near in the high weeds. But the way she was lying didn't seem natural—face down with her hands crossed behind her back and her legs spread wide. "Something's wrong," said one of the boys as he crept ahead anxiously. When he saw the ropes around her wrists and neck, he bolted away, "She's dead," he yelled. "Murdered!"

The body appeared to have been deliberately displayed by the killer. Because all of her clothing and personal possessions had been removed from the scene, identifying her took a while. She was Ngeun Thi Long, a twenty-year-old Laotian immigrant known to police in Tampa as an exotic dancer at a lounge on Nebraska Avenue. She was into drugs and had not been seen around her apartment near the University of South Florida for two or three days. At some point in that time she'd been strangled with a rope, trussed up with a different kind of cord, and hauled in a car to the place where she was dumped. Plaster impressions of the tracks of the car's tire treads were made. Fibers that had to have come from the vehicle's red carpet were discovered adhering to her body.

Two weeks later, on May 27, 1984, the body of a young white woman was discovered in an isolated area in the eastern part of the county. Nude but with her clothing scattered nearby, she was tied with

85

rope, and a hangman's noose was knotted around her neck. Death, however, appeared to be the result of a slash across her throat. She'd also been battered with a blunt object. Tire tracks were found. Red auto carpet fibers and strands of hair that did not appear to be hers were found. A prostitute who'd worked the Kennedy Boulevard area of Tampa, she was identified as twenty-two-year-old Michelle Denise Simms, originally from California.

For Captain Gary Terry of the Hillsborough County Sheriff's Office, there was no doubt that Simms and Long had run into the same killer, and when double homicide turned into triple with the finding of the corpse of an eighteen-year-old black woman, Chanel Devon Williams, under similar circumstances in October, Captain Terry was certain he was dealing with a serial killer.

Bundling up the evidence in the Long, Simms, and Williams cases, Terry requested a criminal personality profile from the Behavioral Science Unit. Presently, he received a report from Quantico suggesting that the murders of Long and Simms appeared to be the work of the same killer but the death of the black victim was probably not related to the others, who were white. All the forensic evidence pointed to an "organized" pattern that could be profiled as follows:

Race/Age	Caucasian, mid-twenties
Personality	"Macho" image assaultive; inclined to mentally and physically taunt and torture victims
Weapons	Likely to carry weapons
Employment	Difficulty in holding job
Marriage	Probably divorced
Vehicle	"Flashy car"
Geographics	Confined to the Tampa region
Victims	Randomly selected, susceptible to approach

The killings continued. On the morning of October 13, the nude body of twenty-eight-year-old Karen Beth Dinsfriend, a Nebraska Avenue prostitute, was found in an orange grove in the northeastern part of the county. On October 30, the mummified remains of a woman who was not immediately identified were found along Highway 301 just south of the Pasco County line. Eight days later, what was left of a female was discovered near Morris Bridge Road in Pasco County. She was identified as eighteen-year-old Virginia Lee Johnson, another hooker off Nebraska Avenue. On November 24, Kim Marie Swann, a twenty-one-year-old narcotics user, was found dead in Tampa. All of these murders bore the "signature" of the same killer in what was now a multi-jurisdictional investigation involving sheriffs of Hillsborough and Pasco counties, Tampa police, the Florida Department of Law Enforcement, the forensic experts of the FBI crime labs, and the profilers of the BSU.

November provided a break in the case when a North Tampa girl reported being abducted from the vicinity of a doughnut shop and taken to an apartment where she was sexually assaulted for twenty-six hours before being released along an interstate highway. Although she could not provide an address, she bore strands of red carpet fiber that matched those found upon the serial murder victims. Intensively questioned by members of what was now a thirty-member task force, the girl recalled that after leaving the apartment where she'd been held, the man had stopped to use a twenty-four-hour automatic teller machine to obtain money. She also remembered that his car was red with a red interior and red carpeting and "Magnum" on the dashboard.

Immediately, the task force traced Florida motor vehicle registrations in a hunt for a red Dodge Magnum. At the same time, teams of detectives set up stakeouts to observe the Nebraska Avenue strip as prostitutes plied their trade, the object of the police being not the women but the flow of customers and their autos. When a red Magnum cruised past, the police stopped it on the pretext that they were looking for a robbery suspect. The driver of the red-inside, red-outside, red-carpeted car was calm and cooperated by identifying himself as Robert Joe Long.

Meanwhile, others of the task force were checking records of transactions at the automatic teller machine. The name they found for the place, date, and time reported by the young rape victim was Robert Joe Long.

While arrest and search warrants were obtained and Long was put under surveillance, including the use of aircraft to minimize the chances that Long would discover he was being watched, Captain Terry telephone the BSU for advice and counsel on how to conduct the interrogation of Long once they picked him up.

Taken into custody as he left a movie theater, Long was taken back to his apartment in the expectation of questioning him during the search of the place, but when he refused to leave the police car he was driven to the Hillsborough County Sheriff's Office. Waiting there to provide assistance was the agent from the BSU who'd done the criminal personality profile. This suspect would most likely cooperate, he advised the interrogation team, if the officers displayed both their authority and a thorough knowledge of the case.

Few, if any, serial rapists and killers would prove to be as bizarrely twisted by nature *and* nurturing as Bobby Joe Long. Born October 14, 1953 at Kenova, West Virginia, he'd suffered from a rare genetic disorder that produced excessive female hormones and caused him to develop womanlike breasts that had to be surgically reduced. Until he was thirteen he was allowed to sleep in his twice-divorced mother's bed. He married as a teenager and alternately slept with his wife and his mother, both of whom dominated him. Contributing to these problems was a series of head injuries that began at the age of five when he was thrown from a pony. The most recent jolt to the head was a helmet- and skull-fracturing motorcycle crash. Hounded by numbing headaches, he would explode in violent rages. Sex was an obsession—he masturbated five times a day and had sexual intercourse with his wife twice a day. When that proved insufficient, he began trawling the streets for women.

The magnitude of his crimes began slowly unfolding after his questioners painstakingly reviewed and explained the massive amount of evidence they had against him. Confessing, Long gave a brief description of each of the crimes for which he was being charged. The method was virtually a textbook for those who wished to study serial murder—a living prototype of what researchers of the Behavioral Science Unit at Quantico had learned about and described as organized serial killers. He'd talked his victims into his red car. He immediately gained control of them, using a knife and a gun. He bound them. Took them to an area familiar to him. Sexually assaulted them. Killed them. Left them where they'd be hard to find.

Did he match the BSU profile?

	FBI PROFILE	BOBBY JOE LONG
Race	Caucasian	Caucasian
Age	Mid-twenties	Thirty-one
Personality	"Macho" image assaultive	On probation for assault
Weapons	Likely to carry weapons	Gun and knife
Employment	Difficulty in holding job	Recently fired, unemployed
Marriage	Probably divorced	Divorced
Vehicle	"Flashy car"	Red Magnum
Geographics	Confined to the Tampa region	Tampa Bay area
Victims	Randomly selected, and susceptible to approach	Prostitutes

Those whom Long admitted killing in the Tampa Bay region totaled ten, over an eight-month period. But those unfortunate women were but the tip of the Bobby Joe Long iceberg. Between 1980 and 1983 he'd roamed Miami, Ocala, and Fort Lauderdale as the "Classified Ad Rapist," carrying out midday attacks on women in their homes. On the pretext of answering a newspaper classified advertisement, he knocked on doors and, finding a woman at home alone, produced a knife, forced himself into the house, raped, and robbed. He'd done it fifty times. The step up to murder was easy and inevitable.

Charged with nine counts of first-degree murder and felony counts of abduction, rape, and sexual assault on the young woman whose ordeal had led to his arrest, Bobby Joe was convicted and sentenced to die in Florida's electric chair—taking a place on death row along with Ted Bundy in 1985.

On the afternoon of May 29 in that year, the veteran cop with a dream about a violent criminal apprehension program to nab people like Bobby Joe and Ted sat down at a computer keyboard at the BSU at Quantico and entered a command that would bring into reality the kind of program he'd envisioned and started pleading for a quarter-century earlier. For the past nine months—it was just like having a baby—Pierce Brooks had been living at the FBI Academy in order to oversee creation of the new VICAP computer system, which was light-years beyond anything he could have imagined while sitting in the L.A. public library looking for news items about serial killers back in 1958.

Fundamental to the operation of VICAP was a questionnaire made available to the FBI's fifty-nine field divisions whose personnel were trained in its use. But six months later, two problems had become evident. First, the number of cases coming into VICAP was fewer than expected. Second, the reporting form itself proved rather cumbersome, because it provided *too much* detail on the crimes. The role of the people receiving the VICAP information was not to take the role of investigators but to assist them by analyzing a particular case and indicating possibly fruitful avenues to be explored. As a result, the VICAP reporting system was overhauled in 1986, resulting in a considerably more handy and efficient system of paperwork: the VICAP Crime Analysis Report form.

From a blank space for assigning a case number (Item No. 1), the form progressed from "case administration data" to "crime classification" information such as murder and likely related crimes, e.g., "Organized Drug Trafficking," and onward to date and time parameters of the crime, victim data, what was or was not known about the offender, the MO, autopsy data, forsensic evidence, and a request for a profile—a total of 189 queries.

The repository of this accumulation of facts about crimes was the National Center for the Analysis of Violent Crime, where both manual and automated retrieval systems were set up to allow comparisons to be made of crimes and criminals who were reported via VICAP from all levels of law enforcement. Files included persons related to those connected in any manner to FBI investigations and those who were the subjects of the BSU violent crime research studies including, but not limited to, the criminal personality profiles, scholarly journals, and news media references. Also added were names of persons who'd provided unsolicited information (tips) and the subjects of that material, as well as the names of law enforcement personnel who requested assistance and/or made inquiries concerning records. This data bank allowed cross-checking of files and the matching of similar cases from different locations.

In determining priorities for cases to be handled, a pecking order was established, beginning with those in which the FBI had primary jurisdiction. Next came cases in which the FBI and local or state agencies had overlapping claims. Then came all other cases, in which the FBI acted as consultant or provided its scientific expertise (the famed FBI labs, the BSU, and other special units). NCAVC services were provided free of cost to the requesting agency.

Going into the 1990s, the BSU had been renamed Behavioral Science Services and consisted of the Behavioral Science Instruction and Research Unit, with a unit chief (John Henry Campbell), twelve instructors/researchers, administrative support staff, and office management personnel; research support management; and the Investigative Support Unit, headed by Alan E. Burgess and consisting of a Criminal Investigative Analysis Program, computer and engineering support, administrative support staff, and VICAP.

(The organizational chart appears on page 92.)

At the end of 1989, VICAP contained data on approximately 3,700 cases from the United States, Canada, and several other countries. Further worldwide expansion was the subject of a meeting of the VICAP International Homicide Symposium held at the FBI Academy in 1988, and domestic expansion was on the agenda of a conference on implementation of VICAP in all the states of the union.

By using VICAP and the profilers associated with the system it was possible for a local or state law enforcement agency to compare a homicide case it was investigating with hundreds of others. Data in the VICAP/BSU files were arranged on different criteria that included the categories of murder (single, double, triple, mass, spree, serial). Another data bank dealt with the primary intent of the murderer (sexual, criminal enterprise, emotional). The Offender Risk file offered material on the nature and extent of the risks taken by the killer during commission of the murder. Victim Risk was categorized—that is, what was it in the victims' behavior that made them susceptible or vulnera-

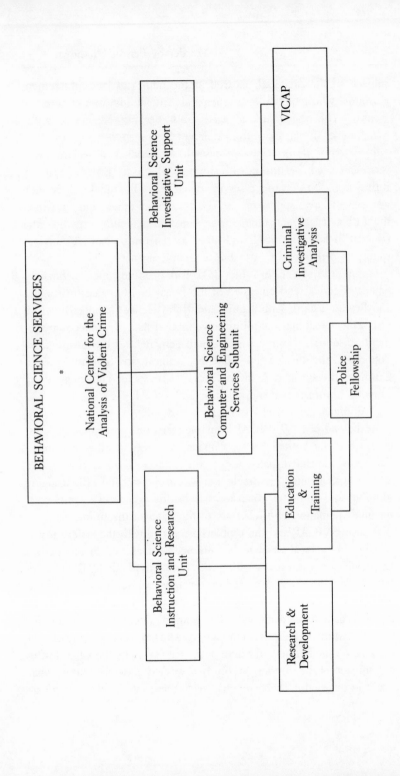

BEHAVIORAL SCIENCE SERVICES

*

National Center for the Analysis of Violent Crime

Behavioral Science Investigative Support Unit

Behavioral Science Computer and Engineering Services Subunit

Behavioral Science Instruction and Research Unit

VICAP

Criminal Investigative Analysis

Police Fellowship

Education & Training

Research & Development

ble to the crime? Information labeled "Escalation" was derived from an analysis of facts and patterns of solved crimes and showed the sequence of acts committed during the crime. The results of analyses of Time and Location Factors were available for comparison. Crime Scene Dynamics were compiled—the *style* of the killer: the symptom of the aberrant behavior, the personality of the killer.

In 1986 a request for a criminal personality profile was made through VICAP by Mel Bailey, sheriff of Jefferson County, Virginia. On July 14 the body of Tracey Schoettlin, clad only in knee-length stockings, had been found by joggers under a bridge in the River Run area. A waitress at the American Café in the town of Five Points South, she was working to earn money so she could return to the study of law at Samford University. She'd been last seen alive after work at 11:00 the night before her body was found. Her broken-down car was found several blocks away. A witness remembered seeing her talking to a man at the Southside Chevron station. Beyond that, Sheriff Bailey had little to go on. "This case took us down so many roads and involved so many avenues to differentiate what was and was not related," he said, all without clearing the case. Then, from Cecil Moses, Special Agent in Charge of the FBI office in Birmingham, Bailey found out about VICAP and the availability of profiling.

Although acceptance through VICAP at that time required the police to have been working on a case for at least six months, Sheriff Bailey's request for assistance was accepted because there was a question as to whether the murder had been done by an area resident or a transient. If the woman had been killed by a man who simply was passing through the area, his arrest would be unlikely. Based on crime-scene data supplied by Bailey, the BSU profilers concluded that Schoettlin had not been murdered by a wanderer but by someone who was very familiar with the region and was probably known and trusted by the victim—possibly a shy and aloof young man with a strong religious belief and suppressed sexuality. The murder appeared to be impulsive rather than planned or one more in a string of killings—the impetuous deed of a local man who out of guilt and fear would be unlikely to slay again and was definitely not a serial killer. Encouraged by the report to look close to home for the perpetrator,

Bailey concentrated his investigation on the town of Center Point and a twenty-six-year-old whose similarity to the profile was, in Bailey's word, "uncanny." An arrest followed quickly.

In announcing the advent of VICAP, FBI Director William S. Sessions had expressed high hopes for the system but warned that "computer technology cannot replace the human element in conducting investigations and analyzing crime." Nonetheless, he saw in VICAP an important new way of helping police not only in cases of serial killers and rapists but "in solving other similar crimes, including drug-related murders and killings that are incidental to other types of offenses."

Pierce Brooks couldn't have agreed more. "It's not going to stop them," he said, "but it could shorten their careers."

In 1989, the Criminal Investigative Analysis Program was an active participant in 793 cases, of which 290 were within direct FBI jurisdiction. In addition to criminal personality profiling and direct aid in the investigation of crimes, that assistance included advice and suggestions regarding pre- and post-arrest interviews and suspect interrogations, proper preparation and execution of search warrants, and advice on strategies in the prosecution of offenders, as John Douglas had provided in the Atlanta Child Murders. In some cases, Special Agents provided on-site assistance in major crime investigations. Agents also were available to testify in court as expert witnesses concerning the process of criminal investigative analysis.

Among the men and women of the NCAVC, graduate degrees were commonplace. In 1989 there were six doctorates and eighteen master's degrees in a personnel list of thirty-four. Affiliated with the University of Virginia, NCAVC staff members were adjunct faculty offering undergraduate and graduate courses ranging from Interpersonal Violence and Community Policing Issues to Futuristics in Law Enforcement. Seminars and conferences were sponsored, including a meeting of investigators who'd been involved in the Ted Bundy case. Beyond the confines of the academy, the staff and faculty of the NCAVC conducted thirty-three courses for police agencies in the United States and training sessions for law enforcement in Portugal, Israel, Italy, Belize, and Costa Rica.

Papers and/or speeches were presented by NCAVC staff and faculty to professional organizations and mental health, legal, medical, academic, and community groups spanning the spectrum from the American Academy of Forensic Sciences to members of Crime Stoppers International.

Writing for publication was encouraged. In 1989, for example, Kenneth Lanning published *Child Sex Rings: A Behavioral Analysis* and collaborated with Ann Wolbert Burgess on "Child Pornography and Sex Rings," a chapter in *Pornography: Research Advances and Policy Considerations*, by D. Zillman and J. Bryant. Nine research papers were presented and seventeen articles were written. Three of those articles were published by Roy Hazelwood, one of the most prolific NCAVC authors. In addition to his 1989 work, Hazelwood's individual titles and collaborations amounted to no less than twenty-four. His subjects included "The Lust Murderer," "Death During Dangerous Autoerotic Practices," interviewing victims of rape, the serial rapist, criminal personality profiling, the NCAVC training program, sexually motivated gynocide and sexual aggression, investigation of sexually sadistic offenses, and the sexual sadist.

Hazelwood was also at the heart of ground-breaking research on "equivocal death." Sometimes called a "psychological autopsy," an equivocal death analysis is conducted in cases in which the means of death was known but the motivation was unresolved, or in cases of "autoerotic" deaths, which were often arranged to appear as accidents or homicides. Conducting an "autopsy" on the victim by analyzing the victim's personality and behavior, Hazelwood was able to render an educated judgment as to whether the death was an accident, a homicide, a suicide-murder, or suicide. In 1983, he reported on his research into equivocal death in a landmark article for the publication of the American Society of Criminology and was collaborating on another definitive analysis of the controversial topic with Special Agent Richard Ault.

And, having achieved considerable success in research into sexual murderers and serial killers in the early 1980s, the scientist/agents at Quantico immediately turned their attention and their research and analytical techniques to a type of criminal who was in much greater abundance in America going into the 1990s than murderers.

SEVEN

The Rapists

Note: to avoid any possibility of identification of rape victims, their names, those of their rapists, and locations have been changed or omitted.

The noise had been muffled and may have been a dream, but she woke up in cold terror. Maggie listened again but heard nothing. Yet something did not seem right. She felt as if someone was nearby. Stirring to reach for the bedside lamp, she heard a quick intake of breath, then felt breath upon her: warm, moist, rapid. A hand clamped tightly upon her mouth and a sharp point dug into the flesh beneath her chin. "Now just be a good girl," whispered a voice out of the darkness, "and I won't use this knife." The rapist was with her less than two minutes. He'd done the same thing in the same town several times before.

Steadily employed at a salary well beyond $30,000 a year, Terry had a measured Full Scale IQ of 139. The way he committed the rapes indicated a great amount of forethought. All took place some distance from where he lived. The residential areas he chose were ones in which he would blend in. In his mind were at least six potential victims. They had been chosen on previous excursions when all he did was look into windows.

Before entering the victim's home, he dressed in his "going-in clothes," consisting of work gloves, a set of loose-fitting coveralls, oversized sneakers, and a ski mask. Using a glass cutter and a suction cup, he slipped quietly through a patio door or window. After making certain that the woman was alone and asleep, he disconnected the telephone. He then opened a window or left a door ajar and exited the house or apartment to change into his "rape clothes," which were coveralls, sneakers in his correct size, the ski mask, and surgical gloves. If upon returning to the residence he found the window or door had been closed, indicating that the intended victim had awakened, he would leave and go to the home of the next victim on his list. If everything was as he'd left it, he went back into the house. Counting to ten in increments of one-half, he moved toward his victim. Reaching the count of ten, he pounced.

"The rape itself was the least enjoyable part," he later told Roy Hazelwood of the FBI. It was the planning and the ritual that thrilled him. If that was so, he was asked, why not just leave without raping the woman? "Pardon the pun," he replied, smirking, "but after all I went through to get there, it would have been a crime not to rape her."

Terry was one of the smartest rapists Hazelwood interviewed as the Behavioral Science Unit began questioning convicted rapists in a twenty-month study funded by a grant from the Office of Juvenile Justice and Delinquency Prevention. Because rape was not a federal crime unless carried out on federal property, the aim of the study was to provide local and state law enforcement with information through the FBI *Law Enforcement Bulletin* and other professional journals and to provide investigative support in specific cases when requested. Led by Dr. Ann Burgess, the team of researchers was the same one that had done the research into serial killers. In this examination of serial rapists in a dozen states, the delving conversations were with forty-one incarcerated men responsible for 837 rapes and more than 400 attempted rapes. They included thirty-five Caucasians, five blacks, and one Hispanic. The number of rapes committed by individuals ranged from ten to fifty. The average age of the rapists was 35.2 years. The time elapsed between the first rape and an arrest ranged from three months to twelve years. When interviewed, fifteen of the forty-one were undergoing some form of treatment program.

At the age of twenty-four, Richard was in a Midwestern prison for murdering five of the twelve women he'd raped over four years in the early 1980s. The youngest of three children whose parents had divorced when he was seven, he'd been a behavior problem to his teachers. Athletic and good at baseball, he was outgoing and popular with a close circle of friends, both male and female. Alcohol and drugs came into the picture in his early teens.

The raping started when he was fourteen. Coming home from a party, he began thinking about the woman next door. A twenty-five-year-old who was divorced, she'd employed Richard from time to time for small errands. Because she surely would recognize him, he wore a ski mask when he scaled her apartment-house wall with the agility of a cat burglar and entered her third-floor apartment through a balcony door. He raped her several times and exited by way of the front door. Evidence found in the apartment linked him to the assault, and he was arrested. His sentence was treatment at an out-of-state psychiatric residential center.

Home from the center for Christmas at the age of sixteen, he raped again, using a knife to subdue a woman in an elevator. Three months later, he accosted a woman in a parking lot and forced her to drive them to her apartment, where he raped her. A third and fourth rape happened while he was free on a weekend pass from the psychiatric residential center, accompanied by two other patients. Three months later in the company of one of the patients he raped a woman in the women's locker room of a local swimming pool. The sixth was the capture of a woman in an elevator. Using an air pistol, he forced her to a storage room, covered her face with a jacket, and assaulted her twice.

Then the killing began. First was a woman whose conversation offended him. "She asked which way I wanted it," he said. This raised suspicions in his mind of her life-style. Then she made the mistake of attempting to escape. "She took off running down the ravine," Richard said. "That's when I grabbed her. I had her in an armlock. She was bigger than me. I started choking her. She stumbled. We rolled down the hill and into the water. I banged her head against the side of a rock and held her head under the water."

His second murder victim also talked too much and made a run for it. "She wanted to know why I wanted to do this; why I picked her. Didn't I have a girlfriend? What was my problem? What was I going to do?" Furious at the incessant questioning, he slammed on the brakes of the car. When it slid to a stop, she bolted. "I go into the woods after her," he said. "I see her run from behind a tree and that's when I go after her. From then on I knew I had to kill her. She trips over a log and that's when I catch up with her and I just start stabbing her." Seventeen times in the chest.

The next woman was not permitted to talk. Shut up and turn on the radio, he ordered. "The more I got to know about the women the softer I got," he explained. He thought about whether to kill the woman. "I was thinking, I've killed two. I might as well kill this one, too. Something in me was wanting to kill." Just for a moment, he wavered. "I tied her up with her stockings and I started to walk away. Then I heard her through the woods kind of rolling around and making muffled sounds. And I turned back and said, 'No, I have to kill her. I've got to do this to preserve and protect myself.'" To the left side of her thorax and upper abdomen he delivered twenty-one stab wounds.

A woman who pleaded with him about her father who was dying of cancer saved her life. 'I thought of my own brother who had cancer," he said. "I couldn't kill her. She had it bad already."

The next woman he raped scratched him across the face. "I got mad," he said. "She started to run. I chased her. She ran into a tree. I caught her. We wrestled, rolled over an embankment into the river. I landed with my face in the water. That's where the idea to drown her came. She was fighting and she was strong but I put her head under the water and just sat there with my hands on her neck."

Next, he feared a woman he raped knew him. "We were walking along, through the culverts, underneath the highway. That's when I pulled out the knife and without even saying anything, I stabbed her . . . maybe fifty or a hundred times."

What Richard did after his crimes interested the team of FBI interviewers. He usually took an item of jewelry from the woman's body for a souvenir. He searched her purse for money and drove her car for an extended period of time, then left it several blocks from his apartment. He avidly searched for news of the discovery of the body in the newspapers and on TV and radio newscasts.

Analyzing this case for the *American Journal of Psychiatry* in January 1983, Robert Ressler, Ann Burgess, and John Douglas noted that "for some rapists there is a progression in the offender's *intent* or decision-making toward killing." The modern view of rape regards it as an act of violence expressing power as one motive, they recorded, but, they wrote: "We suggest that the psychological motive of power expands for the rapist-murderer from a need for power over one person ('It was a real turn-on to realize the victims weren't reporting or identifying me') to a need for power over a collective group ('I'm too slick for them') that included police, judges, psychiatrists, and psychologists."

The lengthy and detailed questioning of the rapists showed that in choosing a method of approaching and subduing his victim a rapist chose one of three categories of attack: con, blitz, or surprise.

In the con approach, the rapist approaches the victim with a subterfuge. "Frequently, he will offer some sort of assistance or will request directions," explained Roy Hazelwood. "Initially, he is pleasant, friendly, and may even be charming. His goal is to gain the victim's confidence until he is in a position to overcome any resistance she might offer. Quite often, for different reasons, he then exhibits a sudden change in attitude toward the victim once she is within his control. In some instances, the motivation for the attitude change is the necessity to convince the victim he is serious about the rape. Other times, it is merely the reflection of a deep inner hostility toward the female gender. This style of approach suggests an individual who has confidence in his ability to interact with women."

This was an exact description of the methods that had been used by Ted Bundy, interviewed on death row at Florida State Prison with the electric chair ("Old Sparky") just down the corridor. In her Senate testimony on serial killers, Ann Rule, before she found out her good-looking and gentlemanly friend was a serial raper and murderer had described Bundy as "kind, caring, and slated for great success in his career as an attorney." Other writers termed Bundy as "the killer next door," the "phantom Prince," and the "deliberate stranger."

The authors of *The Only Living Witness* detailed Bundy's victims and method. "They were all young, and most of them were college girls," wrote Stephen G. Michaud and Hugh Aynesworth. "He often stalked them first, then approached them on a pretext. In a matter of seconds, they were gone."

Just the opposite in his attacks, a rapist employing the "blitz" approach is direct and swift. He permits the woman no opportunity to cope physically or verbally. He frequently will gag, blindfold, or bind his victim. "The use of such an approach suggests hostility toward women," wrote Hazelwood in an *FBI Law Enforcement Bulletin* article. Bundy's charm and affability impressed women like Ann Rule, but the blitz rapist's hostility toward women is generally evident. His interaction with women in nonrape relationships is likely to be selfish and one-sided, resulting in numerous, relatively short involvements with women.

The "surprise" rapist lies in wait for his victim, who may have been previously targeted. This type of offender, according to Hazelwood, "does not feel sufficiently confident to approach the victim either physically or through subterfuge tactics. He uses threats and/or a weapon to subdue her."

If these methods differentiated the forty-one serial rapists who were interviewed, what traits did they share?

54% had generally stable employment.
71% had been married at least once.
51% had served in the armed forces.
52% scored above average on intelligence tests.
54% were raised in average or above-average
   socioeconomic environments.
76% had been sexually abused as children.
36% collected pornography.

Thirty-seven of the forty-one reported having hobbies, and twenty-three of them said they had outdoor pastimes including fishing, hunting, swimming, and baseball. Non-outdoorsmen liked music, building models, woodworking, coin or stamp collecting, chess, antiques, and reading. Fourteen of the readers reported they liked *Playboy, Penthouse,* and other sex magazines. They also read novels.

Ten cited *Time* and *Newsweek* on their reading lists, while only four mentioned comic books.

The vast majority of the rapists could be described as neat and well-groomed men who obviously took pride in their personal appearance, Hazelwood reported. "They exhibited a range of emotions from 'cold and aloof' to 'agitated and tearful' [during the interviews]. The largest proportion of them were observed to be expressive, though guarded and controlled. It was reported by the rapists, and quite obvious to the interviewers, that they were not trustful individuals." They spoke articulately but often punctuated their conversation with profanity. "When asked how their friends would have described them at the time they were committing the assaults, they responded with descriptions such as 'average,' 'friendly,' 'a leader,' and 'willing to help out a friend.'" noted Hazelwood. They showed a good sense of humor but were manipulative and cunning.

Their victims saw them dramatically differently. Many of the women related that they'd detected in their attackers a sense of inadequacy and immaturity.

Noting that people react to stressful situations in various ways, Hazelwood observed five categories of reaction by rapists when confronted with resistance from the woman: ceasing the demand, compromising, fleeing, use of threats, and use of force. He also found significance in the verbal activity of the rapist in the course of an assault. "For example, a rapist who states 'I'm going to hurt you if you don't do what I say' has, in effect, threatened the victim, whereas the rapist who says 'Do what I say and I won't hurt you' may be reassuring the victim in an attempt to alleviate her fear of physical injury and gain her compliance without force," Hazelwood concluded.

The interviews also shed light on the effect of what the women did during the attacks and illuminated the dangers that lie in providing generalized advice on what women ought to do when confronted by a rapist. "Our research and experiences indicate that there is no one specific way to deal with a rape situation," wrote Hazelwood and Supervisory Special Agent Joseph A. Harpold in the June 1986 *FBI Bulletin*. There were three parameters of the sexual assault situation that might assist the potential victim in deciding on a course of action:

(1) confrontational environment, (2) the personality of the victim, and (3) the type and motivation of the rapist (con, blitz, or surprise). Some of the rapists said a victim should "scream, fight, and claw like hell." A number of others recommended that she "pretend that she wants him so he will finish and leave." Others suggested that the victim "bribe" the attacker with money to leave her alone. But Hazelwood and Harpold warned that for law enforcement officers "to generalize the success of one or more instances to all rape cases is not only potentially dangerous to the victim but is also irresponsible and unprofessional" and cited cases from their study to demonstrate how any given suggested means of dealing with a rapist might backfire.

One widely proposed means of defense was for the woman to do something disgusting, such as urinating or defecating. To show how that course could fail, Hazelwood and Harpold related the story of a twenty-year-old woman who was attacked as she was returning home from a movie. Noticing that she was being followed by four males in a car and anxious about her safety, she entered a telephone booth in order to call her parents. But before she could reach them, the four men grabbed her and dragged her into the car. In her panic, she involuntarily defecated and urinated. "This so enraged her captors," Hazelwood said, "that they began pummeling her and forced her to consume her own waste material. Following this, the four took turns assaulting her sexually. Finally, they tied her to the rear bumper of the car and dragged her behind the automobile before releasing her."

In the case of a woman who was being raped in the presence of her tied-up husband by an assailant who thus far had been quite calm, the husband expressed his deep concern by asking his wife if she was all right. "Yes, he's being a gentleman," she replied. With that, the rapist flew into a rage and savagely beat the victim on the breasts. Asked later when he was under arrest why he'd reacted so violently, the young rapist blurted, "Who was she to tell me that I was being a gentleman? I wanted to show her who was in charge, and she found out." Because of the beating, the woman had to undergo a double radical mastectomy.

A third rapist was asked what his reaction might have been if a victim resisted him either physically or verbally. "I don't know," he answered "I might have left, but then again, I might have killed her. I just don't know."

In their book *Sexual Homicide*, Robert Ressler, Ann Burgess, and John Douglas, while noting that their recommendations might be forgotten in the panic of confronting a rapist, plotted a systematic decision-making process for dealing with the attack. "The *first* response should always be an attempt to escape," they wrote. If flight was impossible, the second response ought to be verbal confrontation. If that failed and no weapon was in use, offensive physical resistance was recommended. In the event that method proved ineffective, ceasing the physical resistance and further talk were recommended. "Because there are no reliably safe and effective responses," the authors noted, "the victim must do *anything* necessary to get out of the situation. That may mean feigning participation and, at a critical moment, making maximum use of surprise, attacking the offender's vulnerable areas as viciously as possible. This requires the victim to convert fear and a sense of helplessness into a battle for survival."

What the study of rapists and their victims showed, wrote Hazelwood and Harpold, was the need for the development of a viable training program for victims who might be confronted by a rapist. "We foresee that such a program would provide potential victims with information about the various types of rapists and their unyielding motivations, would teach potential victims to assess their abilities to resist, and would train them to control the environment to their advantage."

That there was a need for a system by which American women might educate and train themselves against violent assault was a sad fact of life in the United States in the 1980s, but as the rising rate of rapes in the nation was noted, some observers were wondering if increasing assaults on women had roots in a dramatic change in society. Was there, as one writer asked, a new breed of terrorist who went after women because the women were *successful*? In a country where women were rapidly assuming more and more power, authority, and prominence, was the nation witnessing the emergence of a new breed of violent criminal?

A profile workshop during the 1986 Police Fellowship Training Seminar at the FBI Academy in Quantico, Virginia.

VICAP ALERT

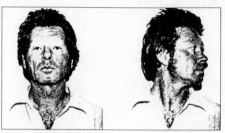

Benjamin Herbert Boyle
RACE: Caucasian; DOB: 7/22/43, Hobart, OK; HEIGHT: 5' 7"; WEIGHT: 170 lbs; HAIR: Red; EYES: Blue; COMPLEXION: Fair; BUILD: Muscular; SSAN: 443-42-4965; FBI NO.: 405 757 EA8; DRIVER'S LICENSE NO.: OK 443-42-4965 (Type: Chauffer).

Crime

Benjamin Herbert Boyle was arrested on October 17, 1985, and has since been in custody in Amarillo, TX, charged with the murder of a white female.

Background

Boyle was in the military from August 1960 to August 1963, and was discharged in Wheeler, IN. From 1969 to 1980, he indicated he lived in Colorado, where he owned an auto body shop. He moved to Las Vegas, NV, in February 1980, where he resided until November 1981, during which time he worked in an auto body shop. Another

move in November 1981, took him to western Oklahoma. From that time until his arrest in October 1985, he was a truck driver for numerous trucking companies, making both local and cross-country hauls. (See map for routes of Boyle's travels.) During those years, he lived in Oklahoma, Texas, and Louisiana.

In addition to the murder charge in Amarillo, Boyle was convicted of attempted kidnaping in Colorado Springs, CO, and a warrant has been issued for his arrest in connection with a rape in Colorado.

Modi Operandi

Described below are three crimes connected with Boyle.

#1 On November 20, 1979, Boyle attempted to kidnap a 28-year-old white female as she was walking along a residential area in Colorado Springs, CO. He tried forcing her into his personal automobile, but the victim pulled a small knife from her pocket, stabbed Boyle 5 times, and fled. Boyle pleaded guilty to attempted kidnaping and was given a 5-year probated sentence.

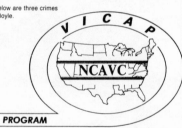

VIOLENT CRIMINAL APPREHENSION PROGRAM

Sample of a VICAP Alert used to broadcast information on apprehended criminals.

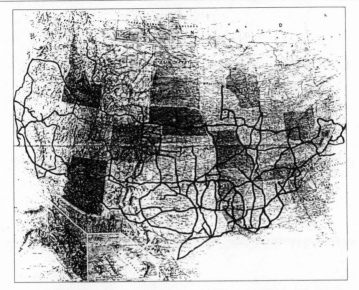

#2 On April 18, 1982, Boyle allegedly picked up by force a 17-year-old white female hitchhiker from a major highway in Colorado Springs, CO. He reportedly pulled his tractor trailer off onto a side road, forced the victim to commit oral sex, vaginally raped her, and then took her back to the highway and released her. A warrant has been issued for Boyle's arrest in this case.

#3 On October 14, 1985, Boyle allegedly picked up a 20-year-old white female hitchhiker north of Fort Worth, TX. The victim's body was found the next day 14 miles north of Amarillo, hidden in a clump of bushes. She had been beaten with a blunt instrument, bound with gray duct tape, and left nude. The victim had been sodomized and semen was found in her mouth. Cause of death was ligature strangulation. Fingerprints of Boyle were found on the sticky side of the duct tape.

In this last incident, Boyle reportedly was driving his distinctive truck—a fire-engine red, 1981 Peterbilt, with a conventional cab and twin chrome stacks.

Alert to Chiefs and Sheriffs

This information should be brought to the attention of all homicide officers. If unsolved cases in your department resemble Boyle's MOs or fit the time frame and routes taken by Boyle (see map pictured above), contact either the National Center for the Analysis of Violent Crime, VICAP, FBI Academy, Quantico, VA 22135 (703-640-1127) or Sgt. Modeina Holmes or Sgt. Walt Yerger, Special Crimes Unit, Amarillo, TX (806-379-2230). When calling Amarillo, refer to file CAS #227,412.

125. The Victim's Last Known Location Was Victim's Residence:
1 ☐ Yes   2 ☐ No   99 ☐ Unknown

126. The Victim's Last Known Location Was Victim's Work Place:
1 ☐ Yes   2 ☐ No   99 ☐ Unknown

EVENTS AT ASSAULT SITE

127. There Is Evidence That the Offender Disabled the Telephone, Other Utilities, or Security Devices:
1 ☐ Yes   2 ☐ No   99 ☐ Unknown

128. The Property at the Crime Scene(s) Was Ransacked, Vandalized, or Burned:
1 ☐ Yes   2 ☐ No   99 ☐ Unknown

129. There Are Indications That the Offender Took Steps to Obliterate or Destroy Evidence at the Scene:
1 ☐ Yes   2 ☐ No   99 ☐ Unknown

OFFENDER'S WRITING OR CARVING ON BODY OF VICTIM

130. Writing or Carving on Body:
1 ☐ Yes (describe): _____   2 ☐ No

131. Instrument Used to Write or Carve on Body:
1 ☐ Knife or Other Sharp Instrument   4 ☐ Writing Instrument (pen, etc.)
2 ☐ Blood   88 ☐ Other (specify): _____
3 ☐ Lipstick

OFFENDER'S WRITING OR DRAWING AT THE CRIME SCENE

132. Writing or Drawing at Crime Scene(s):
1 ☐ Yes (describe): _____   2 ☐ No

133. Instrument Used to Write or Draw at Crime Scene(s):
1 ☐ Knife or Other Sharp Instrument   4 ☐ Writing Instrument (pen, etc.)
2 ☐ Blood   88 ☐ Other (specify): _____
3 ☐ Lipstick

SYMBOLIC ARTIFACTS AT CRIME SCENE

134. Was There Evidence to Suggest a Deliberate or Unusual Ritual/Act/Thing Had Been Performed on, with, or near the Victim (such as an orderly formation of rocks, burnt candles, dead animals, defecation, etc.)?
1 ☐ Yes (describe): _____   2 ☐ No
_____   99 ☐ Unknown

OFFENDER'S COMMUNICATIONS

Item 135 deals with communications initiated by the offender with respect to the crime. Examples would be: an offender sending a letter or tape recording to the police or media claiming responsibility for the crime; a ransom note; or a suspicious communication received by the victim prior to the crime. (This item does not refer to conversation between the offender and victim during commission of the crime.)

135. Was There Any Communication from the Offender Before or After the Crime?
1 ☐ Yes (enclose a copy or synopsis   2 ☐ No
of the communication)   99 ☐ Unknown

Two pages from the fifteen-page VICAP Crime Analysis Report that law enforcement officials must fill out when seeking FBI aid in solving crimes in their areas.

VII.   CONDITION OF VICTIM WHEN FOUND

BODY DISPOSITION

136. There Is Reason to Believe the Offender Moved the Body from the Area of the Death Site to the Area of the Body Recovery Site:
    1 ☐ Yes   2 ☐ No   3 ☐ Unable to Determine

137. Evidence Suggests the Offender Disposed of the Body in the Following Manner:
    1 ☐ Openly Displayed or Otherwise   3 ☐ With an Apparent Lack of
       Placed to Insure Discovery   Concern as to Whether or Not the
    2 ☐ Concealed, Hidden, or Otherwise   Body Was Discovered
       Placed in Order to Prevent Discovery   99 ☐ Unable to Determine

138. It Appears the Body of the Victim Was *Intentionally* Placed in an Unnatural or Unusual Position *after Death* Had Occurred (e.g., staged or posed):
    1 ☐ Yes   2 ☐ No   3 ☐ Unable to Determine

139. Body Was Discovered...
    1 ☐ Buried   5 ☐ In a Container (e.g., dumpster, box
    2 ☐ Covered   refrigerator)
    3 ☐ In a Body of Water (stream, lake, river,   6 ☐ In a Vehicle
       etc.)   7 ☐ Scattered (body parts)
    4 ☐ In a Building   8 ☐ None of the Above

140. If the Body Was Discovered in Water, Was It Weighted?
    1 ☐ Yes —— With What? _____   2 ☐ No

RESTRAINTS USED ON VICTIM

141. Was the Victim Bound?
    1 ☐ Yes   2 ☐ No (go to Item 146)

142. Article(s) Used to Bind or Restrain the Victim or the Body:
    1 ☐ An Article of Clothing   4 ☐ Chain
    2 ☐ Tape   5 ☐ Handcuffs or Thumbcuffs
    3 ☐ Cordage (e.g., rope, string, twine, wire, 88 ☐ Other (specify): _____
       leather thong, etc.)   _____

143. The Evidence Suggests That the Restraining Device(s) Was (check one only):
    1 ☐ Brought to the Scene by the Offender   3 ☐ Both 1 and 2 Above
    2 ☐ An Article Found at the Scene by   99 ☐ Unknown
       the Offender

144. Parts of Body Bound (check as many as apply):
    1 ☐ Hands or Arms   5 ☐ Hands and Ankle(s) Bound Together
    2 ☐ Feet, Ankle(s), or Legs   88 ☐ Other (specify): _____
    3 ☐ Neck   _____
    4 ☐ Arms Bound to Torso

145. The Bindings on the Victim Were Excessive (much more than necessary to control victim's movements):
    1 ☐ Yes   2 ☐ No   3 ☐ Unable to Determine

146. The Body Was Tied to Another Object:
    1 ☐ Yes   2 ☐ No

147. Was a Gag Placed in or on the Victim's Mouth?
    1 ☐ Yes (describe):_____   2 ☐ No
       _____   99 ☐ Unknown

148. Was a Blindfold Placed on or over the Victim's Eyes?
    1 ☐ Yes (describe):_____   2 ☐ No
       _____   99 ☐ Unknown

149. Was Victim's Entire Face Covered?
    1 ☐ Yes —— With What? _____   2 ☐ No
       _____   99 ☐ Unknown

Former FBI Special Agent Robert K. Ressler and Dr. Ann W. Burgess consult with the project staff of the Criminal Personality Research Program at Boston City Hospital.

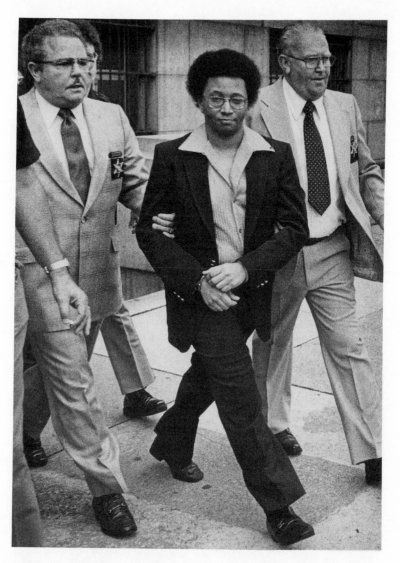

Wayne B. Williams, convicted of two of the Atlanta Child Murders in 1982, was sentenced to a double term of life in prison. (AP/Wide World)

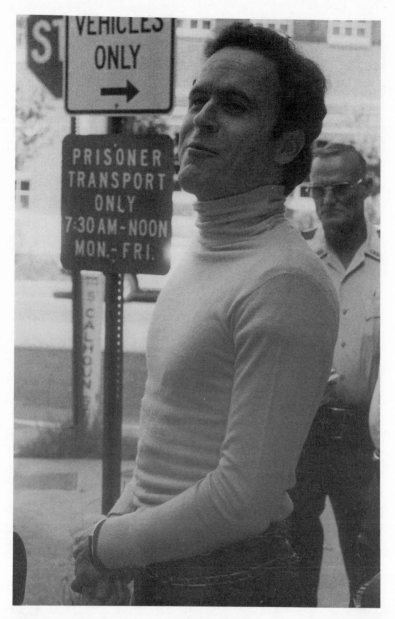

Theodore (Ted) Bundy was convicted and executed in 1989 for the murders of two coeds at Florida State University. (AP/Wide World)

David Berkowitz, the "Son of Sam," was interviewed in prison in 1981 as part of the FBI's program to develop profiles for *known* violent criminal offenders to assist in the apprehension of *unknown* offenders.

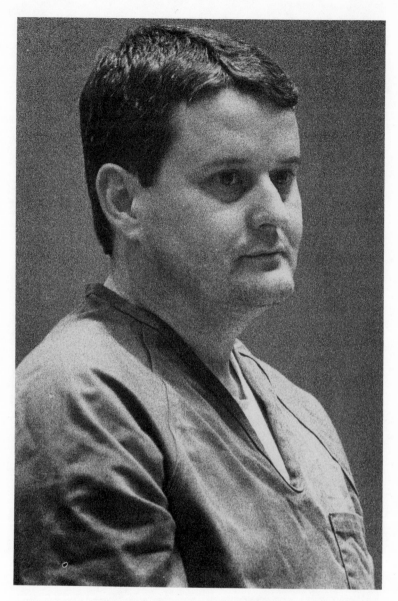

Few, if any, serial rapists or killers would prove to be as bizarrely twisted by nature and nurturing as Bobby Joe Long, convicted of murder and rape in Florida in 1985. (Photograph courtesy *The Tampa Tribune*)

Elmer Wayne Henley was convicted of multiple murders in Houston in 1973, including that of Dean Corll, who headed a sex perversion ring that preyed on young men and boys. (AP/Wide World)

This front page of the June 23, 1990 edition of the *New York Post* during the height of the "Zodiac" crimes shows one of the letters the Zodiac shooter sent to the newspaper.

(Reprinted by permission of *New York Post* copyright 1990 New York Post Co., Inc.)

The motivations of Gunners Mate Clayton Hartwig, one of the forty-seven killed in the explosion on the USS *Iowa*, lay at the heart of the FBI investigation into the incident. (AP/Wide World)

Gunners Mate Kendall Truitt testifies before the House Armed Services Committee in December 1989 during its investigation of the explosion aboard the USS *Iowa*. (AP/Wide World)

John Walsh, host of Fox Network's highly rated program, *America's Most Wanted,* became committed to capturing criminals after the murder of his young son Adam. (Photo courtesy Fox Broadcasting Company)

Accused murderer John List (left), who had been wanted since 1971, in an undated photo and (right) in a sculpture televised in 1989 on *America's Most Wanted*. Made to show what he might look like in 1989, the sculpture led to his location and arrest after more than 350 viewers called the program with tips. (AP/Wide World)

EIGHT

The New Victims

In 1983, the U.S. Justice Department's National Crime Survey Report pointed out what appeared to be a change in the nature of crimes against women. FBI statistics indicated that women who were divorced, separated, or living alone had become the most likely victims of personal violent crime and those who had some college training had a greater likelihood than others of being victimized by strangers.

This trend had also been noted by sociologist Dr. Ann Beuf, the director of women's studies at the University of Pennsylvania when Philadelphia was plagued in 1982 by a series of attacks on successful and affluent young women. "I see it as part of a larger cultural backlash against advances women have made," she said. "Some men feel small and inadequate when faced with women in power. This man thinks, 'What's she doing carrying a briefcase when I can't get a job? I'll teach her a lesson.'"

At the same time, psychiatrist Dr. Robert Seidenberg of Syracuse, New York, first noted male rage at the success of women in a series of assaults on nurses late at night in deserted parking lots or garages. "The attacker was usually underemployed or undereducated," he said. "Contrast the nurse, in her starched, white uniform, driving a car with a ghetto kid or a poor white kid who didn't finish school or have a good job but who had higher, unfulfilled expectations of himself. His pride would be hurt so badly by that nurse that he'd have to get even with women in general."

Seidenberg also detected evidence of male resentment against female success in the "Murder at the Met," in which thirty-one-year-old violinist Helen Hagnes was raped and murdered during intermission at a performance of the Berlin Ballet at the Metropolitan Opera House of New York's Lincoln Center. A child prodigy and graduate of the Juilliard School of Music, she and her husband, sculptor Janis Mintiks, had become a popular pair in the artistic community of the Upper West Side and Lincoln Center. On the night she was to die, July 23, 1980, Hagnes had just finished playing the *pas de deux* from *Don Quixote* and was on her way backstage to have a talk with the famed Russian émigré danger and choreographer Valery Panov.

Instead, in an elevator, the violinist encountered Craig Steven Crimmins, a high school dropout and stagehand whose father had worked as an electrician at the Met the same number of years as his son's age—twenty-one. Following her into the elevator, Crimmins made an off-color remark. "She smacked me on the right side of my face, on the ear," he later told police. Shortly thereafter, she was dead, her supine and nude body discovered the next morning (in the words of the *New York Times*) "dangling on an orange-colored steel ledge, about midway down a sixth-story ventilation shaft" with her arms and legs "bound with a rope and various old rags" and with a gag stuffed in her mouth.

Crimmins was convicted of felony murder and sentenced to twenty years to life. Dr. Seidenberg said, "She was the violinist, the prima donna. He was the 'grip,' a lowly stagehand. He had to get even for that."

As ghastly as that actrocious crime was, it was surpassed in public outrage in April 1989 when a young woman was attacked, bashed with fists, a brick, and a steel pipe, and repeatedly raped by a gang of teenagers who'd invaded the park to rob and pillage. It happened in Central Park and added to the lexicon of crime a new word—*wilding*.

The hapless victim was a twenty-nine-year-old woman who would be known thereafter to the public only as "the Central Park Jogger." The product of an idyllic suburban upbringing, she was an account executive with a Wall Street brokerage firm. Avid about healthful living and being in good physical condition, she regularly ran at night in the park, until she ran into the boys whose nocturnal pastime was rapacious rampaging.

One of those who stood trial for the attack upon the woman said that the gang had been hanging around on a street corner until one of them suggested they go wilding. Heading into Central Park, they had in mind assaulting anyone they came across with the intention of robbery. Bikers were especially targeted in the hope of making off with their bicycles. But after a number of attacks on them and a male jogger, the large gang spotted in the distance the lone figure of a woman runner in a white T-shirt and equipped with what looked like a desirable Walkman-type tape-cassette player. Concealing themselves in bushes, they waited in the blackness until the woman approached, then leaped forward to attack.

"We charged her," one of the youths admitted to police and Manhattan Assistant District Attorney Linda Fairstein in a videotaped confession shown at his 1990 trial. "We got her on the ground. Everybody started hitting her." He grabbed the woman's arm, he said. "This other kid grabbed her arm and we got her legs and stuff, and she's on the ground and everybody's stomping and everything. . . ." He grabbed one arm, he said. "And then we took turns getting on her."

Did someone take off her clothes? asked the DA.

"All of us," was the answer.

"Did a lot of people have sex with her?"

"Yeah."

Another of those tried for the assault was recorded on videotape describing what another of the gang did: "He pinched her arms with his knees. And then he covered her mouth with his hand. And then she was still screaming, so he started smacking her. He was just saying, 'Shut up, bitch,' just smacking her."

"And did she keep screaming?" asked Fairstein.

"Uh hmmmm. And he just kept smacking."

"Did somebody stuff something in her mouth?"

"No. He picked up the brick and he hit her with the brick, twice."

Did the jogger then stop screaming?

"Yeah, 'cause she was liked shocked."

The youth went on to describe watching another of the gang take his turn raping the now still, unconscious, bruised and bleeding woman, who would later lie comatose for months in a hospital and spend more time undergoing several operations for reconstructive facial plastic surgery. Fifteen months after her ordeal, she limped into the courtroom to take the witness stand in the presence of three of her accused attackers and testify that she'd been left with no memory of her ordeal.

When arrested, one of the defendants was quoted as saying to the police, "It was something to do. It was fun."

As this first of the trials in what the news media were now calling the Central Park Jogger Case was unfolding in New York Supreme Court in lower Manhattan, *Newsweek* columnist George F. Will saw a connection between the behavior of those accused of the assault and rape and what Will termed the "coarsening of a community and the desensitizing" of society. Apologizing to his readers for "the offensiveness" of what followed in his column, he cited as an example the lyrics of the popular rap music group 2 Live Crew.

The lyrics of this group, Will charged, "exult in busting women—almost always called bitches—in various ways, forcing anal sex, forcing women to lick feces. 'He'll tear the p——y open 'cause it's satisfaction.' 'Suck my d—k, bitch, it makes you puke.' That's entertainment."

While George Will was finding and deploring the influence of popular entertainers such as 2 Live Crew and comedian Andrew Dice Clay as encouraging devaluation of women and fostering assaults like that upon the Central Park Jogger, others were proffering other explanations for the apparent increase in rapes. Appearing on Cable News Network's *Larry King Live* show as the first Central Park Jogger trial was getting underway, Mel Fein of the National Center for Men saw rape as a manifestation of powerlessness felt by some males. "Male sexual violence," he argued, "is a symptom of male sexual powerlessness and an attack upon female power. His objective is to make that woman feel humiliated and powerless in his presence because that is precisely how he feels in her presence. The rape is an attempt on his part to turn the tables, to knock the woman off her sexual pedestal, to strip her of her power, to force her to feel what he feels. Essentially, rape is an act of sexual vengeance."

In addition to calling attention to the new sort of victim of rape and an apparent new motivation among rapists, federal law enforcement officials reported statistics showing that a growing number of victims of crime were elderly and, because the majority of America's "senior citizens" were women, they were feeling the brunt in this upsurge. Of 18,976 homicides in the United States in 1985, about 12 percent involved victims fifty-five years of age or older, because the elderly, like children, are easy targets for criminal predators. "Their vulnerability allows their victimizers to easily manipulate, dominate, and control them," explained John Douglas, Manager of the Criminal Investigative Analysis Program of NCAVC. "Add the fact that they may be in declining health, living alone, already isolated from others who could be witnesses, and that they have a tendency to keep money in their residences, and they become high-risk."

Crimes against the elderly that were reported to NCAVC indicated that the typical offender was similar to those who were attacking and raping young, successful women—a young male who had achieved only a low level of education and was unemployed. The crimes ignored racial lines and stemmed from a desire for money and an urge to "put the hurt" on someone. "Many times, there is more than one offender," noted Douglas. "One may assault the victim while the other moves around the house looking for valuables. The young man usually has a criminal history, including other burglaries in the neighborhood and perhaps even arson."

The rise in crime against the elderly became the topic of a symposium in 1988 at Quantico, "Violent Crime Against the Aging." More than eighty professionals from various disciplines were invited to the meetings under the combined auspices of the American Association of Retired Persons (AARP), the International Association of Police Chiefs (IACP), and the FBI's NCAVC. The purpose was to improve every aspect of living for older people but especially in the area of the criminal victimization. Of deep concern in this context was the fact that elderly victims of crime, like the victims of rape, often do not report their experience to the police. "The victim believes that sex is not a topic to discuss with others," said Roy Hazelwood in theorizing why the elderly were loath to come forward after they were sexually assaulted. "The victim also fears she may lose her independence; her family may force her to move in with them or to a nursing home. The victim fears her reputation may be damaged. She is afraid the attacker may seek revenge. She may be afraid that police will not believe her."

Following the symposium, the NCAVC laid the groundwork for further research on sexual assault against the aging. Principal investigators taking up the task were Hazelwood, Joseph Harpold, Sharon Smith, and Janet Warren. They began with a search of the literature and a review of case files to identify cases to be studied in the project, following the patterns devised in the studies of killers and rapists.

Unfortunately, there were plenty of cases already on hand. At the symposium, Sergeant Mike Gerhold of the New York Police Department's Manhattan South Senior Citizens Unit related the efforts of the NYPD to apprehend a particularly vicious two-man holdup team responsible for well over one hundred robberies. In several instances, these bullies attempted to bite off the fingers of their victims to get the women's gold wedding rings, he reported. One of these men was arrested, but the second, although shot and wounded escaping a stakeout, fled to South America. There was Richard Angelo, known as "the Angel of Death" because as a male nurse in a Long Island hospital he injected patients, some of them elderly but all of them incapacitated, with doses of potassium chloride in order to "discover" the dying patients and "save them." In Indiana, there was Howard Arthur Allen. Claiming his first elderly victim in 1974, he'd been sentenced to two to twenty-one years but was paroled in 1985. A killing spree that targeted the elderly began in 1987, lasting until his arrest and conviction for murder in 1988. Among the victims he claimed during burglaries was seventy-three-year-old Ernestine Griffin, stabbed eight times and battered with a toaster, all for $10 and a camera. Few at the symposium didn't remember that most of Albert DeSalvo's victims as the Boston Strangler were old women.

A year after the FBI established its project to study crimes against the aging, data had been collected on more then 600 cases of sexual violence involving victims sixty-five years of age or older. To continue the work, a grant proposal was submitted to the National Institute of Justice. As in the studies done on serial killers and rapists, the methodology of this project would include an analysis of solved cases and face-to-face interviews with those who were doing time for what they did to old people.

Just as alarming as the rise in crime against young and successful women and against the aged was the kidnapping, abuse, and murder of children. Since John Walsh testified on Capitol Hill about the killing of his son Adam, an epidemic of child abduction and murder appeared to be unabated. To attempt to come to grips with those burgeoning crimes, the NCAVC in 1984 launched a project focusing on the country's most vulnerable people.

NINE

Suffer the Little Children

*H*ouston, Texas: 1973. Largest city of the Lone Star State and the seventh-biggest in the nation. Former capital of the Republic of Texas, named for the dauntless hero of the fight for independence from Mexico, Sam Houston. Seat of the government of Harris County. Home of the University of Houston, Rice, Southern Methodist. Site of the sprawling Ellington Air Force Base. And, thanks to President Lyndon Baines Johnson and other powerful Texans in the Congress of the United States, the heart of the National Aeronautics and Space Administration. Connected to the Gulf of Mexico by the grand twenty-five-mile-long, 200-foot-wide, thirty-four-foot-deep stretch of the Houston Ship Canal. Oil country. Home to multimillionaires and billionaires living in splendid palaces that spared them from the notorious bake-oven that was south Texas in August.

The heat seemed to slap the faces of detectives rushing to answer a frantic telephone call for help from a man identifying himself as Elmer Wayne Henley and giving an address in suburban Pasadena. "It was self-defense," exclaimed Henley as the cops burst in. "He tried to kill me," he cried, pointing to the crumpled body of a young man whose back was riddled with six mortal bullet wounds.

The dead man's name was Dean Corll, explained Henley, and he'd flown off the handle when Henley showed up at the house for a glue-sniffing party in the company of a girl. This was to be an orgy, Henley continued, and Corll wanted only boys to take part. Young ones.

What Corll liked to do with boys the detectives discovered later that afternoon under the dirt floor of a rented boat shed. They found a total of twenty-seven corpses bearing marks of torture and sadism. If they dug up the sand of the beach at High Island and along the shore of Lake Sam Rayburn, Henley informed the stunned and sickened officers, they'd find more. "Dean seemed to enjoy causing pain," he said.

This was a bizarre contrast to the Dean Arnold Corll known to the police as the respectable owner and operator of a very successful candy-making business and store. Generous with free samples, he'd gotten the nickname "the candy man." But this seeming kindness had been a front, a sham, a means for Corll to befriend young boys.

Born in Indiana on Christmas Eve 1939, Corll had been raised in a quarrelsome home, suffered from rheumatic fever, and missed school a lot. But his health didn't keep him out of the Army, and it was in the service that he first exhibited open, brash homosexuality. At the age of thirty, his Texas friends detected changes in his sunny temperament, an abrupt swing to dark and gloomy moods and hypersensitivity. Preferring the company of teenage boys, he met Henley and another attractive youth, David Owen Brooks, who proved eager to join glue- and paint-sniffing parties at Corll's apartment. Nor did they shy away from Corll's other diversions—sex and sadism with the boys Corll brought home with him and Henley and Brooks were persuaded to recruit.

Most of the victims had been collected while hitchhiking or from the ranks of poor kids in the seedy Houston neighborhood known as the Heights where runaway children were quite common and of only cursory interest to overworked police in the wild and wide-open permissiveness of the 1960s that spilled over into the unbridled 1970s. Corll's three-year span of killings had begun in 1970 with Jeffrey Konen, a college student whom Corll picked up on the road. A pair of victims were friends of Henley's whom Corll demanded be delivered to him. In December 1970, Corll murdered fourteen-year-old James Glass and fifteen-year-old David Yates together. He also had a taste for brothers—Donald and Jerry Waldrop killed at the same time in January of 1971, and Billy and Mike Baulch in May 1972 and July 1973 respectively. The youngest-known victim was a nine-year-old boy who'd lived across the street.

The murders ended with Henley's tearful call to the Pasadena police about his shooting of Corll and the convictions of Henley and Brooks for multiple murder. Upon a booming Houston, these killings bestowed the unpleasant reputation as the place where the largest mass murder in history had taken place, though the killings fell more properly into the "serial" category.

That wasn't the end of it, however. Soon, police discovered that Corll might be connected to the sordid activities of the Odyssey Foundation of Dallas. In investigating Corll, police discovered that Corll had once recommended to a friend the amenities of a homosexual club in Dallas. This led the Dallas police to look into Odyssey, where they discovered records pertaining to 50,000 members whose sole purpose seemed to be trafficking in young boys for sex. A catalog being offered for sale through the mail to the nationwide membership list contained photographs and biographies of hundreds of boys, but there was no proof that Corll had ever solicited any of his victims in that manner—picking them off the streets apparently had been sufficient and satisfying.

Odyssey was owned and operated by a forty-five-year-old former musician and TV-commercial producer who had been arrested twice in Houston for child molesting and sodomy. After being arrested and freed on bond as the Odyssey investigation began, he fled Texas and turned up in Illinois, where presently he was arrested in the small town of Homewood and charged with sexual abuse of boys ranging in age from nine to thirteen.

While there was no way of connecting Corll to the Odyssey Foundation, the Houston police were in for a shocker in March of 1975. During a routine investigation of a stolen bicycle, they discovered a warehouse stuffed with cartons of pornographic photographs and films featuring scores of young men and boys. Of those depicted, eleven appeared to have been among Corll's twenty-seven victims. Again, no direct link was proved, because the Houston authorities chose not to pursue that aspect of the Corll case, feeling the boys' parents had "suffered enough." The material found in Houston led to five men in California and put police onto a source of the boys they'd used in their pornography business. He was a Santa Clara, California, high school teacher and part-time photographer—the man who took the annual class picture.

At about the time Dean Corll was in full swing as a killer of kids, the President's Commission on Obscenity and Pornography was reporting gross sales of sexually oriented material amounting to more than $2.5 billion a year. That there was a big appetite for salacious reading and dirty pictures needed no more proof than the brisk sales of the commission's report when the weighty document was reprinted by an entrepreneur complete with page after page of sex photos added by him to "illustrate" the text.

That the commission's report did little to blunt the flow of sexually explicit material nor to stop the sexual exploitation of children was underscored four years later when *Esquire* magazine devoted its March 1974 issue to the topic "Do Americans Suddenly Hate Kids?" The Dean Corll case was featured in an article titled "The Fate of the Boys Next Door." *Esquire* editors came to the conclusion that a lot of kids in America were taking a beating. Indeed, since 1965, murders resulting from the abuse or neglect of children had increased alarmingly nationally (in Los Angeles by 53.5 percent). By the count of the National Committee for the Prevention of Child Abuse, more than 60,000 children were dying in the United States annually from child abuse. No one knew how many kids had run away from home to escape abuse only to run into the ultimate child abuser—a killer for pleasure such as Dean Corll in Houston or John Wayne Gacy, Jr., of Chicago's Norwood Park Township, who went hunting for young men in an area known as Bughouse Square that was rich in footloose 1970s youths who'd probably never be missed.

Not until 1975 did a Missing Person File become part of the FBI National Crime Information Center, providing law enforcement agencies with a system for filing missing person information and letting them query the file to determine whether a person from their area might be listed. Part of the NCIC Missing Person File was devoted only to missing juveniles, defined as "unemancipated"—that is, minors under the laws of their state of residence. Since the adoption of the 26th Amendment to the Constitution of the United States, that generally meant under eighteen.

Meanwhile, the harvest of children continued. In his 1976 book *For Money or Love*, dealing with boy prostitution in the United States, NBC Television newsman Robin Lloyd recorded that at the time when NCIC was being put into service in the hunt for missing children, five teenagers in St. Louis were arrested for sexually assaulting, beating with frying pans, and mutilating two teenage boys; four men were taken into custody in Missouri for kidnapping a twelve-year-old in Los Angeles and sexually abusing him on their way to Chicago to sell him for sexual purposes; and two men abducted a sixteen-year-old Pennsylvania runaway and castrated him in the back of their station wagon.

Between October 1975 and January 1982, the FBI's Missing Person File swelled to 791,403. That was an average of 10,552 Americans going missing per month. Of that massive total, 76 percent of the files were devoted to missing juveniles. That came to an average of 8,020 kids unaccounted for every month. As of January 1, 1982, there were 23,827 records in the NCIC computers. Of those, 17,983 were in the juvenile category. About two-thirds of those were females. Of the ones age twelve and under, missing boys outnumbered missing girls. Over the age of twelve, girls accounted for more of the missing than boys. Whites made up 82 percent of the total. "If the estimates indicating that there are over one million runaways annually are correct," the FBI noted in its *Law Enforcement Bulletin* in December 1982, "a total of approximately 114,000 juvenile records entered into the Missing Person File per year would indicate that the full potential of the file is not being utilized." This meant that not all the missing were being reported, either to the FBI by local law enforcement or, more likely, to the police by those related to the missing person, either because they didn't care or because they thought the child had left home deliberately.

That not all missing kids had gone willingly was driven home to the American people in two headlined cases: the disappearance from within sight of his home in New York's Greenwich Village of six-year-old Etan Patz, who vanished without a trace on his way to school, and the kidnapping and murder of Adam Walsh, which his grieving and outraged father, John, forged into an unrelenting crusade on behalf of missing children, especially among lawmakers on Capitol Hill and the law-and-order Reaganites landslided by the 1980 election into control of the executive branch.

When President Reagan signed the Missing Children Act into law on October 12, 1982, the FBI was empowered to get involved in the plight of America's missing, exploited, and murdered children as never before. One aspect of the act authorized the collection and dissemination of data on unidentified deceased persons. The result was the creation of the Unidentified Person File in the data bank of the National Crime Information Center. Through these records, those who'd been reported missing could be characterized based on blood type, dental features, broken bones, and other physical anomalies that might aid in identification of unclaimed bodies. The act also required the FBI, when properly requested by a parent, legal guardian, or next of kin, to search the Missing Person File to see if data on a missing child had been entered. This aspect of the law enhanced the ability of agents to connect files on unidentified missing persons with cases that otherwise would remain open.

The act also permitted the FBI to create a file on a missing child on its own, thus opening the door for state and local law enforcement agencies to compare their missing children files with the national data bank. On November 23, 1983 (thirteen months after the act was signed), the Missing Person File contained 19,345 cases of missing juveniles, of which 11,905 were female and 7,440 male.

The Missing Children Act further permitted the FBI's Identification Division to open a fingerprint file for the category of missing persons.

What the act did *not* do was turn the investigation of missing kids over to the FBI. That power rested with the Bureau only in cases in which there had to be federal jurisdiction, as in a confirmed kidnapping. The law also specifically ruled out FBI involvement in the taking of a child by a parent. Unaffected by the law, however, was an existing Fugitive Felony Act allowing FBI intervention in certain circumstances: (1) a state arrest warrant charging a parent with a felony violation, (2) interstate flight accompanied by a warrant issued by a U.S. Attorney, and (3) a specific request by state authorities who agreed to extradite and prosecute the parent being sought.

The system for identifying missing persons established four criteria for FBI entry into a case:

Disability: A person of any age who is missing and under proven physical and/or mental disability or is senile, thereby subjecting that person or others to personal and immediate danger.

Endangered: A person of any age who is missing and is in the company of another person under circumstances indicating the missing person's physical safety is in danger.

Involuntary: A person of any age who is missing under circumstances indicating that the disappearance was not voluntary, i.e., kidnapping or abduction.

Juvenile: A person who is missing and declared unemancipated as defined by the laws of the state of residence and who does not fit the other three categories.

By January 1984, the Behavioral Science Unit at Quantico had amassed chilling statistics on child sexual assault. Based on the data collected over ten years, they reported that one of every four females would be molested or raped by the time she reached the age of twenty and that she would be most likely at risk for sexual victimization by a family member. "Numbers for male victimization are more hidden," wrote BSU Special Agent Kenneth Lanning and Ann Wolbert Burgess. This, they theorized, was because boys "are more reluctant to admit being victimized." However, they added, some clinical data increasingly suggested that "boys may be at equal risk for sexual victimization since they are the preferred target of habitual pedophiles and are victims of child sex rings."

Undertaking a study of child pornography and sex rings, Lanning and Burgess developed a picture of child victims, the perpetrators and the consumers of child pornography, and those involved in sex rings. The study was devised along lines similar to the previous analyses of serial murderers and serial rapists. Initial data from forty cases indicated that none of the children in the cases being looked at had joined in the sexual activities voluntarily. They were, said Lanning and Burgess, "gathered" for sex by an adult who was ten to fifteen years older.

"Although the number of victims actively involved in a ring at a specific time ranged from three to eleven," they wrote, "cases involving hundreds of children could be reported if numbers were added consecutively over the tenure of the adult's operation of the ring."

Cases with one offender fell into three age groups: toddlers (age two to five), prepubescent (six to twelve), and pubescent (thirteen to seventeen). But how did these men find the children? "Almost half the offenders used their occupation as the major access to the child victims," Lanning and Burgess said. "The adult had a legitimate role as an authority figure in the lives of the children selected . . . or was able to survey vulnerable children through access to some type of family records or history."

Sometimes the adult pressured the child to bring others into the group. One sex ring organizer simply posted a notice on a store bulletin board requesting girls to help with housework. The adult's status in the neighborhood sometimes helped to legitimize his presence among and with children. He was viewed as affable, well-liked, and, above all, "trustworthy."

Trust was a fundamental factor in the way pedophiles went about their business, as in the case of a man who took advantage of the trustfulness of the children he picked up in a shopping mall. Pretending to have a broken arm and wearing a sling, he would approach a lone child while holding numerous packages and ask the child to give him a hand carrying them to his car. Once at the car, he shoved the child in and drove off.

"Ralph" was a neighborhood man who hired kids for legitimate work and then seduced them into sex. When his victims talked to police after Ralph was arrested, the kids stated that Ralph had been a very nice man who was concerned with each of them—far more than their parents in some cases. He paid them well for the work he'd hired them to do and he paid them for their sexual activities and photographic sessions. He formed what he called the "88 Club" for boys who completed four different sexual acts. To keep track of all this, he maintained detailed files in his home computer—a treasure of evidence for those who prosecuted him.

After his arrest, the police learned that Ralph had been convicted and imprisoned twenty years earlier in another state on child-sex charges. He also was on probation for molesting a child in another city but had a letter from his psychiatrist to his probation officer stating that "there has been no indication that there has been recurrence of symptoms."

While Ralph had operated on his own, many more molesters of kids carried on their activities through what the FBI called "transition sex rings." In these, there was a network of solo pedophiles who regularly communicated and exchanged materials on their personal sexual experiences with children, including photos. The FBI found that these rings could be expected to evolve into producers of child pornography and perhaps turn into a "syndicate ring." Highly structured and often organized on a national scale, a sex syndicate vigorously recruited children for the production and sale of pornography and to deliver direct sexual service to the eager membership of the web. These operations were found to consist of two to nine adults at the core and involved scores, even hundreds, of children.

To assist local law enforcement in the handling of those who were arrested as sex offenders, the FBI examined how the people accused of the crimes reacted when arrested. First, they denied their involvement. "The offender may act shocked, surprised, or indignant about such an allegation of sexual activity with children," advised Lanning and Burgess. "He might claim it was a misunderstood act of simple affection or he might claim that he does not remember. His denial will be frequently aided by friends, neighbors, relatives, and coworkers, who insist that he is such a wonderful person there is no way he could have done what is alleged." If the evidence is plain and he can't escape it, he will attempt to minimize what he's done in both quantity and quality, they advised.

As the education and training of police officers who handled child sex cases proceeded, it became clear to the experts at the Training Academy that numerous investigators of cases of criminal sexuality were experiencing psychological difficulties. As Roy Hazelwood put it, "Investigating sex crimes is like being a garbage collector. Those who do the dirty job are 'dirty' by association."

Studying the problem with the goal of helping investigators cope, Hazelwood and Kenneth Lanning theorized that one of the major hindrances was the terms most commonly associated with such work—"sex crime unit" or "sex crime investigator." They theorized that when one hears the word "sex" it overwhelms "crime" and thus blurs the seriousness of the work the police are attempting to do. "Criminal sexuality" or "sexual crimes" would be better terms, Hazelwood and Lanning suggested. To find out something about the investigators, they sent out 3,000 questionnaires to police. Of the respondents, 202 were found to be currently involved in the investigation of sexual crimes. They were white men (92 percent) with a mean age of 38.2 years and an average of 13.1 years of law enforcement experience. Eight of ten were married and 54 percent had attended college or held a bachelor's degree.

The study found that common among these veteran officers were symptoms of stress that went beyond the usual strains of police work. "The officers working child sexual abuse, especially in medium or small departments, frequently become isolated from their peer groups," Lanning and Hazelwood reported. "While police officers frequently socialize with each other and talk 'shop,' they don't want to hear about child molesters and child pornography." Nor could sexual crime investigators talk about their work to spouses, family members, loved ones, or friends. "Some officers may not admit, or might even deny, that they work with child sexual abuse," Hazelwood and Lanning found. Delving into the problem, Special Agent James T. Reese of the Behavioral Science Instruction and Research Unit saw the effects of sex crime investigation manifesting themselves in the investigators as apathy, anxiety, irritability, mental fatigue, and denial. They showed restlessness, agitation, defensiveness, and difficulty in concentrating. They might become arrogant, argumentative, hostile, and even insubordinate. Depression was common and chronic.

Strategies for coping, as suggested by Reese, included a limit on an investigator's exposure to sexual crime cases—there had to be a set time when an investigator moved on to something else. A sense of humor was deemed essential. The officer who was naturally glum or lacking in humor would be a bad choice for investigating the grim facts of criminal sexuality. Peer support was seen as vital.

The FBI experts at Quantico also alerted the police to a startling phenomenon which they'd run across in interviewing victims of sexual crimes—the frequent reluctance or outright refusal of those who'd been molested to assist the police. The offender often had the cooperation of his victims. Kids often played down the magnitude of what happened, stating that it happened only thirty times when in fact it was a hundred. A victim might admit to having sex but not to taking money for it. Why would the victim not want to assist in punishing the man who victimized him? Lanning and Burgess reported: "Child victims frequently have mixed feelings about the discovery. They do not necessarily want the offender to be punished and sent to jail. They may describe him as a nice man. They may be embarrassed about others discovering what they have been doing." But not all victims felt that way; many welcomed the discovery of what was going on and welcomed the intervention of police.

From the data collected, shocking truths about the crime of sexual molestation of children emerged. Perhaps chief among them was the conclusion that child molestation wasn't being carried out by sex-starved maniacs. Instead, like rape, it was an offense committed not for sexual gratification but as a result of other psychological factors. It is a crime that happens anywhere. Child molestation is not limited to the street, playgrounds, or near schools but is found in homes, schools, juvenile programs, and day-care centers. Single incidents are not isolated but often involve or are connected to a number of other offenders and victims. The child molester is not a "dirty old man who wears a raincoat." He may be a well-respected, prominent member of the community or come from any walk of life or social stratum. In the majority of molestation cases, the offender is not a stranger to the child. Girls and boys can be victims.

To those who believed that the only way a child could be molested or involved in a sex ring or pornography was by force, the FBI's study revealed an unpleasant reality that underscored the ugly truth about the position of some children in America in the mid-1980s. Many who were victims of molestation had not been forced, compelled, or enticed into sex by threats of harm. They were, in many cases, willing, noncomplaining victims. Some children even described their molesters as their "best friends."

Like rape, child molestation was one of the most underreported crimes in the nation, with only 1 to 10 percent of the incidents being disclosed, according to statistics in 1984. The American Humane Association estimated there were between 200,000 and 300,000 molestations of females each year. Other estimates were much higher.

What of punishment? According to the Lanning and Burgess report of January 1984, it was estimated that 95 percent of the child molesters in California did not go to prison. The same appeared to be true elsewhere. Mental health facilities, counseling, and psychiatric help were often the recourse of courts. Further, the easy availability of parole was returning sexual offenders to the streets to repeat their offenses—a situation that did not change much in succeeding years. Case in point: Randy Breer, age twenty-nine, who was sentenced to prison in Virginia for sexual assaults including the abduction, rape, and sodomizing of a ten-year-old girl. In his testimony in court, psychiatrist Dr. Fred Berlin stated that Breer was a danger because of his biological craving for young girls and "recurrent eroticized cravings for children." If Breer was released, said Berlin, the chances that he would commit these crimes again would be "exquisitely high." In the sentence handed down by the court, Breer was ordered to a prison where he could obtain treatment. Breer had pleaded guilty under a plea-bargaining agreement in which two rape charges were dropped to allow Breer the possibility of . . . parole.

TEN

The Fire Starters

The place was way overcrowded. Elbow-to-elbow people. So jammed together were they that dancing was something you pretty much did standing in one spot—more bouncing up and down than moving around. Yet folks in their best "night out" clothes kept pouring up the narrow stairway from the street door and somehow managed to sardine their way into the club. Happy Land, it was called, and that was a good name, because everybody packed inside the small rooms on the second floor of the building that housed it was having a *real* good time—except for Julio Gonzalez. He was down by the door yelling at his on-again, off-again girlfriend, who worked at the only social club available to the folks of the Hispanic and Caribbean neighborhood around Southern Boulevard in the Bronx.

There was really only one way in . . . and out: the front door where Gonzalez's lady collected the admission fees, checked hats and coats, and did anything else that needed doing on that chilly March evening. Finally, she'd gotten rid of Julio, who'd stormed away cursing. Drunk, he'd been impossible to talk to. But now he was gone.

But not for long. Having left the club and fetched from his home a generous container, Gonzalez walked to a service station not far away and bought enough gasoline to fill it. Now he was back, glaring at the door to Happy Land. He flung the gasoline, lit a match, and tossed it into the running, pooling liquid.

Firemen who quelled the inferno and made their way up the narrow stairway to the second floor found bodies piled like logs, the life smothered out of them by the roiling, impenetrable smoke that had been sucked upward by the chimneylike stairs. When the counting was done, there were eighty-seven corpses. Though it was the worst fire of its kind in the history of New York City, the Happy Land toll fell short of the ninety-eight killed in a fire in 1986 at the Dupont Plaza hotel in San Juan, Puerto Rico. Like the Happy Land blaze, it had been set.

Why do some people start fires? What sort of person is an arsonist? One might suppose that these questions would have been answered long ago, yet the earliest large-scale scientific study detailing the motives of arsonists was not published until 1951. More than thirty years passed before there was another. Conducted by the FBI Behavioral Science Unit in association with the Prince Georges County, Maryland, Fire Department (PGFD), it analyzed data from 1,016 interviews of juveniles and adults arrested for arson during the years 1980 through 1984.

This intense FBI interest in arson was the result of the mandate of Congress, which had noted an apparent increase in arson across the nation. To probe arson-for-hire, hearings were held by the Senate Permanent Subcommittee on Investigations, chaired by Senator Sam Nunn of Georgia. "Arson is our costliest crime," he noted, "with losses estimated at $2 billion a year and rising at a rate of 25 percent annually." Arson-for-profit, he warned, was "the fastest-growing crime in this country," accounting for $10 billion a year if you added in the indirect costs of increased taxes, higher insurance premiums, medical costs, and the price paid for fire services.

The hearings resulted in legislation that required of the FBI a far more substantial commitment to arson than ever before and the upgrading of arson in the FBI's Uniform Crime Reports, issued annually. Further legislation, the Anti-Arson Act of 1982, took the FBI even deeper into arson as a field for research into and analysis of the incidence of the crime itself, kinds of arson in terms of the motive of the firesetter, and the psychological profile of each type of arsonist.

Chief Statistician Dr. Yoshio Akiyama and Peter C. Pfeiffer, survey statistician, Uniform Crime Reporting Section, provided information comparing the frequency of arson arrests compared to those for homicide, showing that they were quite similar. And the data dramatically demonstrated that arson was significant among the young. Almost one-fourth of arson arrests in 1983 involved persons under the age of fifteen. More than 60 percent were among persons under twenty-five.

Would those findings also show up in the arson survey that had been carried out by the PGFD from 1980 to 1984? To find out, the FBI's Technical Services Division loaded the data into the NCAVC computers at Quantico. Poring over the information gleaned from the 1,016 offenders were Dr. David J. Icove, senior systems analyst, and M. H. (Jim) Estepp, fire chief of the PGFD. Writing in the *FBI Law Enforcement Bulletin* in April 1987, they reported that among other reasons for starting fires, arson-for-profit amounted to only 1 percent of the cases. The main motive of firesetters was vandalism (49 percent), followed by "excitement" (25 percent), revenge (14 percent), and other reasons, such as crime concealment (10 percent).

Preferred targets of these firebugs, in order, were homes and other residential properties (44 percent), schools and other educational properties (31 percent), fields and forests (10 percent), structures of other sorts (10 percent), and vehicles (6 percent).

The main motive in starting fires in homes was revenge and excitement-seeking (26 percent). In an article for the *Bulletin* in 1980, Special Agent Anthony Olen Rider of the BSU noted that arson was associated with love, aggression, hostility, destruction, sadism, revenge, and other psychological factors. "In fact, revenge seems to run like a thread throughout motivational research," he noted. He also pinpointed a type of arsonist who resorted to arson as a means of attracting attention to himself, such as the young man in Scott Spencer's best-selling novel *Endless Love*. Published in 1979, it became a movie by director Franco Zeffirelli starring Brooke Shields and Martin Hewitt as the love-sick arsonist David Axelrod with a plan: "This was my strategy: as soon as the papers catch fire, I hop off the porch and run down the block. When I'm at a safe distance, I stop to catch my breath and begin strolling back toward the Butterfields', hoping to time my arrival with their emergence from the house. I'm not sure what I planned to do then. Either jump right in and help put out the little fire, or stand transfixed, as if surprised to see them, and hope that Jade or Ann would see me, wave, invite me in. The point was not to allow them to go another day without seeing me."

The attention-seeking or would-be hero depicted in the novel was one classification of arsonist identified by Special Agent Rider in his 1980 article "The Firesetter: A Psychological Profile." Excluding profit-seekers, others were the Adult Revenge Firesetter, the Jealousy-Motivated Adult Male, the Volunteer Fireman Solitary Firesetter, the Fire "Buff," the Pyromaniac, the Schizophrenic Male, the Excitement Firesetter, the Female Firesetter, the Child, and the Adolescent—each with his or her own motive for wanting to start a blaze. Ironically, the arson research that was set in motion by a concern over arson-for-profit had found that monetary gain was much less significant than anticipated. Nonetheless, the FBI/PGFD research into arson provided valuable insights into the overall problem of arson and how law enforcement might cope with it.

Icove and Estepp found that race did not appear to be a correlate with arson and fire-related activities. Use of alcohol and drugs was found to be significant in arsonists because they "loosen an offender's inhibitions at the crime scene." Firesetters often had previous contact with the fire or police authorities. Arsonists frequently live close to the crime scene. They do not always act alone but often have companions, especially when juveniles are involved. A large number of the offenders interviewed admitted to staying at the scene of their blaze or returning to it as the fire-fighting equipment arrived. This finding prompted Icove and Estepp to advise fire and police departments to take pictures of the crowds of onlookers at fires.

Arson may be a prelude to other violent behavior, noted Special Agent Anthony Olen Rider, citing the Son of Sam case as a prime example of how the setting of fires could be a warning signal of worse to come. Before David Berkowitz started shooting couples necking in cars, he'd set more than 2,000 fires and triggered 137 false alarms. Calling in to report the fires he'd started, Berkowitz frequently identified himself as the "Phantom of the Bronx." Searching Berkowitz's possessions, detectives reportedly found note pads listing the details of more than 1,400 fires, including the date and time, street, borough, weather, number of the fire box, the building or property burned, and the fire department code indicating the type of equipment that responded. The transformation from well-organized and methodical "phantom" to the cold-blooded gunman called Son of Sam took less than two years.

Of course, not all arsonists go on to become killers, but in the blazes they set, death often occurs, as Julio Gonzalez found out at the Happy Land social club.

While some people seeking excitement will start fires or turn in false alarms, others were like the five teenagers in Dyersburg, Tennessee, who in September 1975 tore pages out of a Sears, Roebuck catalog that illustrated items they wanted and enclosed a note informing the store manager that if they didn't get the items, along with three Peterbilt trucks, they'd bomb the store. Police easily traced the package and collared the kids, who claimed it was just a prank.

Perhaps so, but in America since the 1960s, threats of bombings, assassinations, and other terroristic acts weren't funny. Indeed, they had become a major concern and cause for investigation, study, and research by the men and women of NCAVC.

ELEVEN

Angry Words

As usual, he'd wowed them with his speech. But why wouldn't he? He'd been charming audiences all his life, whether on the silver screen in fifty-three movies—more than a few of them pretty good pictures—or talking politics. He'd logged thousands of miles on what he called the "mashed potato" circuit on behalf of others, then on his own running for the governor of California and in two bids for "the big enchilada." Running for Republican nomination in 1976 and losing, then running again in 1980 and winning both nomination and election, he'd advocated his brand of conservatism—less government, a foreign policy of unbending anti-Communism and thwarting the Evil Empire of the USSR around the world, and law-and-order at home.

Espoused in a kind of "aw, shucks" manner that reminded his audiences of the heroes and boy-next-door roles he'd played, such as Notre Dame football legend George Gipp, he called on voters to "put America back on the right track" and to "win one for the Gipper." He'd been elected President in a historic landslide. Now when Ronald Wilson Reagan walked into the ballroom of a hotel for yet another speech, a band struck up "Hail to the Chief," and nobody walked out on the speech and no one left the place before he did.

On the afternoon of March 20, 1981, Reagan strode from the Washington Hilton Hotel through a side door much preferred by his Secret Service protectors because it afforded easy access to the presidential limousine. A small crowd waited across the street and an even smaller one around the exit, presumably members of the White House security force, reporters, and news photographers. As he flashed a grin and thrust up an arm to wave at the cheering spectators, shots rang out.

The .22-caliber Röhm revolver in the hand of the youth who was immediately wrestled to the ground by machine-gun-toting Secret Service men had been manufactured in the West German town of Sontheim and purchased legally at Rocky's Pawn Shop on Elm Street in Dallas, Texas, not far from the site where President John F. Kennedy was assassinated in 1963. The small gun cost its purchaser $47. Bullets for it were bought in Lubbock. Known as Devastators, the slugs contained a small aluminum canister filled with an explosive compound. Costing twelve times as much as ordinary .22 ammunition, the bullets had been developed for the use of sky marshals in hijackings, and their only purpose was to harm humans. That Reagan and three others who'd been hit by them weren't killed was attributed to the ammo's inexplicably not functioning as it was supposed to.

On the radio in the President's car as it sped away from the hotel, Secret Service Agent Jerry Parr informed his command post at the White House: "Rawhide is heading for George Washington." "Rawhide" was the code name for Reagan. The car was Stagecoach." George Washington was the nearest hospital. "I guess I should've ducked," quipped Reagan as he was escorted in. How close he was to death wouldn't be known in detail by him or the American public until much, much later.

Why and how John Warnock Hinckley, Jr., nearly succeeded in assassinating the President would also be a long time in being explained, but two weeks after the attempt on Reagan's life, *Time* magazine had a headline that got it right: "A Drifter Who Stalked Success."

Hinckley was born in Ardmore, Oklahoma, on May 29, 1955, where his father worked as a petroleum engineer, a vocation that provided the family with a comfortable life, although a somewhat mobile one. In 1957 the Hinckleys moved to a suburb of Dallas where the lawns were broad and the houses handsome. In 1966 they traded up to top-of-the-line Highland Park. In 1975 the parents moved once more, this time to Evergreen, Colorado, but left their youngest child behind.

Since 1973, John had been studying business courses at Texas Tech in Lubbock, smack in the middle of the high plains of the Texas panhandle, but when he gave it up no one there would remember him as more than a weird standoffish kid with a blank expression directed at a TV screen. In late 1976, he landed in Los Angeles with the avowed intention of "crashing Hollywood." By now he'd developed a penchant for the crazies who infested the underside of society and spent a lot of time prowling the whore-and-hustler-populated streets in the seamy Selma district of L.A. His chief interests appeared to be Nazis and the pretty teenage movie actress in the film *Taxi Driver*.

For Jodie Foster, the movie was a career breakthrough. Her role was that of a street prostitute. Robert De Niro played the title role. A loner incapable of communicating who usually spent his off-hours in a dingy room eating junk food, Travis Brickle was obsessed with the young prostitute. Scorned by her, he hoped that by killing a presidential candidate he might win the girl's heart. A story that had been suggested by the events in the life of Arthur Bremer, who'd tried to kill Governor George Wallace in 1972, it and its star now became Hinckley's obsession.

Learning that she was enrolled at Yale University, Hinckley traveled to New Haven in the autumn of 1979, boasting that he and Foster were lovers and leaving notes for her at her dormitory. A few days later, he was arrested in Nashville, Tennessee, while attempting to board a plane for New York with three guns and fifty rounds of ammunition in his carry-on luggage. Perhaps not so coincidentally, visiting Nashville that day was President Jimmy Carter, but authorities never notified the Secret Service about a strange kid with guns in his bags. "This may be the first clear, though unheeded, signal of Hinckley as stalker," noted *Time* in its coverage of the attempt on the life of President Reagan.

Between visiting Nashville in 1979 and taking up a shooter's stance at the Washington Hilton in 1981, Hinckley paid repeated visits to New Haven to leave letters for Foster and also made excursions to the nation's capital, the last on March 25 for his fateful encounter with Reagan five days later.

Time's journalistic profile of Hinckley would find parallels in what the FBI behavioral scientists at Quantico define as a "disorganized" assassin, one whose one motive is to be linked personally in history with a celebrated target. In contrast, an attempt against the life of a prominent figure or against a group by one or several persons for a politico-military motive in which great secrecy is involved is categorized as "organized." These are usually terrorists and assassination is but one method.

Following the attempt on Reagan's life, in order to explore what compelled assassins, the FBI opened an exhaustive ongoing study modeled on the research patterns established with serial killers, rapists, child molesters, and arsonists and spearheaded by John Douglas and Kenneth B. Baker. The purpose of studying the assassins was to identify and analyze common characteristics of themselves and their crimes; to identify what *differentiated* them; to denote their personal characteristics and methods of operation; to focus on and attempt to identify and understand the behavior of assassins in the weeks and days prior to their attacks; and to construct an "artificial intelligence" rule-based expert computer system that would provide investigative consultations with law agencies in potential assassination investigations and prosecutions. It was a short list of political assassins: Sirhan Sirhan, the killer of Senator Robert F. Kennedy; Arthur Bremer, the attacker of Governor George Wallace; David Hinckley, the youth who tried to assassinate President Reagan; and a pair of women who went gunning for President Gerald Ford.

Those attempts on the life of a President went into the history books as double "firsts." They were the first time that two attempts had been made on the life of the chief executive in less than three weeks and were the first carried out by women. While their common target was Gerald R. Ford during a visit to California in December 1975, the motives of the assailants were quite different.

Lynette (Squeaky) Fromme was a disciple of Charles Manson acting in a bizarre belief that if she was put on trial for shooting Ford she could call Manson as a witness and permit Charlie to preach his "message." Residing in Sacramento, California, while Manson was in prison, Fromme shared an apartment with two other Manson followers. "We're nuns now, and we wear red robes," she said. "We're waiting for our Lord [Charles Manson] and there's only one thing to do before he comes off the cross [out of prison], and that's clean up the earth. Our red robes are an example of new morality. They're red with sacrifice, the blood of sacrifice."

Rebuffed in repeated bizarre attempts to obtain news media coverage for Manson, Squeaky warned members of the press that if Manson wasn't allowed to speak "there will be many young murderers, beginning with the person typing this letter." When this shrill communication went unanswered, she turned her warped attention to news reports that President Ford and his entourage were in Sacramento and ensconced nearby in the Senator Hotel.

Donning a fresh red robe and packing a borrowed .45-caliber automatic under it, she walked to the hotel on September 5, 1975. Soon, Ford stood before her. Jovial and beaming as he waved at the welcoming crowd, the former congressman and Vice-President who'd served on the Warren Commission that investigated the 1963 assassination of President Kennedy noticed the small childlike woman on his left, about two feet away. As he smiled toward her, she drew the gun from the robe and aimed it at Ford's genitals. In that instant, a Secret Service agent grabbed the weapon and wrenched it out of her hand. Finding himself abruptly in the middle of a flying wedge of guards, Ford was hustled away unharmed. Asked why she'd gone out gunning for Ford, Fromme shrugged and said, "Well, you know when people around you treat you like a child and pay no attention to the things you say you have to do something."

As for why Sarah Jane Moore, the second female would-be assassin to strike in less than three weeks, took aim on President Ford, she declared, "There comes a point when the only way you can make a statement is to pick up a gun." Moore's attempt took place in San Francisco. A heavy-set, middle-aged figure, Sally, as she preferred to be called, shot at Ford as he was leaving the St. Francis Hotel. Though the President clutched his chest as he was whisked away by guards, he was not injured.

Moore had led a politically confused life during which she took part in leftist and radical activities, including involvement with the violent Symbionese Liberation Army, and coincidentally became an informant for the FBI. Repenting the FBI connection, she made another sudden switch in her ideological direction only to be brusquely shunned by the people she'd spied on. Believing that shooting the President of the United States would somehow expiate her feelings of guilt, she did so. But unlike the Manson-obsessed Squeaky Fromme, whose attempt on Ford's life had been impetuous, Moore plotted what she intended and engaged in several target practices. Still, right up to the climactic moment, she was ambivalent—a sure sign of being "disorganized." "There was a point when anything could have stopped me and almost did," she said. "The most trivial little thing and I would have said, 'Oh, this is ludicrous. What am I doing standing here? What the hell am I doing here, getting ready to shoot the President?' I turned around to leave. Couldn't get through the crowd." At 3:30 P.M., as Ford appeared from the hotel, she fired.

Three years earlier in the parking lot of a shopping center in Maryland on the scorching day of May 15, 1972, a deliberate planner had blasted George Wallace, the governor of Alabama and putative candidate for President. Born in 1950, Arthur Herman Bremer had been a compliant little boy with a wicked, domineering mother who punished him and his older siblings often and hard. At the age of twenty-two, he was rejected by a young woman after he took her to see a pornographic film. Devastated, Bremer brooded in his apartment, living on cold cereal, bread, and peanut butter. He shaved his head in Mohawk style. Much of this behavior became the model for the taxi driver in the Martin Scorsese film. The fictional Travis Brickle then became a role model for Hinckley in the stalking of President Reagan.

Once, Bremer put a noose around his neck and wrote "KILLER" on his forehead with a blue felt marker. He thought about tying a rope around his neck as he stood on a bridge spanning a highway, shooting himself, and falling over to dangle above the whizzing cars. He fantasized hijacking an armored truck. Shooting people at random from a high place as had Texas Tower shooter Charles Whitman appealed to him. Finally, he decided to assassinate President Richard M. Nixon. Thwarted in that goal, he stalked George Wallace in order to etch a name for himself in history. Shooting Wallace was his way of grabbing the world by the lapels and compelling its attention. In his diary, he'd written: "Hey world! Come here! I wanna talk to ya!"

While a common trait in Hinckley, Fromme, Moore, and Bremer

was an obsessive thirst for attention, the fixation propelling Sirhan B. Sirhan to plot a murder was wholly political. "Robert F. Kennedy must be assassinated before 5 June 1968," he scribbled in a diary on May 18. The date was significant to him because it was the first anniversary of the defeat of Arab armies in the Six-Day War with Israel. Senator Kennedy was viewed by Sirhan as a symbol of the commitment of the United States to Israel at the expense of Arabs and Palestinians. "RFK must die," he wrote. "Robert F. Kennedy must be assassinated."

From that moment on, Sirhan was a calculating stalker. He was seen at a Pomona restaurant where Kennedy spoke on May 20. On the 24th he was on the fringes of an RFK rally at the Los Angeles Sports Arena. The following day, after hours of pistol practice at a firing range in Corona, he stalked lobbies and banquet halls of the Ambassador Hotel in Los Angeles, where there was a Kennedy campaign event. The next day, the Monday before the California Democratic primary, he drove down to San Diego for another rally at the El Cortez Hotel. On election day, he practiced rapid-fire marksmanship at the San Gabriel Valley Gun Club's firing rage until five in the afternoon, ate a hamburger at a Bob's Big Boy restaurant, and drove again to the Ambassador, where Kennedy and his supporters planned to celebrate his certain triumph in the primary.

Stationing himself in a pantry area on the assumption that Kennedy would leave the rally through the kitchen, Sirhan waited.

After shooting Kennedy and being taken into custody with the gun still in his hand, he was asked by Jesse Unruh, a California Democratic leader, why he'd shot Senator Kennedy. "I did it for my country," said Sirhan. Later, he'd boast: "I have achieved in one day what it took Robert Kennedy all his life to do. I am famous." Asked why he didn't shoot the President, Sirhan took note of what many Americans had been expecting to occur come November—the election of Bobby Kennedy as President. Smirking, Sirhan answered, "I did shoot the President."

Of the two other assassinations of political figures, that of President John F. Kennedy in 1963 by Lee Harvey Oswald and the 1968 sniper killing of Dr. Martin Luther King, Jr., by James Earl Ray, there have been persistent theories put forward that each had been a pawn in a carefully plotted scheme involving others with a political agenda, rather than a lone gunman driven by personal, if obscure, motives. These "conspiracy" enthusiasts' pointed out that both Oswald and Ray were unsophisticated and financially limited individuals, incapable of the acts they were accused of carrying out. But Oswald was himself shot and killed before he could be questioned at length and in depth, and no convincing evidence was found to refute the evidence that put Ray in prison as the lone killer of the Nobel Peace Prize–winning civil rights leader, leaving the "conspiracies" in the realm of speculation.

No conspiracy scenario has ever been put forward concerning the killer of John Lennon. Like Hinckley, Mark David Chapman was a classic celebrity-fixated stalker who'd had delusions about the former Beatle and came to New York in December 1980 from Hawaii with a .38-caliber Charter Arms pistol intent on using it to link his name forever to John Lennon in history. Assuming a combat stance as Lennon stepped from a limousine to enter the Dakota apartments where he lived, Chapman called out, "Mr. Lennon?" and opened fire. When arrested, Chapman had tapes of the Beatles in his pockets, including a copy of Lennon's new album, which Lennon had autographed for Chapman hours before he was murdered.

Fan obsession with a show-business celebrity blasted into the news headlines in several ways in the 1980s: late-night TV star Johnny Carson's home was invaded, later-night television talk-show host David Letterman's house and car were commandeered time and time again by a zealous female fan, and, tragically, twenty-one-year-old promising actress Rebecca Schaeffer was shot to death by Robert John Bardo as she answered the door of her home in Los Angeles. Neighbors said that Bardo had been seen around the actress's address for several hours and had asked at least one neighbor where she lived.

So acute had become the problem for well-known personalities in the celebrity-worship decade since Lennon was shot that many were forced to hire security forces and bodyguards and to engage companies that specialized in screening their mail for letters that appeared to go beyond simple, harmless fan mail and to be serious threats of harm.

At Quantico, the psychological sleuths of the National Center for the Analysis of Violent Crime had begun looking at those who wrote or voiced threats of all types. Chief researcher in this relatively new field, known as "psycholinguistics," was Dr. Murray S. Miron of Syracuse University. Undertaking the "semantic analysis of threat communications," he hoped to achieve an understanding of the personality of those individuals who used threats of violence or property damage as the central part of their criminal behavior. The aim was to produce data that would form a computerized threat analysis dictionary.

The idea was to scan threat communications as they were received in an attempt to identify the predicted outcome and courses of action contained within the threat as deduced from the language used. The system was sketched by Dr. Miron in an article written with Special Agent John Douglas of the Behavioral Science Unit for the *FBI Law Enforcement Bulletin*. Storing summaries of more than fifteen million words in written and spoken English, the system categorized the content of threat communications and printed out a profile of the message and the "signature" of the person responsible.

An impressive example of the value of psycholinguistics was a case involving an unidentified subject (UNSUB) who'd threatened an airline flight from New York to Geneva, Switzerland. Through analysis of the handwriting, Dr. Miron projected that the UNSUB was a German-born male at least fifty years old, an immigrant to the United States as an adult, and a twenty-year-resident. He had probably sent threats to prominent officials in Germany and the United States.

In carrying out his mischief, UNSUB felt compelled to leave clues in his threats regarding his identity. The clue in the case of the New York–Geneva flight was a code consisting of sets of three digits preceding the spelled-out name of what appeared to be a terrorist organization called "Alliance for Peace, Justice and Freedom Everywhere." Analyzing the code, Miron rearranged the digits so that each group was written in columns rather than serially, as follows:

$$6 \; 2 \; 9 \; 3 \; 7 \; 4 \; 9 \; 8 \; 9$$
$$0 \; 4 \; 4 \; 0 \; 3 \; 3 \; 1 \; 3 \; 0$$
$$4 \; 7 \; 5 \; 5 \; 4 \; 0 \; 5 \; 7 \; 7$$

Correlating the vertical columns of numbers to letters of the alphabet, Miron found that "6 2 9" correlated to "F B I." By using a standard coding device which employs a displacement key for the remaining text, the next code groups were translated to "IM." Two groups of initials followed: "JK JK." Put together, the letters were a message: "FBI, I'm JK."

A check of the names of passengers on the threatened flight revealed that one traveler matched the personality profile and part of the initials in the cracked code. Examination of threats received regarding other flights unmistakably linked the mystery man's handwriting to all the messages. Thus, airlines and police were provided with ample data on which to send alerts to be on the lookout for the man described and now known as JK.

For the Los Angeles Police Department, a case of identity struck close to home. With frustrating regularity, appearing on television news programs was a man who always wore a mask and called himself the "Masked Marvel," claiming to be a member of the LAPD and alleging that there were "death squads" in the police whose goal was to assassinate minority citizens. When analyzed psycholinguistically by Miron, the tapes provided a profile of the Masked Marvel, including evidence that he was, indeed, a cop. Using these conclusions, the LAPD was able to narrow its search for him from 7,000 members of the force to five. When the Masked Marvel ultimately resigned from the force, he admitted his identity publicly and confessed that the charges of death squads were false.

In the case of the kidnapping of newspaper heiress Patty Hearst by the Symbionese Liberation Army, Dr. Miron was able to deduce from SLA communications that its leader, calling himself "Cinque," was likely to turn out to be a known radical named Donald DeFreeze. Even more startling, however, was Professor Miron's prediction that Hearst would join the SLA and commit some criminal acts with them. (She did, assisting in a bank robbery.) All of this would come to a violent end, Miron forecast, based on his analysis that DeFreeze and his gang were suicidal and if trapped would choose to die in a shootout rather than surrender. All of this happened on May 17, 1974, when DeFreeze and five SLA members fought the Los Angeles police and the FBI, dying when the house where they were holed up caught fire and burned down.

By studying the SLA, the Special Operations and Research Unit at the FBI Academy produced a psychological profile of a terrorist organization that became a basis for continuing studies by specialists of the NCAVC in arson, bombings, threat analysis, and assassinations. In "A Terrorist Psychosocial Profile: Past and Present," published in the *FBI Law Enforcement Bulletin* in 1988, Special Agent Thomas Strentz noted that the nature of terrorism had changed since the heyday of the SLA: "Terrorism is different today than it was yesterday, and it will, like every dynamic organization, change again by tomorrow. Terrorists learn new tactics and adapt and adjust to countermeasures developed by governments or airlines, or they die and are replaced by more dynamic individuals."

The "Terrorist Organization Profile" constructed by the FBI found that all groups regardless of their ideological slant include individuals with three different personalities: the leader, the opportunist, and the idealist. In hostage-taking situations, the person or persons captured and held could be expected to encounter all three. The activist operator (opportunist) seizes the hostage, the leader interrogates, and the idealists guard and feed. Of these three individuals, the one most likely to change is the idealist, as so many of the "radicals" of the 1960s who matured to become the "yuppies" of the 1980s proved. The message for law enforcement was clear. Don't focus efforts toward the arrest, incarceration, and interrogation of the idealist, who knows little and will be reluctant to betray his idealism. Similarly, the leader will be equally resistant to pressure. It's in the opportunist that the best chance for success lies. Being nobody's friend and out for himself, he is most likely to open up and spill secrets. Indeed, that is exactly what has happened in cases in which terrorists have been captured in Europe and the Middle East; the "soldiers" talked, providing valuable intelligence on their organizations.

The study of terrorists was not limited to the left of the political spectrum. The right wing was also analyzed. Except for the motivating ideology, the profile of the leader of a leftist terrorist group operating in the Middle East was found not to differ much from the leader of a right-wing group in the United States. Each was male. The leftist had no specific religion, while the right-winger was Protestant. Both had

been to college. Age was thirty to fifty or more. Middle-class, urban/
sophisticated, and possessing high verbal skills, each had a strong
personality and was well trained in terror tactics carried out with a
compulsion for perfection.

"The radical left enjoys the planning operations," Strentz noted.
"Those on the radical right express their fantasies of power and control
through their collection of great caches of weapons. They tend to plan
less and shoot more." But the threat was not so much in what they
did, he concluded, as in the perception they created. What the FBI's
analysis of terrorism demonstrated was that Lenin was right when he
taught, "Terrorism is theater."

Terrorists were a concern in the United States, Strentz pointed
out, because of their potential rather than their actual performance,
for as the crime statistics demonstrated, it was not terrorists on the
loose that kept American law enforcement busy but murderers such as
the prolific message-writer and serial killer who had been plaguing the
San Francisco area since the late 1960s and calling himself "Zodiac."

On the basis of nineteen of Zodiac's letters shown to Dr. Murray
Miron when police called upon him for assistance in 1974, Zodiac
was profiled as a Caucasian unmarried male in his twenties with some
exposure to training in codes and cryptology. Not much of a reader, a
loner, quiet and unprepossessing in his disposition, he liked TV shows
and movies. Magical thinking fascinated him. He showed narcissistic
infantilism typical of schizophrenics. He needed to be in control and
would shun the inhibiting effects of alcohol by not drinking. Detecting
a tone of moralism in a 1974-dated letter, Miron surmised that Zodiac
might kill himself or just stop his activities because he would burn out
as he got older. (The last suspected Zodiac attack occurred in 1981.)

Enthusiastic about psycholinguistics and faced with the mounting
problem of those who used threatening behavior in their criminal and
terroristic endeavors, the NCAVC committed itself in coordination
with other FBI units to a Threat Analysis Project with implications
reaching into cases of arson, bombings, and the intimidation of and
retaliation against witnesses in narcotics investigations and prosecutions.

From what was learned from the messages provided by the criminals
who felt compelled to communicate, it was possible for law enforce-

ment to open direct or indirect dialogues in the hope of enticing the criminal into a trap. Known as "pro-active," it's a controversial tactic that has by no means been proved flawless. Using the pro-active approach depended first upon development of a criminal personality profile. If the portrait that emerged was one of a criminal who seemed jumpy or under a great deal of stress as a result of his crimes, going pro-active might be advised. This most often required involving the news media—generally without the press's awareness that manipulation was taking place. Eager to have a follow-up story or a new angle, reporters and editors can be rather easily seduced into running an item that they have no way of knowing is a pro-active device, a trick. Just such a ploy was used by Sherlock Holmes in *The Adventure of the Six Napoleons* as the sleuth of Baker Street contrived to feed a fake story to journalist Horace Harker. When the trick worked, Holmes quipped to his faithful companion and biographer Dr. John Watson, "The Press, Watson, is a most valuable institution, if you only know how to use it."

Whether the pro-active technique actually results in the arrest of the criminal, it can be an effective means by which to collect evidence for use at trial. As in the case of Son of Sam, in which David Berkowitz reacted to "insulting" comments on television news broadcasts by the detective in charge of the investigation by writing a chastising letter, a response holds out the prospect that information will be inadvertently provided that will lead to capture or that the criminal will blunder.

During a baffling series of assaults on men in New York City in 1990, the pro-active approach was tried along with many other tactics, as the NYPD, led by the same detective whose appearance on the TV news stirred the ire of Son of Sam and impelled him to write an outraged but revealing letter, went after New York's own version of an astrology-oriented Zodiac Killer.

TWELVE

"You Know My Methods"

*I*f you were in charge of casting a movie about reporters, you'd hire Jerry Nachman without a moment's hesitation even if he didn't have a couple of decades behind him as one of the sharpest journalists in a "naked city" that an earlier-day newshound, Mark Hellinger, found brimming with eight million stories. Built like a keg of nails, Nachman had covered all the things that people did that were newsworthy as he pounded beats for radio and TV news departments and newspapers. He'd bossed a few newsrooms as well, and now, in the summer of 1990, he was editor of the *New York Post* and holding in his hands a most peculiar letter:

> This is the *Zodiac* the twelve sign
> will die when the belts in the heaven
> are seen
> the *first sign* is dead on march 8 1990 1:45 AM
> white man with cane shoot on the back in street
> the *second sign* is dead on march 29 1990 2:57 AM
> white man with black coat shoot in side front of house
> the *third sign* is dead on May 31 1990 2:04 am
> white old man with can shoot   *Faust*
> in front of house
> no more games pigs
> all shoot in *Brooklyn* with .380 RNL or 9mm
>   no grooves on bullet

Emblazoned on the note were drawings of the cross hairs of a gunsight and a circle segmented with three pielike wedges each of which bore a symbol of a sign of the Zodiac: Scorpio, Gemini, and Taurus (these would be found to correspond to the birthdates of the men "Zodiac" claimed to have killed).

For as long as Nachman had been prowling the streets of New York digging up news stories, Joseph Borrelli had been a member of the New York Police Department. Having risen in the ranks of "the finest" to carry the gold shield of a detective, he'd seen plenty of Nachman during the Son of Sam reign of terror in the mid-seventies when, then age fifty and a captain, he was the commanding officer of the Manhattan D.A. Squad. Now he was chief of detectives.

"I don't know what we have yet," he said when shown the letter to the *Post*. "If we have a person going around shooting people, I'm worried. We're obviously dealing with someone seeking publicity."

The letter which Nachman had turned over to Borrelli seemed to be, in the words of the immortal baseball player Yogi Berra, "*déjà vu* all over again." Was it Son of Sam all over again? Might there now be a stream of taunting letters sent to the news media and to the police from Zodiac? And more attacks? Killings? Was it possible that the writer of this note was the same Zodiac who'd started on a murder spree in California twenty years ago only to drop out of sight a decade past? Had that Zodiac settled in New York?

First things first! Was any of what Zodiac claimed in the note true? To an extent, yes, police found out. Records showed that three men fitting the descriptions in the note had been shot on the dates and times indicated, but the sender of the note was also wrong: although each had been shot as claimed, none had been killed.

Confirmation that the writer of the note to the *Post* and an identical one mailed to the CBS-TV program *60 Minutes* was the person who'd shot two of the men in the East New York section of Brooklyn and the third in nearby Woodhaven, Queens, came with the discovery in a case file of a message that had been left beside the body of the third victim. "This is the Zodiac," it said in the same blocky lettering. "The belts in the heaven" were also mentioned. At the time, the note's meaning and significance could not be known. "To anybody who reads it, it's scary," Borrelli said to the *Post*. "And the one that you got is even worse."

With the contents of Zodiac's letter verified, Nachman's paper broke the story with a full front page featuring a reproduction of the letter, thus announcing to already crime-weary citizens of New York on June 19 in big, bold, black letters that they had a "shooter" in their midst who'd given himself the task of killing one person for each of the twelve astrological signs and assigned to himself the snappy headline-fitting name "Zodiac."

That evening, the news programs of the city's television stations ran with the story as only local TV could—a mixture of fact and fright in which excerpts from Borrelli's news conference were interlaced with interviews of scared citizens in the area of the shootings and ominous-sounding narrations by reporters and anchorpeople. Comparing the new Zodiac with the West Coast's variety and recalling the rampages of Son of Sam, they stirred the specter of a dawn of a new reign of terror in America's premier city.

In his remarks behind a forest of news microphones, Borrelli again expressed the view that Zodiac was looking for publicity. "In the first two shootings there was no publicity, no record of it," he said. "The third shooting, he left a note so he could identify himself and then the letters were sent to the news media."

If headlines and TV coverage were what Zodiac sought, he got them in spades.

That sort of individual was nothing new to Borrelli, who'd become a favorite correspondent of Son of Sam when Borrelli was running the task force set up to catch the .44-caliber killer.

So far in the Zodiac case, no one had been killed, but there was no doubt in anyone's mind, including Zodiac's, that homicide had been intended. With the prevention of Zodiac's success his immediate goal, Borrelli returned to the techniques used in the hunt for Son of Sam, beginning with the organization of a task force of the city's best detectives. Rather than setting up the group in the massive pile of red brick at One Police Plaza that was headquarters of the NYPD in the middle of the helter-skelter jumble of atherosclerotic streets feeding the heart of New York City's government center in Lower Manhattan, the Zodiac Task Force assembled, safe from nosy reporters, in the serenity of an unoccupied portion of the Brooklyn Navy Yard not very far from the scenes of the shootings.

The only hard evidence available to them aside from Zodiac's letters concerned the weapon he'd used in the three attacks. The firearm was likely to be, according to ballistics experts, either a low-quality gun like a "Saturday-night special" or a homemade device, commonly called a "zip gun." The bullets, however, had been professionally made—.380 and 9mm round-nose lead (RNL)—and their only purpose was to do serious harm. That Zodiac knew something about guns and ammo was evident from his mention of bullet calibers, "no grooves," and "RNL" in his notes.

The detectives also had a description of Zodiac given by one of his victims: a black man, thirty to thirty-five years of age, six feet tall and 180 pounds, with a mustache and beard, wearing dark clothes and with an unkempt appearance. While better than nothing, it happened to fit a lot of men in New York, and the police artist's sketch of the suspect even bore a close resemblance to the Reverend Al Sharpton, a controversial activist. As the sketch circulated, scores of men were questioned—one of them so frequently that the police had to give him a letter certifying he was not Zodiac.

What the task force did not have was an insight into the personality of Zodiac. To begin acquiring that, they welcomed back from an overseas business trip the NYPD's resident expert on personality profiling of criminals. A veteran of homicide cases, broad-shouldered, bulldog-like Detective Ray Pierce was a star graduate of the NCAVC Police Fellowship program, Class of 1985.

Mandated by FBI Director William H. Webster to provide intensive training on the behavioral analysis of violent crime to the nation's law enforcement community, the training program in criminal profiling got off the ground when Roger Depue of the BSU surveyed several large police agencies to find out if there might be an interest in such a training program. The favorable response was overwhelming, and the program was established in 1983. The first fellowship was awarded in

1984 to Detective Sam Bowerman of the Baltimore County Police Department. In 1985, four fellows were picked, including Pierce.

The ten-month course was made available at no cost to the officers or their agencies (other than the salaries and benefits which the officers got anyway). The fellows were chosen on the basis of the size of their police agency (the number of sworn officers), the size of the population served by the agency, the rate of violent crime in that area, and the agency's willingness to allow the one chosen from its ranks to provide behavioral science assistance to neighboring departments. As to students, a proposed fellow had to be a sworn officer with an outstanding record of investigative experience, at least three years of which were devoted to major cases. Good physical conditioning was expected. A bachelor's degree, preferably in behavioral sciences, was required. An ability to write well and a proven record of success in public speaking were on the list of criteria, because the graduates would have to agree to conduct classes in crime analysis for their colleagues and prepare profiles for at least three years after completion of the course.

Centered at the FBI Training Academy at Quantico, Virginia, the course began with three months of intensive training and academic programs designed to prepare the students for the next phase—a kind of "basic training" in the "art" and science of criminal behavior. The classes were conducted at the academy and at the University of Virginia, the Armed Forces Institute of Pathology, and various police academies. Content: homicide and rape investigation, the sexual exploitation of children, abnormal psychology, equivocal death evaluation, and criminal personality profiling. The second phase was practical application of what they'd learned, with an emphasis on analyzing and consulting on ongoing and unsolved crimes of violence. These were hands-on exercises alongside NCAVC profilers—six to nine months of immersion in the techniques of profiling. Working in groups, the students operated in the manner of "think tanks" in tackling problems, often with the guidance of Dr. James Luke, consulting forensic pathologist for the NCAVC. Six fellows took part in 1986, four in 1987, five in 1988, and six in 1989.

As Ray Pierce returned from an assignment abroad to his fifth-floor office at One Police Plaza at the beginning of the Zodiac case, among the mementoes of his police career was a photo of him and the other 1984–87 Police Fellowship recipients in the December 1986 issue of the *FBI Law Enforcement Bulletin*, accompanying an article on the NCAVC training program written by its manager, Roy Hazelwood. Now, for the first time since Pierce had completed the course, he was being called upon to put all that he'd learned to the test in what appeared to be a puzzle whose resolution might lie in the stars.

How much did Zodiac really know about astrology? Not very much, replied recognized experts in the field. His knowledge was no more profound than what might be learned from the most cursory books on the subject. Attempting to "read" Zodiac's own celestial pattern, one expert ventured that it was "very likely" the Zodiac would make two attempts soon.

While a crash course in horoscopes was definitely in the future for Pierce and the fifty members of the Zodiac Task Force settling into quarters at the Navy Yard, so were the wizardries of the Computer Age. Almost instantly, technicians and installers were at work setting up data banks. Declaring to Richard D. Lyons of the *New York Times* that "we have to educate ourselves" about astrology, Police Commissioner Lee Brown was not overlooking the marvels of high tech. Nor was Chief of Detectives Borrelli. Both had firsthand experience with computers as a tool in this type of case. Borrelli had used them effectively in the Son of Sam case. Brown had their help when he was chief of police in Atlanta during the Child Murders. For the newly appointed commissioner who'd been plucked from the job of commissioner of police in Houston, Texas, by freshly elected Mayor David Dinkins, the Zodiac case shaped up as his first real challenge as head of a police force whose rank and file were already harboring grave doubts about his abilities and the capabilities of the city's first black mayor in coping with the city's epidemic of violent crime.

Along with the keyboards, video display terminals, and data banks of the computers, the task force was providing itself with old-fashioned devices, starting with huge maps of the city with the scenes of Zodiac's crimes pinpointed. "Seek ye patterns," went an old police adage. What were Zodiac's patterns?

In devising a criminal personality profile, the researchers of the

NCAVC had learned and taught, one always begins with the victims. In choosing his, Zodiac immediately demonstrated that he was not going to fit neatly into an "off-the-shelf" profile. To begin with, his victims were men, whereas most men committing serial violent crime picked women as victims. The males chosen by Zodiac had also been either old or infirm or perceived that way.

How were they assaulted? The fifty-year-old cane-using man who'd been shot on March 8 said, "He was across the street from me and crossed to meet me." Mario Orozco said Zodiac had worn a brown ski mask and gloves. "He just put a gun against my back and then, bang. He shot me in the spine," he said. "Then he reached down and held the gun to my face for about one or two minutes. He said nothing to me. I froze, because I thought he was going to kill me." When Orozco shouted for help, Zodiac walked away wordlessly.

The second of the victims was shot while walking away from a subway exit. Jermaine Montenesdro, age thirty-four, had been drinking and staggered a bit, suggesting infirmity.

Number three was seventy-seven-year-old Joseph Proce, approached by a man who asked, "You got a dollar?" and, in the next instant, shot.

Most amazing about these attacks was that the birthdays of these men coincided with the astrological signs attributed to them in Zodiac's letters. None of the victims recalled telling the attacker his birthdate. How did Zodiac know them? From day one of Pierce's work, that would be the enduring unanswered question hanging over him and the task force.

Was New York's Zodiac the one who plagued the San Francisco area? To check that out, the New Yorkers requested the complete file on the never-arrested West Coast Zodiac. Conclusion after comparing the facts: New York's Zodiac was not San Francisco's. This fact was trumpeted by Jerry Nachman's *Post*.

By mid-June, Ray Pierce was ready to provide his profile of the personality of the object of the task force's efforts. It seemed safe to assume that Zodiac would have one thing in common with nearly all violent serial criminals: childhood roots in a broken, fatherless home. His attacks demonstrated that he'd done a lot of planning, so, obviously, he was a cunning and careful individual, but the fact that he was seeking publicity for his crimes showed that he was likely to be an underachiever in his everyday world. Because of that, all his jobs would be tedious and repetitious. That he struck at night pointed toward one of the traditional night-owl jobs, perhaps a night watchman or a cleaning man. Because he'd waited in hiding for his opportunity to shoot the men whose "sign" he'd chosen, he was quite patient and probably enjoyed tedium—the kind of guy who could sit and watch the sunset for four or five hours. He would prefer to live by himself. He used the subway to get around (he'd followed his first two victims from the train before shooting them), so he was not likely to have a car. That he chose not to assault children and women pointed to a certain sensitivity. Women were likely to be reminders of his mother. His ease of movement and escape indicated that he'd be a resident of the area where he carried out his crimes.

Because an analysis of Zodiac's pattern indicated that his attacks had been carried out at either twenty-one-day intervals or a combination of twenty-one-day periods, the police and the people of the city braced themselves for what might occur on Friday, June 21, the start of the astrological sign of Cancer. Expecting a fresh attack where the others had taken place, hundreds of police flooded the area.

Zodiac struck as expected, but his fourth assault broke a part of his usual pattern. This victim was a homeless man sleeping in Central Park, miles away from the area of the first three shootings. His astrological sign was Cancer. That it was Zodiac who'd shot him and not a copycat was proved by analysis of a new note left under a rock beside his wounded fourth victim. "This opens up a whole new Pandora's box," said Chief Borrelli in frustration. "Now we've got the whole city to be looking at."

The day after the Central Park shooting, Zodiac demonstrated a classic behavior of the serial killer. He revealed that he was following the reporting of his exploits in the press by firing off an outraged letter to the *Post*:

This is the *Zodiac* I have seen the Post and you say the note sent to the Post not similar to any of the San Francisco Zodiac letters

you are wrong the hand writing look different it is one of the
same *Zodiac one Zodiac*

At the end of the note, he claimed responsibility for the fourth
shooting:

Fourth sign dead shoot in Central Park white man sleeping on
bench with little black dog shoot in chest

This occurred, he wrote correctly, on June 21, 1990, at 3:52 in the
morning. But he got the man's race wrong; the victim was a black
man. Because his previous victims were white or Hispanic, the
Central Park victim may have been attacked in error or simply because
Zodiac could find no one else.

Three days after the Central Park assault, Zodiac became a killer
when his third victim, Joseph Proce, died of his wounds.

"Zodiac jitters have gripped the city," wrote *Post* reporters Anne E.
Murray and Marsha Kranes. "The police, newspapers and radio and
TV stations have been besieged by phone callers eager to talk about
the Zodiac Killer—offering their tips, theories, fears and suggestions."
One task force investigator grumbled, "People are going crazy over
this." Chief Borrelli sighed, "We've had about a thousand suggestions
about where we should be looking. We're investigating every lead."

Coincidental with Zodiac, another serial attacker was carrying out
assaults on women in midtown Manhattan. His weapons were homemade darts. Pins or needles with paper wings launched through some
kind of blowgun, they were aimed at the buttocks of young women who
appeared to be dressed in business-type clothing. That this nettlesome
character might be Zodiac could not be overlooked, but when an arrest
was made on July 12 of a young black man working as a midtown
messenger, the individual whom Channel 7 news producer Ed Rickards
had named "Dart Man" was stricken from the list of Zodiac suspects.

Using their twenty-one-day reckoning, the task force calculated that
Zodiac would strike for a fifth time on Thursday, July 12. In anticipa-
tion, the NYPD inundated the city with cops. A reporter asked if

Borrelli thought Zodiac would appear on that rainy night. "I have no friggin' idea," grumbled the chief of detectives.

On the eve of the expected reappearance of Zodiac, the police appeared to be trying a bit of "pro-active" psychology by telling the news media that because Zodiac was known to use the subways in making his escapes, at the first sign of a new attack the entire city subway system would be shut down and searched. Whether this information got to Zodiac and caused him to cancel his plans could not be known at the time, but that night the Zodiac did not put in an appearance.

When he didn't show at the next twenty-one-day interval, the second of August, the men and women of the Zodiac "Operation Watchdog" Task Force fixed their eyes on the calendar on the wall of their Brooklyn Navy Yard headquarters, counted off multiples of twenty-one, and pressed on.

Meanwhile, they were soliciting the help of Dr. Murray Miron in deciphering Zodiac's letters. Although presented with far fewer examples of the latter-day Zodiac's writing than had been available to him from the San Francisco Zodiac or Son of Sam, Miron detected some "scholarly achievement" on the part of the New Yorker as demonstrated by Latin and French phrases in the letter left at the scene of the shooting in Central Park. "It's very difficult to pretend to be stupid when you're intelligent and vice versa," said Miron. "At some point the writer makes a slip somewhere and reveals he is pretending."

In running Zodiac's words and phrases through the psycholinguistic computers, Miron found no files to assist the New York police in their manhunt as the next likely date for a strike by Zodiac approached—Thursday, August 23, 1990, the last day in the astrological sign of Leo.

Dispersed across the city, the police again waited through the night.

Zodiac disappointed them.

So long as he remained active, the odds of his being caught increased, but weeks had passed since his last attack, and now the police, facing a horrifying upsurge in murders that were not the work of serial killers, began cutting back on the number of investigators assigned to Zodiac. The leads were few. Tips weren't coming in. The trail was cold. By October, it was frozen. The task force was disbanded.

Of course, the case was not closed. Nor would it be. The only option for Ray Pierce and the others and their boss, Chief Borrelli, was to wait. Perhaps Zodiac was following the pattern of his West Coast predecessor by stopping the killings and disappearing. Maybe he was in jail for some other offense. He might be dead. But if he was just biding his time until he was compelled to shoot again, he'd find Pierce waiting. And if he surfaced again, he was bound to reveal himself by way of his behavior, and in doing so, he would be providing additional bits of the puzzle. This was a case of identity, and, as Sherlock Holmes said in an adventure with that title, "It has long been an axiom of mine that the little things are infinitely the most important."

That had been the central lesson of Pierce's NCAVC training program. Look for the little things, the symptoms. In *The Hound of the Baskervilles*, Sherlock Holmes's words might have been Roy Hazelwood's teaching a class of FBI Fellows at Quantico: "The very point which appears to complicate a case is, when duly considered and scientifically handled, the one which is most likely to elucidate it." And like Holmes speaking to Watson, Hazelwood and the others at NCAVC in effect said to the graduates of the Police Fellowship Program: "You know my methods—apply them!"

While Hazelwood and the others teaching profiling believed in the process, they were careful to warn their students not to make it the basis of their entire investigation. There was always the possibility of being wrong, as Hazelwood had been in a case in Georgia. Look for a man who came from a broken home, he told the local police. He would also be a high school dropout, holding a low-skill job, an habitué of honky-tonk bars, living far from the crime scene, and divorced. When the criminal was arrested, he was found to be a college graduate, a top executive, a nondrinker, living nearby, and happily married. "I keep that profile around," Hazelwood admitted, "as a reminder that we're still in the stage where profiling is an art rather than a science."

THIRTEEN

"We've Got a Problem Here"

What a day! What a weekend: the official celebration of the centennial of the Statue of Liberty with its rededication set to coincide with a four-day observance of the Fourth of July, 1986. The bright sun of a flawless sky glinted off the fresh gold leaf of the statue's brand-new torch and reflected brilliantly from the crisp white uniforms and jaunty round caps of the proud crew of the flagship of the armada arrayed in New York Harbor—the long, gray, graceful, glory- and history-laden battleship *Iowa*.

As ramrod-straight as he'd ever been portraying a youthful George Armstrong Custer in *They Died with Their Boots On* or in *Hellcats of the Navy*, Commander in Chief Ronald Reagan stood on the red-white-and-blue-bedecked reviewing platform constructed atop Gun Turret No. 1.

Looming above him were the three massive barrels of the 16-inch naval rifles of Turret No. 2.

At parade rest along the sides of the ship from bow to stern stood the 1,500 sailors in their dress whites as the great vessel glided down the Hudson River to take the salute of the fleet of warships, pleasure boats, dinghies, and elegantly masted and full-canvased tall ships all signaling, tooting their horns, and ringing their bells in the busy, churning waters of the great harbor and seaport that surrounded the gleaming, refurbished Miss Liberty, beckoning her welcome to tired, poor, and huddled masses as she had been for a hundred years.

On a day ripe with symbolism, the *Iowa* represented the fulfillment of Reagan's 1980 campaign pledge to reconstruct and revitalize the armed services and to create a 600-ship navy that would ensure that the United States was unchallenged on the high seas. A previous proposal to bring Iowa-class battleships out of mothballs in 1979 had been sunk by the personal opposition of the nuclear-navy man Jimmy Carter—a short-lived victory. To run the Navy Department in the stiffening of the nation's defense, Reagan chose John Lehman, a former naval aviator who had chaired the Republican Party's 1980 campaign committee on defense. Himself a battleship enthusiast, Lehman fought against often derisive and scornful opposition of powerful figures in the Congress who saw the big guns of the big ships as outmoded and anachronistic in the age of nuclear-tipped missiles, and who much preferred the money Reagan was spending on the military to go to the social programs traditionally favored by Congressional Democrats.

On the strength of a Republican Senate and the enhanced GOP rolls in the House of Representatives, the new administration won approval for bringing back the Iowa-class battleship *New Jersey* in the spring of 1981, and the ship was commissioned in December 1982. *Iowa* was next, brought into service with a commissioning ceremony on April 28, 1984, that was presided over by a veteran of naval service in World War II, Vice-President George Bush.

The building of the *Iowa* had been authorized by a war-wary Congress in 1938, and its keel was laid down two years later. The launching was at the Brooklyn Navy Yard on August 27, 1942, eight months after the Japanese attack on Pearl Harbor thrust America into a two-ocean war. After service in both hemispheres, *Iowa* was the radio communications ship during the surrender of the Japanese aboard the *Missouri*, another Iowa-class battlewagon.

In the Korean War, *Iowa* bombarded targets along the North Korean coast, lobbing its giant shells for the first time near Chaho on April 8, 1952. In a nine-day period it fired 549 main battery projectiles, and in an all-day shoot off Chongjin on May 25 it blasted its 16-inch guns 202 times in eleven hours with savage accuracy. By the end of 1952, four Iowa-class battleships had seen action in Korea and had demonstrated forcefully their great utility in a limited war in the atomic age. In the cruise book containing the comments of crew members during the Korean action, an *Iowa* sailor wrote: "There is no ship that sails the seven seas whose guns are mightier than ours."

The most powerful rifle ever mounted in an American ship, the 16"/50 gun was sixty-eight feet long, weighed 120 tons, and was capable of firing two shells, weighing 2,700 pounds each, per minute to a distance of 22.8 miles. Three of these enormously potent weapons were housed in each of the two forward turrets and the aft No. 3 turret. Designed by the Navy's Bureau of Ordnance along revolutionary lines, the triple-gunned firing platforms featured better protection, a lower silhouette, and more compartmentation than in earlier-vintage dreadnaughts. The new gun turrets also afforded enormously increased protection for the crew in the gun room and others working in the powder-handling magazine four decks below in the multitiered turret complex.

Designers also increased safety by devising a system of concentric rotating rings on the projectiles and a system of interlocks between the gunhouse and the magazine area, where the bags of powder used to fire the shells were stored and loaded onto hoists. Raised to the gunhouse level, five of the bags of powder were placed on a cradle equipped with a driving mechanism that thrust the propellant into the barrel of the gun and up against the shell. A crew of seventy-seven in the gunhouse and below in the powder-handling room was required to carry out these tasks in one of the most intricate and complicated weapon systems ever devised (the manual of operation totaled 500 pages). Yet in the three-war history of Iowa-class battleships there'd never been a fatal firing accident in either battle action or gunnery practice.

The first of the Iowas brought back on line under Reagan was the *New Jersey*, which was pressed into service off Lebanon on December 14, 1983. Two weeks short of the fortieth anniversary of her first battle, she fired eleven rounds of 16-inch ammunition against Syrian antiaircraft batteries that had downed a pair of Navy A-6 Intruders two days earlier. On February 8, 1984, she lobbed nearly 300 shells toward terrorist camps deep inland.

By the time the *Iowa* was ready to relieve *New Jersey*, the situation in Lebanon no longer required its deployment in that area of the world, so the ship steamed out for gunnery training at Vieques Island east of Puerto Rico. Then came exercises off Nicaragua. In September 1985, she joined a month-long NATO naval exercise called Ocean Safari. The training highlight of this mission was pulverizing an iceberg off Greenland with six 16-inch rounds.

Between these alternating sea exercises of varying lengths the ship was home-ported at Norfolk, Virginia, under the command of Captain Fred Moosally. At age forty-five he was a twenty-three-year veteran of the Navy who'd graduated from the Naval Academy in 1966 and now stood on the bridge of the ship that had won the Battenberg Cup in 1985 as the best all-around ship in the Atlantic Fleet. From her mast as she returned from sea exercises in late 1985 flew the coveted Battle "E" Efficiency pennant.

One of the crewmen who snapped a smart salute as he reported aboard for duty in January 1986 had been Kendall Truitt, a fair-haired, handsome teenager. Having enlisted in the Navy with the intention of going into nuclear electronics, he was disappointed at being dropped because of an insufficient grade average. Given a choice between duty on an aircraft carrier or a battleship, he chose the latter and was assigned to the *Iowa* with the expectation of being assigned to routine duties with the deck crew. But in a review of his record the Navy discerned qualifications suitable for a post in weapons. His assignments exposed him to all facets of the work in the gun room, the magazine, and the projectile decks. After two and a half years, he'd done it all, except being gun captain. Offered an opportunity to qualify as a gunner's mate, he took it.

Although he had the physical attractiveness to recommend him as a model for a Navy recruiting poster, the naturally quiet and retiring Truitt was not the boisterous, hell-for-leather, girl-in-every-port stereotype of a sailor. Nor was another *Iowa* crew member who befriended him—Clayton Michael Hartwig. At the age of twenty-four, Hartwig hailed from Ohio and was, in the words of his sister Kathy, "a loner, a quiet and shy, religious kid" who "wasn't your typical sailor." Rare among their *Iowa* shipmates, Clay and Ken were not drinkers and didn't care for carousing in nightspots. They spent time together, went to movies together, palled around together in overseas ports. "We didn't go out and get trashed," said Truitt. "We had a lot in common."

To the others on the ship, these best buddies and kindred spirits seemed rather odd. Some suspected they were homosexuals. An incident aboard ship which contributed to this was described later by Truitt as "the wrestling match." It happened when they were sharing the midnight-to-4:00 watch and Truitt, violating procedures, was taking a catnap. "Clay was military," he said of the incident. "He started hitting me a couple of times to keep me awake. We started wrestling. I had taken judo lessons and they teach you two ways to do each movement. I went to throw him down, but I held on to his collar so I would not bang his head. When I did this, he grabbed me and tried to flip me. About this time, two guys on the port side were walking there and shined the light on us and said, 'What are you guys doing?'"

What some crewmen believed they were doing was kissing. Though being thought of as gay apparently upset Hartwig, Truitt did not let the scuttlebutt about them worry him. "I knew it was not true," Truitt stated. "He knew it was not true. It didn't bother me. It bothered him a little more. Obviously, he didn't like people to talk about him."

An event that was said to have bothered Hartwig a great deal was Truitt getting married in December 1988 and not inviting Hartwig to the ceremony. Following the marriage, Hartwig seemed sulky and resentful and spoke to Truitt only when necessary in the line of duty.

The mission of the crew and officers during this time was to maintain a state of readiness that would permit a quick response should the international climate require one. Of all the world's hot spots in which the Navy could play an effective role, the Persian Gulf was at the top of the list. Since the outset of a war between Iraq and Iran, oil shipments through the vital waterway were always vulnerable. When attacks were launched on tankers, the United States responded by beefing up a naval presence nearby and by providing U.S. Navy ships as escorts. Dispatch of the *Iowa* into those troubled waters seemed imminent. Then word came down from Captain Moosally's bridge to prepare for a six-month cruise.

For the sailors, that meant square away your affairs, get your savings allotments in order, take care of your financial responsibilities. In pursuit of those goals, Hartwig went to the Navy Federal Credit Union across the street from the base to take out a savings allotment. In connection with it he was offered a life insurance policy at a nominal rate. Signing up, he listed his friend Ken Truitt as beneficiary of a $50,000 policy with a double-indemnity clause that would raise the value to $100,000 in the event of Hartwig's accidental death. He did not inform Truitt of the policy until they were well out to sea. "Hey, Ken," he said, "if I ever die you are going to be a rich man."

Truitt answered, "Ya, ya, ya, what are you talking about?" Surprised at what he was hearing and puzzled because Hartwig hadn't named his parents as the beneficiaries, he asked, "Isn't this a little weird?" Hartwig replied that it was something his father had done when he was in the Navy—naming a buddy in "servicemen's life insurance." Truitt recalled thinking, "He was twenty-four and I'm twenty. We're going to live forever."

In mid-April 1989, Captain Moosally brought the *Iowa* into position for gunnery exercises 300 miles north of Puerto Rico. Assignments for the gun room of Turret No. 2 had been made in March, but in the intervening period personnel changes had taken place, so shifts in manning were required. Because Turret No. 2's gun room crew was one man short, the man who was to be the cradle operator was moved into the position of powder hoist operator and Petty Officer Eric Lawrence, who was listed to be gun captain for his first shoot, was shifted to the hoist position. Brought in to replace him was a qualified gun captain—GMG2 Hartwig.

Kendall Truitt was stationed below in the magazine.

Turret No. 1 opened up first, firing four rounds of reduced-charge projectiles from the center and right guns before having a misfire in the left. Ordered to load, the crew in Turret No. 2 rammed D881 projectiles and five-bag charges into the left and right guns and closed the breeches. These were standard operating procedures followed since the Iowa-class battleships slid down the ways half a century earlier and sailed off to global war, a "police action" in Korea, an undeclared and unwon contest of wills in Vietnam, and action off the beaches of Beirut. From the depths of the magazine, an elevator lifted bulky silk bags of gunpowder. These bags being fed up to Hartwig's crew from Truitt's magazine had been loaded aboard the *Iowa* from open barges where they'd been stored for some time in hot weather. Packed in the form of grains that were either stacked (for full charges) or dumped (partial charges, such as on this occasion), five bags were used for each projectile. Closed on each end like the puckered tip of a hot dog, every bag had a black-powder ignition bag which had to be loaded facing the rear of the gun and fired either by percussion or more usually by electricity. Loaded onto a cradle, the bags were then pushed into the gun. During this process, the gun captain placed between the first two bags two lead foils that served as a de-coppering agent and helped clean the gun. The rammer fed the powder bags into the gun, shoving them against the already-loaded projectile. The breech was closed. The gun was fired.

So it had always been and so it was to have been as GMG2 Clayton Hartwig directed the process on April 19, but at about 9:53 A.M., Eric Lawrence's voice crackled over the communications system: "Hold up just a minute, we've got a problem here."

At 9:55, Turret No. 2 exploded.

Deep below in the magazine, Kendall Truitt and John Mullahy heard it, were rocked by it. They looked at each other in astonishment. Mullahy tried the phone to the gun room. No one answered. Hurrying to investigate, he and Truitt found powder bags on fire. Mullahy ordered everybody out of the magazine. There was a lot of smoke. They flooded the magazines and got the hell out.

By that time, bodies were being pulled from the gun room. Just by looking at them it was possible to deduce where they'd been at the time they were hit by a blast that came at them at 2,000 feet per second, with a force of 4,000 pounds per square inch and a temperature of 3,000 degrees Fahrenheit. Someone who had been sitting was ripped and scorched from the waist up. Eric Lawrence's wounds clearly showed that he'd been standing and wearing a communications headset. Clay Hartwig, leaning across the loading cradle and rammer and facing the open breech, had his legs blown off and arms ripped away in varying lengths, considerable damage to the trunk, head, and face but less wounding of the back. These injury patterns, along with the postmortem process called anthropometrics, blood grouping, the men's personal possessions and identity tags, and what ship records showed to be the personnel assigned to the gun room and their jobs would confirm who was where, doing what, when the explosion occurred. There were forty-seven bodies.

Five days later at Norfolk Naval Station, the man who'd had the happy assignment as Vice-President of officiating at the recommissioning of the *Iowa* was now President of the United States with the grim task of consoling the loved ones of those who'd died in Turret No. 2. With brimming eyes, George Bush said, "Your men are under a different command now, one that knows no rank, only love; knows no danger, only peace. May God bless them all."

Following the explosion, the Navy declared a moratorium on the firing of 16-inch guns by the four battleships in service (*Iowa, New Jersey, Wisconsin, Missouri*) even as the old debate over the place of battleships in the modern Navy erupted anew on Capitol Hill. In one of the more remarkable interpretations of recent history that must have come as surprise to those who'd served on battlewagons and those who'd been on the receiving end of 16-inch guns in the European and Pacific theaters of war, Senator James Exon, a Democrat from the landlocked state of Nebraska, asserted, "The battleship was obsolete in World War II."

Meanwhile, the Navy was starting an inquiry by appointing Rear Admiral Richard D. Milligan, a former battleship skipper, to search out the cause of the incident so that action could be taken to ensure that something like it couldn't happen again. He arrived aboard *Iowa* the day after the explosion and found a scene of utmost horror and devastation. He found that in fighting fire in the gun room and in the removal of the bodies a considerable amount of debris had been dumped overboard. This was not thought significant at the time, when the farthest thing from anyone's mind was the likelihood of a criminal investigation. "The turret was in pretty bad shape with hydraulic oil all over the place," Milligan reported. "When I first went down through the turret, which was still flooded at the lower level to some degree, it was rather a hazardous journey. It was very dangerous to move in the turret." Because the area contained materials that might easily ignite, Milligan ordered a further cleanup.

The most important indicator of what might have caused the explosion was buried deep in the barrel of the middle gun—the 16-inch projectile with its rotating band of soft copper. In the twenty microseconds of the firing of a shell, a narrow gap in the band closes. Microscopically examined, it might be a "snapshot" of what chemical processes were taking place in the firing chamber at the time of the explosion. It would take a technical assistance team headed by Captain Joseph D. Micelli a month to coax the shell from the rifling of the big gun.

All avenues that might provide a technical explanation for the blast were followed, including tests on the powder bags. They were rammed at normal speed and as fast as possible. They were crushed and ruptured. They were dropped, split open, and spilt. But nothing Micelli's experts could do could create an eruption.

While Micelli was making his technical probe, Milligan talked to witnesses aboard and associated with the ship and reviewed relevant documents relating to ship's personnel, conditions, and procedures that might have contributed to an accident. These included reviewing both shipboard safety and ordnance handling procedures, manning and crew training, powder stability, and mechanical issues. He found much that was troubling—the ship was undermanned, and there was some slackness in discipline—but nothing to even hint that the Turret No. 2 disaster was anything but a tragic mishap.

That perspective shifted dramatically on May 8 with the receipt of a letter from Katherine Kubicina, Clayton Hartwig's sister. Discussing the insurance policy taken out by Hartwig with Kendall Truitt as the sole beneficiary, she asked whether her parents could share in the $100,000.

For Milligan, Truitt's name rang a bell. Noted passingly in the review of his personnel record as part of the examination of all pertinent crew files had been an item about Truitt having been investigated by police in connection with an auto theft. At first look, the incident seemed inconsequential, but in the new light of Truitt's being the beneficiary of a life insurance policy taken out by the man who was gun captain of Turret No. 2 on the day of the explosion, and with as yet no plausible theory as to how the explosion could have been accidental, Admiral Milligan felt a responsibility to probe deeper into the personal relationship between Truitt and Hartwig. In order to follow that troubling thread, he called in the Naval Investigative Service (NIS).

Meeting on May 9 with NIS representatives, Milligan advised the NIS team that because no accidental cause for the explosion had been found, he now wanted a criminal investigation. NIS was to give it top priority. Indeed, it turned into one of the largest and most comprehensive efforts in NIS annals, involving more than one hundred agents, who gathered physical evidence such as the letters Hartwig had written to friends and family, the contents of his locker, and material from his room in his parents' home, and interviewed hundreds of individuals. On the list were Hartwig's family and acquaintances and *Iowa* crew members who knew both Hartwig and Truitt.

Almost immediately, intimations of a possible homosexual relationship between Hartwig and Truitt surfaced. Credible? If so, might there have been a falling-out between gay lovers? Had one of the men the type of personality capable of committing an act of vengeful murder? Murder-suicide? Suicide?

For reasons that could only be speculated upon, somebody with an insider's knowledge of the NIS investigation let this troublesome cat out of the bag. In Washington parlance, that's called a leak. In this instance, one leak was to NBC Television investigative reporter Brian Ross, who went on the air with a startling story of a possible sex-related crime, of jealousy and betrayal in Navy blue that may have led to a murderous plot that seemed to come straight from the pages of a lurid detective novel. Among others following up the story was *Newsweek* magazine, which published a full-page story on June 5 under the headline "Foul Play on the Iowa? A suspicious friendship."

The magazine also quoted an anonymous source: "A working theory is that it was a suicide, and there's a fair amount of evidence. Murder cannot be ruled out either, but it's far down the list." The news accounts based on the unidentified navy source noted that the Navy had traced the lethal explosion to the space between the first and second powder bags where the foil cleaning packets were customarily inserted before firing the big guns—a task carried out by the gun captain, in this instance, Hartwig. "What began as a routine probe into such problems as equipment malfunction or personnel failures aboard the *Iowa*," said *Newsweek*, "has turned into a bizarre criminal investigation."

FOURTEEN

An Equivocal Death

Was either GMG2 Clayton Hartwig or GMG3 Kendall Truitt the sort of person who could cause an explosion that would take his life, that of his shipmate, and anyone else unlucky enough to be inside the gun room of Turret No. 2 of the *Iowa* on April 19, 1989?

In sifting the data collected about both men, the probers of the Naval Investigative Service found considerably more testimony and circumstantial evidence pointing toward Hartwig than pointing toward Truitt, but to obtain a further evaluation of this material, the NIS turned to the FBI Behavioral Science Unit for psychological and personality profiles of Hartwig and Truitt.

In a meeting on May 23, photocopies of memo and steno pads which had passed between Hartwig and Truitt were provided, and on June 2, NIS handed over files relating to:

Mark D. Freeman, a shipmate and friend of both men
Mark S. Elkins, also a shipmate and friend
Edward J. Stark, shipmate and friend of Truitt
D. P. McElyea, friend of Hartwig during a port call by the *Iowa* at
   the U.S. Navy base at Guantanamo Bay, Cuba
John Glynn, shipmate and friend of Hartwig
John Mullahy, heroic crew member serving beside Truitt in the
   powder magazine at the time of the explosion

Adam Jason Zion, a survivor of Turret No. 2, friend of Truitt and
   former friend of Hartwig
Charlene Meter, who'd received numerous letters from Hartwig
Pam G. Hartman, friend of Hartwig
Angel Baker, friend of Hartwig
Michelle Poling, friend of Hartwig and recipient of many letters
   from him
Carol Truitt, Kendall Truitt's wife
Katherine Kubicina, Hartwig's sister
Brian Hoover, close high school friend of Hartwig

On June 15, NIS turned over to the BSU its file on another of
Hartwig's shipmates, David Smith, and a copy of a poem which had
been found tacked to a bulletin board on the *Iowa*. Believed to have
been placed there by Hartwig, its title was "Disposable Heroes." Part of
it read: "Sailor boy made of clay, the deceased, we grieve his death,
you coward, you servant, you patriot, more death means another
crow."
In all, more than 300 investigative dossiers and all other forensic
and photographic records were provided to Roy Hazelwood and Richard
Ault.
A lanky "Air Force brat" from California, Ault had opted not to go
for wings in the military but to enlist for four years in the Marine
Corps, including a year in Vietnam, before devoting twenty-plus years
to the FBI, fourteen of them in the BSU, where one of his interests
was foreign counterintelligence. In earning his Ph.D. in counseling
and development, he'd written a dissertation on stress and risk-taking.
He was currently in charge of the NCAVC research program, including a project on suicide. With his bushy mustache, casual clothing,
and relaxed manner, he was clearly of the new breed of FBI Special
Agent since J. Edgar Hoover's day and was somewhat of a contrast to
his partner.
Roy Hazelwood's attire ran more to the conservative business suit,
although his eyeglasses were of the aviator style. With an undergraduate degree in sociology and a master's in psychological counseling, he,
like Ault, was a member of the adjunct faculty at the University of

Virginia. He also was associated with the University of Pennsylvania, the National College of District Attorneys, and a long list of learned societies and professional law enforcement associations. For a year he'd held a fellowship with the Armed Forces Institute of Pathology, and he'd been appointed to the faculty of the Army Criminal Investigation Division School. His military service was spent in the Army military police (eleven years). An eighteen-year FBI veteran, he'd clocked a dozen years with the BSU and was recognized worldwide as an expert on interpersonal violence and violent death; he had lectured on the subject before the National Association of Medical Examiners, the International Association of Coroners and Medical Examiners, the American Academy of Psychiatry and the Law, the University of Virginia Institute of Psychiatry and the Law, and the Johns Hopkins University School of Medicine. Most recently, he'd been carrying out pioneering research into equivocal death, that is, deducing from all available evidence whether unexplained deaths had been the result of accidents, murders, suicides, or murder-suicide—exactly the kind of case the Navy had brought to Ault and him.

"We were advised by the naval authorities that they had ruled out the possibility of an accidental explosion," Hazelwood recalled. His and Ault's lack of experience in the technical aspects of such occurrences disqualified them from either supporting or disagreeing with the Navy opinion, he added, nor were they being asked to do so. In terms of the customary work of the BSU, they were being presented with all the pertinent information related to an equivocal death in which an accidental cause was excluded. Although the *Iowa* disaster had been an especially dramatic and tragic occurrence of national importance, the death of Clayton Hartwig was, from the BSU standpoint, like many other equivocal deaths the unit had examined. The question before Hazelwood and Ault was simple and straightforward: was it (1) a homicide on the part of Truitt as a means of collecting the $100,000 insurance, (2) a suicide-and-homicide attempt by Hartwig to wreak revenge on Truitt for getting married, or (3) a suicide by Hartwig because of a variety of personal reasons?

Immediately, Hazelwood and Ault discarded the murder option, because it made no sense. For Truitt to attempt the murder of Hartwig by arranging an explosion that was certain to kill all the men in the gun room and likely to kill everyone else in the turret, including Truitt himself, was beyond belief, and in any case there was no supporting data to suggest that Truitt wanted to kill Hartwig. Whether Hartwig had intended to murder Truitt or anyone else while taking his own life appeared to Hazelwood and Ault to be irrelevant, inasmuch as Hartwig was dead and so were forty-six others; it was beside the point whom he might have intended to murder.

The central issue was whether Hartwig intended suicide.

Was there any evidence to indicate that he might have harbored suicidal tendencies in his past and, especially, recently? Did he possess the psychological capability for it? Did he have the knowledge and the skills to cause the explosion in Turret No. 2? Was there any evidence to indicate that he was planning something? Were there clues to what he intended to achieve by the act of suicide?

In approaching a case of equivocal death, it was basic to address the three fundamental criteria that were explored in a murder case. Did the suspect have at the time of the deed motive, means, and opportunity? Did the material provided by the Navy add up to the conclusion that Clayton Hartwig *could have* and *probably did* kill himself and forty-six others by arranging for what would seem to be an accidental explosion in the middle gun of Turret No. 2?

As in all such profiling, Hazelwood and Ault went back to the beginning by reviewing Navy interviews with Hartwig's parents, siblings, and schoolmates for information on his childhood and teenage interests and activities and his personality as a boy and a youth. The youngest of three children, Hartwig was born twelve years after the second child. His two siblings were girls. According to one of them (Kathy), he'd spent a lot of time in his room and was considered to be a loner with no friends. He was also aloof and estranged from his family. His interests did not lie in athletics. Rather, he showed a great deal of interest in collecting combat-style knives. He had a smaller collection of guns and a large library of male adventure magazines such as *Soldier of Fortune* and books on World War II and warships.

Not until he was in the eleventh grade of a private school did he develop a close male friend, Brian Hoover, who was in the ninth grade, and a girl, Michelle Poling, a seventh-grader. According to the navy investigators who'd interviewed Hoover, one day Hoover had looked into Hartwig's room, had seen that Hartwig appeared to be running the blade of one of his knives across his wrist, and had snatched it away. Following the incident, Hartwig believed that Hoover had saved him from taking his life. To show his gratitude, he wrote a last will and testament naming Hoover as his heir. The Navy's NIS investigators found the document tucked between the pages of a Bible in Hartwig's room at his parents' house.

After joining the Navy, Hartwig made out a $200-a-month allotment to Hoover. These payments continued for a year and a half, when they were cut off, apparently because Hartwig had been told by another male friend that Hoover had had sex with Poling. Hartwig felt betrayed.

His next known close male friend was Daniel McElyea, a sailor whom he met at Guantanamo Bay. In December 1986 he met Kendall Truitt and maintained a close friendship with him until Truitt married, at which time their communication with each other was limited to what they had to say in line of duty.

In view of this apparent estrangement, why did Hartwig make Truitt beneficiary of a double-indemnity life insurance policy? To prove to Truitt—after Hartwig's death—that he loved him? ("Hey, Ken, if I ever die you are going to be a rich man.")

If Hartwig planned to take his own life, why not just jump off the ship? Arrange it in a way that harmed no one else? Might he have *wanted* to take others with him? If so, why? Perhaps sink the ship? Did he harbor a fantasy of a Viking death—sinking into the depths in a blazing vessel? Navy evidence contained reports of Hartwig's having had conversations with shipmates about suicide. The subject reportedly came up in a chat with a crewman only hours before the explosion.

How did Hartwig see himself? To seek that understanding, Hazelwood and Ault had a mountain of written material to go through. Hartwig had been a prolific letter-writer. Brian Hoover had gotten more than a thousand over three years. Several women had corresponded with Hartwig. In these missives Hazelwood and Ault detected feelings of rejection, alienation, and threatening pressure (one of the women wrote to him that she expected sexual relations with him after his return from sea duty; was that a powerful and perhaps threatening message for one who'd apparently been asexual all his life?).

"As a young adult, Hartwig was reticent in close personal relationships with either men or women, preferring to utilize letters and notes for intimate communications," Hazelwood reported. "His letters reflect a great deal of egocentricity, and he described himself as being shy. In the Navy, he was described as not sufficiently aggressive to be a good leader, immature, and lacking in other leadership skills. He had low self-esteem and was unable to verbally express his emotions."

Poring over the results of the NIS investigation into the life of Hartwig, Hazelwood and Ault discerned a troubled young man who was dissatisfied with his life as he lived it. He often expressed a desire to be a law enforcement officer or FBI agent or voiced expectations of being given an important assignment in the Navy that would station him in London. He told shipmates and others that he was looking toward this change of duty after the training cruise, but, in fact, no such assignment appeared likely in his future. Was Hartwig fantasizing himself in positions of power and prestige? Did he think that a job in the Navy that many would consider glamorous and exciting—a gun captain on one of the greatest warships ever built—was beneath him?

Getting off the *Iowa* seemed to be an important goal to him. "He disliked the ship, and once referred to it as a 'damn pig,'" Hazelwood said. "He also disliked the ship's previous captain. He had been the object of ridicule and rejection by many of the shipmates who knew him." He had been before a captain's mast and been reduced one grade. He was also upset about not receiving an achievement medal and stated that the individual who had attained the medal got it for making chocolate-chip cookies. He'd resented the rumors and scuttlebutt about him being gay, about him and Truitt being lovers.

Then he had the falling-out with Truitt. "It seems to me my world is changing around me," he wrote in a letter eleven days before the explosion that killed him. "I have lost friends who are closest to me." He griped that every time he turned around, there was more shocking news for him. Furthermore, his enlistment was up; he would have to decide whether to stay in the Navy.

In the opinion of Hazelwood and Ault, because of all these stresses, Hartwig felt he had good reasons for not returning from the training cruise. But did he evidence thinking or any outward behavior that he was making plans not to return? Was Clay Hartwig *suicidal?* There'd been the incident with the knife that Brian Hoover attested to. But that had been a few years ago. Was there anything in the record about Hartwig's interest in the subject of suicide . . . recently? In NIS interviews were the words of a shipmate concerning a chat he and Hartwig had had about the shipmate's own fretful ruminations about suicide: "We came to the conclusion that the quickest way we had ever seen anybody die was by explosion. He just said he had imagined that he wouldn't feel a thing and he would never know it. He said he kind of knew what I was going through, because he had tried to commit suicide at one time, so we kept talking and talking. Then he confided in me that you know, he still thinks about it sometimes."

What about the idea of "going down with the ship," the death of a Viking? Among Hartwig's possessions, NIS agents had found an album of newspaper clippings concerning ship disasters during the 1979–80 period. He'd once checked out a book entitled *Glorious Ways to Die: Kamikaze Missions of Battleship "Yamamoto," April of 1945.* According to one *Iowa* shipmate, Hartwig had said he wanted to die in the line of duty and be buried at Arlington National Cemetery.

If all of this pointed to motive, did Clayton Hartwig have the ability to arrange what would appear to be an accidental explosion in the gun room in which he served as gun captain? In the conversation with the sailor about his desire to die in the line of duty, Hartwig was reportedly asked what would happen if an explosion occurred in the gun room. He answered that the blast would be confined to the room and that it would take only five pounds of pressure on the ignition pads of the powder bags to set them off.

According to the NIS, Hartwig's sister Kathy Kubicina had told them her brother had talked about what would happen if there was an explosion in the gun room, saying that no one would live to tell the story. The NIS said she also reported that in the summer of 1988 when her brother had visited home, he'd brought some explosives from the ship. She further advised that after his death, she went to his room and found in his typewriter a list of men permanently assigned to Turret No. 2.

In the NIS material were other data about Hartwig's familiarity with explosives. His friend Brian Hoover spoke of Hartwig's having told him that he'd made pipe bombs and blown up trees and that he and Hartwig had once made a Molotov cocktail and thrown it into a field. With a shipmate he'd discussed how to set off the powder bags by hitting them with a hammer. He also had a manual entitled *Improvised Munitions* and a small book on the subject of how to get even with someone. Kendall Truitt was on record as telling the NIS that Hartwig showed him how to make pipe bombs and other improvised explosives and assorted trip-wire devices. Another *Iowa* crewman had told the NIS investigators that in a glimpse at Hartwig's locker he'd seen off-the-shelf materials such as a timer that could be turned into a detonation device.

Did the weight of all this come down on Clayton Hartwig as a man who by some ingenious sleight of hand had placed a homemade explosive device between the silk powder bags as they were being loaded into the middle gun and thereby killed himself and forty-six shipmates? Did all the bits and pieces turned up by the NIS fit together into a jigsaw picture puzzle of a twenty-four-year-old loner in a sailor suit who'd reached a point in his life where he'd believed the only choice confronting him was to blow himself to pieces and perhaps the *Iowa* as well? And Ken Truitt?

The plain reality facing Hazelwood and Ault as they sat down together at Quantico to hash all this out, debate it, weigh it, ponder it, and write their report for the Navy was that no one could ever state with certainty that Hartwig deliberately caused the explosion. Only the men who were there had that answer, and they were dead. But it was possible to form an *opinion*. It was possible—indeed it was their duty—to give the Navy an answer based on all the data available to them and what they came to believe out of their years of training and experience in the examination of human behavior, especially criminal behavior.

Their answer was that Gunner's Mate Second Class Clayton Michael Hartwig was "a very troubled young man who had low self-esteem and coveted power and authority he felt he could not possess. The real and perceived rejections of significant others emotionally devastated him. This, combined with the inability to verbally express anger and faced with a multitude of stressors had he returned from the cruise, virtually ensured some type of reaction. In this case, in our opinion, it was a suicide. He did so in a place and manner designed to give him the recognition and respect that he felt was denied him."

Admiral Milligan signed off on the investigative report, which relied heavily on the FBI profile, and then forwarded it to the Commander, Naval Surface Force, U.S. Atlantic Fleet on July 15, 1989—although technical tests were still going on. On September 7, with the testing still not finished, Milligan stepped before an enormous battery of microphones and told reporters, "The explosion in center gun, Turret 20, U.S.S. *Iowa*, on 19 April 1989 resulted from a wrongful intentional act." He went on boldly, "Based on this investigative report and after full review of all Naval Investigative Service's reports to date, the wrongful intentional act that caused this incident was most probably committed by GMG2 Clayton M. Hartwig, USN."

In the salty words of an old Navy saying, the shit hit the fan.

Truitt called a news conference. "I think the Navy is at a loss," he asserted. "They are looking for scapegoats."

Outraged, too, were members of Hartwig's family. For the woman who'd triggered the investigation of Hartwig with her letter to Admiral Milligan, Kathy Kubicina, another letter was in order. This one went to Mary Rose Oakar, the feisty liberal Democrat who represented the Kubicinas and the other residents of the west side of Cleveland in the U.S. House of Representatives. First elected to the Congress in 1976, Oakar had a voting record that scored high among such liberal groups as the Americans for Democratic Action and the American Civil Liberties Union. On issues dear to the hearts of defense-oriented and anticommunist Reaganites in the House, she was almost uniformly opposed. She had voted to deny aid to the Contras in Nicaragua, to cancel the MX missile, and to support a nuclear freeze. She took a hard line and a dim view of increased military budgets and looked at the Navy's buildup (battleships included) with deep skepticism and trepidation. While she held no memberships on committees directly related to the subject of Kathy Kubicina's letter, she was an influential and resourceful member of Congress capable of opening doors.

Reaction to Admiral Milligan's announcement of the Navy's findings was not confined to Hartwig's family, Kendall Truitt, and Representative Oakar. The CBS-TV program 60 Minutes did a show to "set out to see whether the admiral was right in fingering Hartwig," in the words of correspondent Mike Wallace.

Having thus implied that the 60 Minutes staff had all the evidence in the case available to it in order to render a verdict and subtly telegraphed what the show's point of view was going to be in the choice of the pejorative word "fingering," Wallace proceeded to conduct his customary cut-and-slash, raised-eyebrows presentation in which Admiral Milligan was called upon to justify the Navy's report. "Do you think that the case that the Navy makes against Hartwig would be sufficient to obtain a criminal indictment against Clayton Hartwig?" asked Wallace for openers. Milligan answered affirmatively. His voice brimming with incredulity, Wallace said, "You do?"

Alone on the screen, Wallace then posed several rhetorical questions. What was Hartwig's motive? Did he have the opportunity to blow up the gun? What method did he employ? Was the explosion a criminal act at all, or was it an accident?"

Although Milligan answered Wallace generally, based on the Hazelwood/Ault profile and the NIS investigation, Wallace went on to present results of the 60 Minutes staff's "investigation" in the form of interviews with persons who'd found the Navy's report unacceptable. These included Truitt, who suggested the Navy was engaged in a coverup; John Mullahy, who spoke of Hartwig's looking forward to duty in London and Mullahy's belief that it would have been impossible for Hartwig to have placed a detonator between powder bags without provoking a struggle in the gun room or some commotion that Mullahy would have heard in his role as communicator between the magazine and the gun room; Iowa crewman David Smith, who described in unflattering terms the NIS investigators who had interviewed him; the widow of Iowa crewman Jack Thompson, who said her husband had told her that Turret No. 2 was a "potential death trap";

and Earl Hartwig, Clayton's father. Of him, Wallace asked, "What could be in it for the Navy to point the finger at Clay?"

"Four battleships that are on the line right now would be the main reason," answered Earl Hartwig.

"So you mean you believe it's just self-interest on the part of the Navy that wants to hold on to its battleships and they're willing to point the finger at Clayton Hartwig, if necessary, to save their battleships?" asked an astonished and troubled-looking Wallace.

"That's right," said Hartwig. As he saw it, if Iowa-class battleships were found to be defective, "I don't think the government would support an antiquated piece of equipment that may kill hundreds of other people down the line."

Was Clayton Hartwig the scapegoat? The fall guy? Was all of this a desperate ploy by the Navy to protect its battleships from members of Congress who would like nothing better than to scuttle the Reagan administration's defense buildup?

Near the conclusion of the 60 Minutes broadcast, Mary Rose Oakar told Wallace, "You have the most flimsy circumstantial, so-called evidence pinpointing this young man as having done this ill deed and he's not here to defend himself. It's the family against the United States Navy."

Not quite.

On September 12, 1989, she met with Admiral Milligan for a briefing on the investigation. She was impressed with "the thoroughness of its technical testing, its examination of personnel and operating procedures," but "nevertheless" found "several aspects" of the Iowa situation that caused her serious concern. These matters pertained to "material about the character and personality of Petty Officer Second Class Hartwig of Cleveland [that] appeared in the press in advance of the Navy's report in this matter," she wrote in a "Dear Nick" letter to Democratic Congressman Nicholas Mavroules of Massachusetts, chairman of the Armed Services Subcommittee on Investigations, immediately after meeting with Milligan. "Since some of this information could be considered adverse, it caused a great deal of anguish to the Hartwig family," she wrote, "particularly since the individual concerned was killed in the explosion and could not defend himself." In addition to her concerns about the press leak, she voiced alarm about the "circumstantial" nature of the Navy's evidence. These worries led her to request in her letter that Mavroules's subcommittee look into the entire affair.

In the Capitol Hill tradition of committee chairmen who never met a problem they didn't feel the need to hold hearings on, Mavroules announced an investigation.

On the other side of the Capitol Building in what members of the House prefer to call "the other body," Senator John Glenn, the hero-astronaut-turned-senator-turned-defeated-presidential-hopeful, requested of Senator Sam Nunn, chairman of the Senate Armed Services Committee, a parallel inquiry. Inevitably, both panels would be demanding to know how and why the disaster on the *Iowa* could have been the deed of a suicidal sailor. For the Navy, the FBI Behavioral Science Unit, and the NCAVC in general and Dick Ault and Roy Hazelwood in particular, this gathering of clouds of doubt over Capitol Hill was a harbinger of very heavy weather on the horizon.

FIFTEEN

*I*nquest on the *H*ill

*I*n the typical lingo found in government documents, the Navy Technical Support Team headed by Captain Joseph Micelli in its report to Admiral Milligan of the findings of its investigation into possible causes for the *Iowa* explosion stated, "Ignition by deliberate personnel action should not be discounted." In other words, someone in the gun room might have set off the blast on purpose. How? By placing an electronic detonation device within the powder bags as they were being loaded into the gun. Was there any evidence that anyone working in the gun room on April 19 may have had access to such a device? The NIS criminal investigators had testimony from a crewman that he'd seen such a device in Clayton Hartwig's locker. Based on the statement, the technical team evaluated the feasibility of placing a similar detonator between powder bags and found that it was possible to do so. A simulation of the manner in which it might have been done was made and videotaped.

The crucial question now was whether there was any physical evidence of foreign matter within Turret No. 2 and its gun that might be remnants of a detonating device. If such evidence was found and combined with the FBI psychological profile of Hartwig, that would amount to reasonable cause to believe that Hartwig was the cause of the disaster. Beginning on June 11, the Naval Surface Weapons Center conducted thirteen feasibility tests that demonstrated that compression and timer-activated devices of the kind that the NIS had in mind *could* cause an explosion like that of April 19.

Now the Navy asked the FBI Laboratory Explosives Unit to take a look at portions of the rotating bands associated with the shells that were fired by Iowa-class 16-inch guns. Two of these bands were known to have been involved in test detonations using timing devices, one was not, and the fourth band was a part of a rotating band from the center gun of the *Iowa*. The FBI tests found some 1,200 particles but could not determine whether any of those particles originated in a timing device without "additional scientific scrutiny."

The Navy decided to conduct further tests in its own labs and, in Admiral Milligan's words, "confirmed the FBI suggestion" that the device which the NIS suspected was used "did not cause the explosion." But there remained the presence of "unexplained foreign material present on the *Iowa* projectile." More tests were carried out in the hope of determining the nature of the foreign material. Results showed that the material was "unique to the *Iowa* projectile and its presence could not be duplicated by simple contamination such as steel wool or chemicals routinely located in the gun turrets." But the report indicated that some types of nonelectrical explosive devices would produce these foreign materials.

As two Capitol Hill investigations were being organized, Admiral Milligan found "nothing in the final Technical Team report that caused me to alter the opinions I expressed in my earlier investigative report," that is, that the explosion was not an accident and that the individual who "most probably" committed "the wrongful intentional act" that caused the blast was GMG2 Clayton Hartwig.

On October 26, House Investigations Subcommittee chairman Mavroules released information that the FBI labs had found "no trace elements" of an explosive device in the center gun of Turret No. 2. That same day, Milt Ahleric, FBI assistant director, Office of Public Affairs, confirmed that Bureau technicians had not discovered any evidence of a timing device. Navy spokesman Mark Baker stated, "The Navy is sure that foreign material was in that propellant charge."

In the meantime, the Navy had found itself on the defensive in the matter of the news leaks regarding the relationship between Hartwig and Truitt. Its response was a report dated October 6 from the Inspector General for the Department of Defense to Secretary of the Navy Lawrence H. Garrett III that absolved the NIS from charges that NIS had maligned Truitt. Inspector General June Gibbs Brown found the NIS probe to have been "thorough, complete, and expeditious" in covering all "logical investigative leads" that "required examining the backgrounds of persons closest to the explosion."

While this report was viewed in some quarters as a whitewash of the NIS on the matter of leaks, the House subcommittee that investigated the case ultimately concluded that the NIS investigation of the possibility of a homosexual relationship between Hartwig and Truitt had been justified and noted that the Defense Department's internal probe of the source of the news leaks showed they did not come from the NIS but from others higher up in the Navy who were briefed by the NIS. When those briefings were stopped, the leaks ended.

However, gushing from the corridors of Capitol Hill and pouring down the grand prospect of Pennsylvania Avenue to the headquarters of the FBI were intimations that the House and Senate investigators who soon would begin a public probe of the *Iowa* disaster already were privately persuaded that the Navy had botched the affair and was now hanging on to its position with the tenacity of a sailor grasping a lifeline in a hurricane. If there were any doubts that the hearings were going to be intensely adversarial in nature, the opening statement by subcommittee chairman Nicholas Mavroules on the morning of Tuesday, December 12, 1989, dispelled them. "What we have put together," he declared ominously, "is a substantially different picture from the one painted by the Navy."

That Roy Hazelwood and Dick Ault were going to be on the hot seat was also obvious in Mavroules's opening: "While the FBI's 'equivocal death analysis' is the linchpin document in concluding that Hartwig committed suicide and murder, witnesses . . . will portray a very different picture of Hartwig." Because of the "significance" of the subcommittee's findings regarding Clayton Hartwig's personality, he declared, a full day would be devoted to testimony on that issue alone.

No single witness addressing Hartwig's nature compelled more attention as he sat down to testify than Kendall Truitt. "I would just like to start off and say for the record," he began, "this is my opinion, that Clayton Michael Hartwig did not cause the explosion. I do not think he committed suicide."

Presently, Congressman Larry J. Hopkins of Kentucky peered across the space between himself and Truitt and got down to the nitty-gritty of the Trutt/Hartwig relationship. "I have a lot of sympathy for where you find yourself today," he said. "I look at you sitting there in your uniform. You could be on a poster anywhere for the United States Navy. I think some of the questions that have to be asked here are not very comfortable perhaps for any of us, but I think they need to be asked. Let me ask you, yes or no, do you consider yourself a celebrity?"

"No."

"Do you consider yourself a hero?"

"No."

"Are you a homosexual?"

"No."

Truitt and Clay Hartwig were "good friends, best of friends," Truitt went on. "I think Clay cared a lot. He had no brothers and I was kind of like a brother to him. I have two brothers. If this were the NIS [asking the question] I would say no, I don't think he loved me, but since it is you [Congressman Hopkins], I think he loved me as a brother, but nothing sexual or anything."

Hopkins was a former sailor himself. "I was an enlisted man," he said in tones sympathetic to Truitt. Not a whole lot of enlisted men came to testify before Congress, he pointed out. "All the generals and admirals who come in here didn't know me then [when he was an enlisted man]. They call me 'sir' now," he said. "Sometimes things have a way of reversing themselves." The former enlisted man explained that he had to ask Truitt about "the wrestling match" between Truitt and Hartwig when they were supposed to be on watch. Truitt told Hopkins he was outraged that the incident had been construed as possibly a homosexual act. "In other words," Hopkins interjected, "rather than what was being described as rolling around, you were scuffling, you were playing, in the vernacular of the ship, a little grab-ass."

"That's right," said Truitt. "I threw him down, and he threw me down."

"But no sexual moves, one on the other?"

"No."

Again, Truitt asserted his belief that the United States Navy was protecting itself. "I really believe this is a cover-up," he said. "I still can't believe the way they are doing this." Again and again in his testimony, Truitt expressed his conviction that the Navy had seized upon Hartwig as a means of diverting the attention of the nation from the Navy's shortcomings. And he saw himself as a victim. Asked if he had an explanation for why the Navy hadn't cited him as a hero for his actions following the gun-room explosion, he said, "I think the Navy is not too proud of me right now. They said I was gay. They said I was probably a suspect. They said a lot of things. Obviously, I have not just stood by and said, sure, you can say that about me. It is not true, and I am fighting it. With as many of the rumors and lies that have surfaced, my wife and I took it upon ourselves to go out and get as much publicity, if you will, to turn the heads of the people who have already been influenced."

Asked to explain why he'd not invited his friend Hartwig to his wedding, which was interpreted in the FBI profile of Hartwig as one of the causes of Hartwig's suicidal ideation, Truitt said that he knew Hartwig would not have attended if invited, so he saved a little money by not sending an invitation. "He did not especially care for my wife," he said. "He thought she was going to hurt me like my previous girlfriend did."

Chairman Mavroules asked Truitt if he believed that his marriage could have had such an adverse effect upon Hartwig that he would commit suicide. "No," said Truitt. "He would not have gone in the gun room and risked being caught. I don't think he could have built the detonator they are describing. If he really wanted to do it... he could have opened the can [of gun powder] and taken a Bic lighter and lit a bag of powder. There is one hundred percent success, and the whole ship would go."

On that point, Mavroules had a colloquy with Vice Admiral Joseph S. Donnell III, who'd approved Admiral Milligan's report concluding that Hartwig most probably caused the explosion. "What bothers me," Mavroules said, "is that you can point your finger when, indeed, there is that little chance that maybe it isn't so. I just think it's wrong."

With that tone established, the subcommittee reconvened at ten the next morning to take the testimony of Hazelwood and Ault, who were accompanied by FBI Assistant Director Anthony Daniels, who was in charge of the Training Academy, the entity of which the NCAVC and

BSU were part. Coming to the witness table, the three FBI men found themselves in an extraordinary—perhaps unprecedented—moment in the history of the Federal Bureau of Investigation. As they prepared to give their testimony, they knew that imemdiately following them to the very same chairs would be representatives of a panel of fourteen behavioral scientists who'd been engaged by the subcommittee to analyze the FBI equivocal death analysis and personality profile of Hartwig. That they would provide views different from those of Ault and Hazelwood was anticipated. Had these dozen psychologists and two psychiatrists reported substantial agreement with the FBI, they would not have been likely to be invited to take part in the proceedings. From the outset, it was quite clear that the hearings had been set up to challenge the Navy' findings in the *Iowa* investigation and to undermine the credibility of the "linchpin" of the Navy's report, the FBI profile of Hartwig. This was a radical departure from previous instances in which the FBI had been called to give testimony on the Hill. Heretofore, Special Agents of the FBI who were witnesses before Congressional panels were viewed as highly qualified experts whose work and judgments were accepted without challenge. If a member of the House or the Senate had a fight to pick with the FBI in public, it had been the top man, the FBI Director, who was called to answer, not the Special Agent.

Any doubt about the hostile tenor of the investigation was laid to rest immediately by the opening remarks of the chairman of the Armed Services Committee, Les Aspin of Wisconsin. "Given the serious defects in the Navy investigation that we have uncovered in our previous hearings," he stated darkly, referring to evidence presented the preceding Monday on the Navy's technical testing, "today's testimony becomes even more crucial to the Navy's case against Hartwig. If the psychological assessment compiled by the FBI is flawed, then exactly what is left with which to support its conclusions?"

With that opening salvo, Assistant Director Daniels and Special Agents Hazelwood and Ault might be forgiven if at that moment they were reminded of a passage in Lewis Carroll's *Alice in Wonderland*. "'I'll be judge, I'll be jury,' said cunning old Fury; 'I'll try the whole cause and condemn you to death.'"

After explanations of FBI procedures in equivocal death cases from

Daniels and Ault and a summary by Hazelwood of what they'd determined about Hartwig, the questioning began. Aspin wanted to know if they ever qualified their judgment. "I mean, how definitive do you have your judgments in these cases? Are you always as definitive as you are in this case?" he asked Hazelwood.

"Yes, sir."

"You feel you have to come down yes or no, is that right?"

"No, sir. We say yes, no, or we don't know."

"But there is no probably?"

"No, sir."

"Here is the statement," said an obviously dubious Aspin. "It is the opinion of Mr. Hazelwood and Dr. Ault that the victim, Clayton Hartwig, died as a result of his own actions, staging his death in the way that it would appear to be an accident. You don't give a judgment that says, well, probably he did it, or we think that the chances are that this is what happened or possibly, or on a scale of one to ten, we give this a possible six. It is none of that. It is either yes or no?"

"That is correct," answered Hazelwood. "One of your staff reviewed our previous equivocal death analysis [record]. He reviewed about fifteen; all of them were exactly like that."

"So you would come down yes or no," said Aspin.

"Yes, sir."

"I guess I am a little wary of that," Aspin declared. "It is nice, because I know that in a lot of other parts of law enforcement you get a lot of mush, and so I understand the desire to be definitive in these things. I worry a little about being able to be quite so definitive in a conclusion, especially when you are not being able to interview the prime suspect in this case, who is dead."

"We feel comfortable with that opinion," answered Hazelwood. "It can be used or discarded or discounted. That is simply our opinion."

Ault interjected, "Even if you could interview the principal [Hartwig], you would still only receive probables and maybes."

"You do not configure it as your job to put in qualifiers," said Aspin. "The world is full of qualifiers, and you come down yes or no."

"Yes, sir," said Ault.

Taking over the questioning, subcommittee chairman Mavroules was interested in knowing whether Ault and Hazelwood regarded the "average NIS agent" as "capable of eliciting meaningful responses in a clinical sense that would validate a psychological profile."

"We don't know what an average NIS agent is, sir," retorted Hazelwood.

"You had to take their word for it," said Mavroules testily. "How was the interview bias-controlled? How was the interviewer bias-controlled in NIS interviews?"

"It wasn't a research project," said a puzzled Ault, "and I don't have the foggiest idea."

"This is a criminal investigation, sir," added Hazelwood. "You are asking about bias controls, which refers to research."

Mavroules persisted. "How did you select the [interviews] that you base your decision on?"

"We looked at the whole process," explained Ault. "The conclusion was fairly easy to form and fairly unanimous. Not just among the two of us, but other members [of the BSU] who had been there for quite some time, and then we went back without regard for who had done the interviews or what kind of bias there may have been in the interviews [and] selected out the statements that supported what we were saying."

"An expert in forensic psychology has noted that the interviews with Hartwig's family and friends should have been conducted only by senior clinicians experienced in interviewing persons under stress," said Mavroules.

"Well, first of all, I certainly appreciate that wonderful academic approach to a practical problem," bristled Ault. "It is typical of what we find when we see people who have not had the experience of investigating either crime scenes, victims, criminals, and so forth in active, ongoing investigations. Second, in the real world, you just can't work that way with the NIS. So, we have to take the information as we get it."

How were Ault and Hazelwood able to base their opinion that Hartwig killed himself, asked Mavroules, when there was testimony from key witnesses such as his closest shipboard friends, Truitt, John Mullahy, and Daniel McElyea, that Hartwig was not suicidal?

"Sir, key witnesses in whose opinion?" snapped Hazelwood. "We have a lot of other witnesses who say exactly the opposite."

Admitting that "a lot of what you [Ault and Hazelwood] do is above me," Congressman Norman Sisisky of Virginia wanted to know if it was an official FBI opinion. "Yes, sir," answered Ault. "This is done by our unit. It has been done for fourteen years, and we stand by it."

Mavroules returned to the style of the NIS investigators whose interviews contributed substantially to the data from which Ault and Hazelwood derived their profile of Hartwig. "It all depends on how you conduct the interview," he suggested. "Are you an intimidator, and perhaps I am not?"

"You sound pretty intimidating to me," quipped Congressman Sisisky, adding a rare spark of levity.

In perhaps the most snide and insulting remark of the proceedings directed to the two longtime veterans of the FBI, who were holders of graduate degrees in behavioral psychology, Frank McCloskey, an Indiana Democrat, said that he didn't "doubt that you have great law enforcement experience, and I don't doubt your competence per se, although I would question maybe the scope of your conclusions, but it would seem to me that in many ways politicians, teachers, or people in the insurance business would have similar outstanding psychological skills. I don't know that that certifies them to make some of these judgments."

Did Hazelwood think "it is all that unusual for a person who works around explosives many hours a day to possibly think that he or she could die by explosives?" McCloskey asked.

"No, sir, but it is unusual for them to say 'I want to die in the line of duty,' not 'I may die,' not 'I am in danger of dying,' but 'I want to die in the line of duty,' to two different people. That is unusual, yes sir," replied Hazelwood.

Loftily, McCloskey asked if Hazelwood had been published in national journals on the subject of equivocal death.

"In the book that I wrote," answered one of the nation's leading authorities and researchers on equivocal death, "there is a chapter dedicated to equivocal deaths."

"That is not a national journal," sniffed McCloskey, adding, "I would love to have a copy of your book if we could. I will pay the market rate, no autographing."

Chairman Mavroules inquired why the FBI did not set aside the results of the NIS investigation and conduct one of its own. Assistant Director Daniels answered: "That would indicate that the NIS investigation was flawed, and we had no reason to believe it was flawed."

That the participants in the joint hearings before the Investigations Subcommittee and the House Defense Policy Panel of the Committee on Armed Services of the 101st Congress believed the FBI's profile and conclusions regarding GMG2 Hartwig were flawed had been made clear even before the hearings began. Weeks before, the committee had invited the American Psychological Association to select a panel of noted psychologists to provide input regarding the development of the FBI profile of Hartwig.

Their verdict was officially delivered shortly after Hazelwood and Ault had answered the last of the questions put to them by the subcommittee. While much was made in the news media of the views of the majority of the panel (ten out of fourteen) as presented in person to the subcommittee and in detailed written analyses of and dissents from the FBI's work, the essence of their contribution can be found in an on-the-record question from William T. Fleshman, Jr., a member of the staff of the Armed Services Committee, and APA panelist Dr. Norman G. Poythress, professor of psychology, American University.

MR. FLESHMAN: We have spent some time this afternoon talking or examining the procedure for conduct of a proper psychological autopsy, and we have certainly questioned the FBI's procedures. And I believe the conclusion most of you provided questioned the conclusion that the FBI reached. I am not sure how I am going to ask the question, but are you going as far as to say that based on what we reviewed, we do not believe Clayton Hartwig to have been a suicidal murderer?

DR. POYTHRESS: My answer would be couched in the manner that I think psychologists are able to answer that question, in relative probability terms. I think it a relatively low probability, but I can't dismiss it out of hand.

Flat-out assertions that Hartwig didn't kill himself and forty-six others on the *Iowa* were made by Dr. Robert P. Archer, Department of Psychiatry and Behavioral Sciences, Eastern Virginia Medical School; Dr. David Trachtenberg, Woodmont Psychiatric Associates, Bethesda, Maryland; and Dr. Alex B. Caldwell, president of Caldwell Report and associated with the University of California at Los Angeles. Also in dissent from the FBI's profile was Dr. Ronald S. Ebert, who was the one cited by Mavroules as having raised the propriety of interviews having been conducted by NIS criminal investigators rather than by senior clinicians, and therefore believed they were faulty and unreliable.

While the report on the hearings gave great weight to the dissents by this panel, an objective analysis of the reports they submitted reveals many points of agreement with the FBI profile or qualifications of their disagreements:

Dr. Alan L. Berman, Washington Psychological Center: "It is most reasonable, based on the preponderance of the evidence, to conclude that Hartwig sacrificed his own life in a planned suicide-mass homicide to accomplish a variety of ends."

Dr. Stanley L. Brodsky, professor of psychology, University of Alabama: "Yes, he may have done it. No, the investigation does not present clear, cogent, and compelling evidence that he did do it."

James N. Butcher, Department of Psychology, University of Minnesota: "I believe that the conclusions drawn by the FBI investigators concerning Hartwig's psychological adjustment are plausible and based upon sound inferences from the behavioral profile contained in the report. . . . However, it is impossible to conclude with certainty that he actually committed suicide by causing the explosion on the *Iowa*."

Dr. John E. Exner, Jr., executive director, Rorschach Workshops, Asheville, North Carolina: "The conclusion that Hartwig died as a result of his own actions seems reasonable and logical in the light of the material on which it was based."

Dr. Roger L. Greene, Department of Psychology, Texas Tech University: "It appears that there are a number of potential problems with the logical links between the evidence and conclusions drawn in the FBI equivocal death analysis."

Dr. Kirk Heilbrun, Forensic Service, Florida State Hospital: "After reviewing the letters and interviews, as well as the equivocal death analysis... the suicide explanation does strike me as the most plausible. I am comfortable reaching a conclusion about its likelihood based on the available evidence."

Dr. Douglas Jacobs, director, Suicide Education Institute of Boston, professor of psychiatry, Harvard Medical School: "Although one cannot conclusively rule out an underlying psychiatric disturbance, or an acute undetected psychological state precipitating suicide, the preponderance of evidence does not point to a suicidal/homicidal death."

Dr. Norman G. Poythress, Jr., Alabama Department of Mental Health and Mental Retardation and Department of Psychology, the University of Alabama: "Problems with the FBI psychological analysis notwithstanding, the possibility of a suicide by Hartwig cannot be dismissed out of hand."

Dr. C. J. Rosecrans, professor of psychiatry and psychology, University of Alabama at Birmingham: "[Hartwig] would appear to be at high risk for self destruction *but* in a specific manner which afforded him an opportunity to achieve that which evaded him in life."

Dr. Elliott M. Silverstein, Diplomate in Forensic Psychology, American Board of Professional Psychology, Chapel Hill, North Carolina: "Assuming all the evidence presented is true, the psychological profile drafted by the FBI is very plausible."

In reporting on its investigation, the House Subcommittee relied heavily on the analyses by these distinguished experts to declare that "if there was a single major fault in [the Navy's] investigation, it was the FBI system for producing the equivocal death analysis." As a result, said the report, "the subcommittee believes the evidentiary materials are simply not present to permit the Navy to accuse the late GMG2 Clayton M. Hartwig of being a suicidal mass-murderer." But although a careful reading of the written assessments by the panel of experts does not appear to be as definitive in undermining the FBI equivocal death analysis as the subcommittee claimed, the report was unstinting in its harshness in discussing the FBI profile of Hartwig and the BSU profiling system:

"The FBI psychological analysis procedures are of doubtful professionalism. The false air of certainty generated by the FBI analysis was probably the single major factor inducing the Navy to single out Clayton Hartwig as the likely guilty party. The FBI should consider revamping its entire equivocal death analysis system."

The report argued that "by the standards of the U.S. Justice system, the subcommittee does not believe that Clayton Hartwig could be convicted of any crime." Should it have been possible to conduct a trial in which a jury would have to have been persuaded beyond a reasonable doubt, the author of the subcommittee report might prove correct. But neither the FBI behavioral scientists nor the Navy declared that there was conclusive proof that GMG2 Hartwig killed himself and murdered forty-six crewmates. What the FBI's equivocal death analysis enabled Admiral Milligan to do was offer the sort of evidence that a prosecutor would first present to a grand jury. In that context, all that is required is sufficient evidence to persuade the grand jurors that there existed sufficient evidence to determine "probable cause" to believe a crime had been committed and vote a true bill—an indictment. What did the Navy say? "The explosion in center gun, Turret 2, U.S.S. *Iowa* on 19 April 1989 resulted from a wrongful intentional act. Based on this investigative report and after full review of all Naval Investigative Service's reports to date, the wrongful intentional act that caused this incident was most probably committed by GMG2 Clayton M. Hartwig, USN."

The House investigators concluded that by its standards, and the standards that the subcommittee felt should have applied in the Navy's investigation, there was only a hypothesis, and a tenuous one at that, that Clayton Hartwig was a suicidal mass killer. "By the more subjective standards of history," stated the report, "there will likely always be a case to make against him."

The House subcommittee's strong criticism of its methods and conclusions notwithstanding, the FBI stood by its findings, prepared to let history have the final say. However, one more chapter in the saga of what happened in the gun room of Turret No. 2 of the *Iowa* on April 19, 1989, remained to be written.

SIXTEEN

The Unquiet Death of GMG2
Clayton Hartwig

*T*he report by the Investigations Subcommittee of the House Armed Services was titled: "U.S.S. *Iowa* Tragedy: An Investigative Failure." Above its editorial on the report, the *New York Times* headlined: "The Navy's Disloyalty to Its Own." Praising the report for its "clear, dry prose," the editorial chastised the Navy for clinging to "its unproven, probably unprovable charge that one dead crew member was the culprit." The FBI equivocal death analysis of Hartwig was described as "a sci-fi psychological profile of the gunner-suspect based on the Navy's supply of biased evidence." The Navy's record, the *Times* went on, "adds up to repeated breaches of professionalism, sound command, and the loyalty the Navy's leadership owes 'down,' to its lower ranks. Even in peacetime, Navy crews must be alert for danger at sea, with only seconds to decide whether an oncoming plane is friend or foe. No such pressures confronted the Navy's high command as it reviewed the *Iowa* tragedy; there is no imaginable excuse for the wild flights of pseudo-science and calculated character assassination. Worse than having an unsolved mystery on its hands, the Navy has a bogus solution, which means it can't even begin to solve the *Iowa* case until it reverses course."

The *Times*'s language about the FBI profile of Hartwig was tame compared to the column written by Lars-Erik Nelson following the testimony by Ault and Hazelwood to the Senate committee that investigated the disaster. Nelson wrote, "Deep within the FBI there exists a unit of people who—without ever talking to you or anyone who knows you—are prepared to go into court and testify that you are a homicidal maniac." He then hoped that "any defense lawyer, any judge, any jury would laugh this kind of quack evidence out of court."

When Hazelwood and Ault were called upon to testify before the Senate committee running a parallel investigation to that of the House, they also met rough going from some dubious senators, but the main thrust of the Senate committee's interest in the explosion in Turret No. 2 was along technical lines and deep questioning of the Navy's conclusion that the blast was not simply an accident. These probers sat on the Armed Services Committee, led by San Nunn, Democrat of Georgia, who was regarded by admirals and generals of the Pentagon as a man to be respected for his power over the Defense Department budget. Unlike some of Nunn's predecessors in the center chair of the Armed Services Committee's hearing room, he was not known as a constant friend who could be counted on to grant rubber-stamp approval to what the chiefs of the armed forces desired. Similarly, he could not be relied upon to go easy on the Navy in the *Iowa* investigation.

Accordingly, Nunn on behalf of the Armed Services Committee turned to the General Accounting Office, an investigative and research body available to the Congress, to arrange independent technical tests of Iowa-class battleship powder bags to see if it was possible for there to have been an accidental explosion, as well as scenarios in which the powder bags might have been set off intentionally, as the Navy suggested Hartwig had done. The tests were carried out by Sandia National Laboratory, a federally financed research center in New Mexico.

First to be tested was the Navy's contention that a chemical detonator had been used. This conclusion was based on the finding of traces of calcium, chlorine, brake lubricants, and cleaning fluids in the middle gun rifle. The Sandia investigators found nothing unusual in the presence of these elements. Microscopic bits of steel wool that were also found in the gun and that the Navy suggested were evidence of a detonator couldn't be accounted for by Sandia, but neither did

Sandia say it could endorse the Navy's idea that the steel wool could have been remnants of an explosive device.

Next, Sandia testers found that an explosion could have been the result of the powder bags being unintentionally rammed into the gun too quickly, perhaps as much as seven times the normal speed. Using laboratory simulations, the researchers found that under extreme compression, the powder could ignite prematurely. No one disputed that in the center gun of Turret No. 2 the rammer had been driven too far into the gun, and some dissenters from the "no accident" theory believed it was an overram that Eric Lawrence referred to when he said, "We have a problem here."

Prompted by Senator Nunn to conduct new tests along the lines of the Sandia experiments, the Navy at first dismissed the Sandia findings because the tests hadn't been done in a 16-inch gun, but the Navy relented (probably because it knew that Nunn was about to go public with the Sandia findings) and on May 24 conducted a simulated high-speed ramming test—not using a 16-inch gun. The test was done by putting an 800-pound weight on top of five bags of gunpowder and then dropping them thirty-six inches onto a steel plate. On the eighteenth try, the powder bags began to burn.

Announcing the result immediately, the Navy declared that it was reopening the *Iowa* investigation. The timing of this turnabout by the Navy was significant in that it preempted Nunn, who convened his hearing the next day (May 25) to reveal the Sandia findings.

Among those who packed the available seats in the hearing room that Friday was Captain Fred Moosally. Skipper on the *Iowa* on the fateful April 19 when Turret No. 2 was devastated, he was now retired, having taken his last salute from the 1,500-man *Iowa* crew on May 4 at Norfolk. In the wake of the investigation, he'd been given a nonpunitive letter of caution for what the letter called administrative deficiencies as captain of the battleship. And he was cited for "a failure of leadership" and "marked deficiency in command over-sight." In his brief retirement-ceremony remarks, he fired what the Associated Press called a "broadside" at the way the Navy had handled things from the beginning. "It is too bad the *Iowa* investigation team consisted of managers, and apparently not very good managers at that," he said. In civilian clothes at Nunn's hurried hearing, the balding ex-skipper was asked by the ubiquitous inquisitive reporter why he was attending the hearing. "I'm only here to listen," said Moosally.

Also there to hear what she regarded as a vindication of her brother was Kathy Kubicina, dressed in a blue-and-white blouse with a red anchor on the pocket. She was thrilled at what she saw as the lifting of the cloud from her brother's reputation. "I'm really bitter," she'd told *New York Times* reporter Dirk Johnson in her home in Cleveland. "The Navy took away my brother and then tried to destroy his name." She hoped the Navy would express some sorrow. "When they say they're sorry," she said, "we'll feel a whole lot better."

The irony in Kubicina's role, of course, lies in the fact that it had been her letter to the Navy regarding the insurance policy taken out by her brother with Kendall Truitt as the beneficiary which first pointed the Navy's attention toward her brother. Had that letter not been sent to Admiral Mulligan it is quite unlikely that a criminal investigation would have been ordered. In the *Times* interview Kubicina was quoted as saying that if she had it to do over again, she would not cooperate with the Navy investigators. "When they asked me if it were possible that Clayton was a homosexual, I said it didn't matter. The investigators really went to town with that statement," she said. After listening to testimony before Senator Nunn's committee based on the Sandia experiments, she appeared that evening on CNN's *Crossfire* program with the glint of vindication in her eyes.

In fact, the Sandia report and the Navy's new battery of tests were not the final word on what happened in the middle gun of Turret No. 2. The Navy had had to drop powder bags eighteen times to get a fire that could have become an explosion. This was a situation that did not replicate overramming a 16-inch gun. Neither did the Sandia tests. The report to the Senate Armed Services Committee by the GAO stated that "these experiments must be extended to actual 16-inch gun conditions." It stated: "We cannot prove nor disprove the presence of a chemical igniter as proposed by the USN." And, most significant, the report said: "The cause of the explosion was not conclusively determined."

Though the Sandia testing could not conclusively determine the cause of the explosion of April 19, 1989, there were those who were prepared to be definitive. Representative of the views of many observers, commentators, and editorial writers was the editorial in the *New York Times*. "When the Navy managed to ignite five bags of gunpowder at its Dahlgren, Va., weapons station, it exploded more than the official story that a gunner's mate had sabotaged the battleship Iowa, killing himself and forty-six other sailors. It blew open a tight naval mind-set that demands blame. It's a mind-set so incapable of accepting uncertainty that the Navy couldn't let the baffling tragedy go unexplained but had to smear a crewman's memory on flimsy evidence." Noting that the Navy had "silenced its ancient 16-inch guns," the *Times* took aim at "the libelous psychological profile of Mr. Hartwig" and called for "a prompt and full-throated apology, and not just from some investigating admiral." Presumably from the FBI.

In the aftermath of all this Congressional attention to its means and methods, a letter traveled down the Hill on behalf of those who'd investigated the FBI's role. It was addressed to the Attorney General, Richard Thornburgh, and suggested that the people in the FBI headquarters across Pennsylvania Avenue from the Justice Department get their "act" together.

The response that went back up the Hill informed Congress that the FBI considered its "act" to be quite nicely in order at the National Center for Analysis of Violent Crime at Quantico.

Was the storm of criticism of the equivocal death analysis done by Ault and Hazelwood justified? Did the Behavioral Science Unit botch its work on the *Iowa* case? Did the FBI fail?

The answer to these questions is: no.

Time and time again, Ault and Hazelwood in their testimony with deliberate, painstaking, and extremely patient explanations spelled out quite clearly for those who cared to pay attention and to think about what they were hearing exactly what they'd been engaged to do in the *Iowa* case. What was that? First, they were not asked to conduct an independent criminal investigation of the explosion; had they been, they were the wrong FBI unit to call upon—they had neither the mandate, personnel, nor budget to investigate the *Iowa* case on their own. Second, they had been informed authoritatively by the Navy that its investigators had ruled out an accident as the cause of the disaster.

Third, they were presented with the Naval Investigative Service's complete files on the remaining three possible causes of the explosion: murder, murder-suicide, suicide. All the information and evidence available to the Navy was handed over—hundreds of pieces of data including forensic reports, Hartwig's personal history, letters, note-books, transcripts of interviews with his family and friends, and numerous personal items. Based on this material, what the Navy sought from the FBI was an *opinion* as to the most likely scenario of the three causes, murder-suicide, murder, suicide—not FBI proof. Ault and Hazelwood responded with their opinion that Hartwig committed suicide.

All of this was made abundantly plain in their testimony, as the following excerpts from the Senate hearing show. Concerning the Navy assertion that its investigation ruled out an accident, Senator William Cohen, Republican of Maine, asked Ault, "And you accepted that?" Ault answered, "We accepted it."

How and why could they not accept the Navy's judgment that there'd been no accidental explosion? First, they always operated on the basis of the evidence provided them by a duly constituted investigative agency. On what basis might they have challenged the NIS? It was an investigative service authorized by Congress and had a long history of credible work. Its standing was no less valid than the FBI's.

Still, Senator Alan Dixon, Democrat of Illinois and a former prosecutor, struggled to grasp the obvious. "You interviewed nobody, analyzed no fingerprints, analyzed no handwriting, otherwise did any investigation concerning an accident, an explosion; none of that was done?"

"We don't do that type of investigation in this type of request, sir," said Hazelwood patiently. Again, striving to break through an apparent cloud of nonperception, Hazelwood told the seemingly baffled Senator Cohen, "Whenever we are requested to do a case for an investigative agency, we make the assumption we are dealing with professional investigators."

Outside the hearing room, Cohen remarked, "The Navy came to the FBI with a preordained conclusion, and the FBI comes back with the Good Housekeeping Seal of Approval." It was a snappy quote and it found its way into at least one newspaper column, but that is not what had occurred. The Navy had not come to Ault and Hazelwood with a "preordained conclusion" but with an opinion founded on its technical investigation that the explosion had not been an accident. By anyone's logic, that left only three alternatives, which Ault and Hazelwood analyzed as they had done in dozens of equivocal death cases.

Seemingly lacking information on the way the BSU worked and not knowing that Ault and Hazelwood were not a pair of crime-scene probers in rumpled trench coats and snap-brim hats of the kind Senator Dixon had been familiar with when he was a prosecutor, Dixon asked, "Do you have any hard evidence that would support the idea that Hartwig actually carried out this act?"

Ault replied, "We're not detectives ourselves. We don't pretend to be. We're professionals in the area of behavioral sciences."

Had Ault and Hazelwood been testifying before members of the House and Senate judiciary committees, they might have had a much easier time getting across their point. Of the four senators of the full Armed Services Committee who attended the hearing (Nunn, Cohen, Dixon, and John Warner of Virginia), only Warner (former Secretary of the Navy) expressed anything less than scorn for the FBI testimony. Had questions been asked by Senator Arlen Specter, who had years of experience in oversight of the activities of the FBI and who understood the role and limitations of psychological profiling, and his counterparts in the House, the work that Ault and Hazelwood performed in the *Iowa* investigation might not have run into quite the myopia and befuddlement that greeted them among the two bodies which heard their testimony.

It must have seemed ironic to Ault, Hazelwood, and the others at Quantico reading the scathing accounts of themselves that were blooming in a sizable portion of the press that these same news media critics for years had been praising the BSU's system of criminal personality profiling. That the "psychological sleuths" who were written up glowingly in cases of serial murder and other violent crimes should suddenly be described as amateurs, sci-fi fantasists, off-the-wall theorists, and pseudo-scientific lackies of the Navy caused a lot of head-scratching at Quantico.

Were Hazelwood and Ault right about Clayton Hartwig? Was he all they said he was? Had he been capable of, and driven to, the awful act of April 19, 1989? Did Hartwig possess all the motivations and personality quirks ascribed to him? In the *opinion* of Hazelwood and Ault, expressed to the Navy and to the two Congressional committees *as* opinion—yes.

But what if the explosion *was* an accident after all?

Such a finding would certainly clear GMG2 Clayton Hartwig of suicide and murder.

But would the definitive evidence that the explosion in the middle gun of Turret No. 2 on that fateful day was accidental alter in any way the psychological profile of him as deduced by Ault and Hazelwood? Could incontrovertible evidence that Hartwig did not commit suicide change in any way what Hartwig was in life? Would it alter the facts about his life that had led Ault and Hazelwood to depict him in the manner they did?

Answers to those questions will be rooted in whether the one being asked affords any credence to psychological profiling. If one accepts that a trained observer and analyst can from the evidence presented come to a logical conclusion, that person will not find fault in the psychological autopsy of Clayton Hartwig, even if he did not kill himself.

If one rejects psychological profiling and the technique of indirect personality assessment as so much mumbo-jumbo and pseudo-science fit only for pages of thrillers or the Saturday-night mystery movie on TV, flights of angels swearing otherwise will not change that mind.

One doubter was Lester Bernstein, a free-lance writer and editorial consultant and a veteran of the *New York Times, Time,* and *Newsweek,* who wrote in a column for New York's *Newsday* on June 12, 1990, "The U.S. Navy's scapegoating of a gunner's mate for the April 19, 1989, explosion that took forty-seven lives on the battleship Iowa is now being exploded itself. Still intact, however, is an older, more stubborn Navy myth—that the battleship class, long obsolete in every other navy in the world, still carries its weight in a modern fleet."

Bernstein contended it was the Navy's "hidebound commitment to its four half-century-old battleships" that "conditioned" its finding on why one of Iowa's 16-inch gun turrets blew up. Without "this malign speculation," speculated Bernstein, the Navy would have had to look harder for a flaw in its equipment, materials, and procedures. "Finding such a flaw might have put the viability of the Iowa and its three sister battleships at risk," he said. "Damn a dead man's reputation; don't give up the ship."

Was that it? Was this the real issue at the heart of the unquiet death of GMG2 Hartwig? Had the Navy been so cynical and self-serving as to try to take an accident and turn it into the work of a suicidal sailor? Has the noisy repercussions of the explosion that killed Hartwig and forty-six others, all the uproar and investigations, been not about the fate of Hartwig but about the future of the four dreadnaughts that had been fetched from oblivion to quench Ronald Reagan's thirst for a 600-ship Navy, the Iowa, New Jersey, Missouri, and Wisconsin?

What made these gargantuan warships something special in the minds of Reagan and others, suggested Bernstein, was a classic "menacing grandeur" that battleship enthusiasts believed could project awesome U.S. might in Third World hot spots. This was faulty and possibly ruinous thinking in Bernstein's view—and in the view of stalwart opponents of battleships in Congress. "For all its modernization with missiles and electronics," he wrote, "each battleship is still a target almost as big as three football fields end to end, and the twenty-three-mile firing range of its big guns has long ceased to confer safety from return missile fire, which can now be swifter and deadlier than the architects of the archaic vessels ever dreamed. The bill for operating the four ships runs only into hundreds of millions of dollars a year—a pittance by Pentagon standards but not to be overlooked by budgeters when every little bit counts."

Indeed, if the Navy had hoped in some bizarre fantasy to preserve its battleships by making Clayton Hartwig the fall guy for the Iowa disaster, the plot failed miserably. Because of massive budget pressures on the Bush administration, it was obvious that the Iowa would not be repaired. Estimates of the cost ran as high as twenty million dollars.

Besides the price tag, there were few people around who knew how to fix 16-inch guns.

A further ironic footnote to the *Iowa* case came in August 1990 when the United States found itself embroiled in a crisis centered on the Persian Gulf after Iraq invaded Kuwait and set off the largest and swiftest American military and naval mobilization since World War II. To help meet the challenge, the Navy announced it was sending the Iowa-class battleships *Wisconsin* and *Missouri* with their intimidating batteries of 16-inch guns to duty stations in the crisis area apparently without fear of accidental explosions.

If anyone sought proof that the Navy maintained its confidence in the safety and reliability of its battleships and their big guns, this surely was it. However, the old fight about their usefulness was far from over. On the very day in November 1990 that the Navy declared its intention of sending the *Missouri* to the Persian Gulf, Representative Oakar was again questioning the reliability of the ships based on a report requested by the Congress from the General Accounting Office (an investigative entity of the Congress) after the *Iowa* disaster. In its seventy-page findings the GAO said that "unless current Middle East operations convincingly demonstrate the unique ability of battleships the *Missouri* and the *Wisconsin* (should) be decommissioned." When Oakar asked GAO analyst Frank Conahan if she should be concerned about the safety of sailors serving aboard battleships Conahan replied, "If the Navy has not taken recent action to improve the conditions (on the ships)... I think you need to be concerned."

As for the *Iowa*, it already lay idle, mothballed once more but now with Turret No. 2 apparently forever frozen facing to starboard with guns one and three elevated and middle gun slanting downward as though observing a perpetual state of mourning.

SEVENTEEN

*E*vidences of the *C*rime

"*I*n the face of misunderstanding and derision, he had tried to trace the criminal, not by the world-old method of the marks he had left on things, but by the evidences which the crime had left on the mind of the criminal himself."

These words might have applied to Roy Hazelwood or Richard Ault going up to Capitol Hill in hope of providing illumination into what they did as detectives of the mind. But, in fact, the words were written about a fictional detective named Luther Trant in a story entitled "The Eleventh Hour" by Edwin Balmer and William MacHarg eight decades before "evidences of the crime" became criminal psychological profiling and an integral part of the work of the FBI.

As violent serial crime surged into the consciousness of the American people, so did the public's interest in the people who had the task of dealing with the problem. Quite suddenly, the men and women in the offices, conference rooms, computer center, and classrooms at the National Center for the Analysis of Violent Crime found themselves being asked to let the public in on what they were doing. Dozens of interviews were sought by newspapers and magazines ranging from the insider's *Law Enforcement News* to *Reader's Digest*. "The public's interest in such crimes has risen each year and the media have been quick to publish articles and books and produce documentaries and fictional films on the subject," noted NCAVC administrator Alan Burgess.

That serial killers were "hot" in the publishing world was duly noted in an article by Rosemary Herbert in the June 1, 1990, issue of *Publishers Weekly*. "Publishers Agree: True Crime Does Pay," declared the headline. In the article, Priscilla Ridgeway, executive secretary of the Mystery Writers of America, reckoned that "media coverage about some pretty dreadful crimes has inured the public to their horror and tweaked interest." The MWA itself acknowledged the growth of interest in the subject by its crime writers when it invited the New York Police Department's chief profiler, Ray Pierce, to speak to the group just weeks before Pierce was called upon to grapple with the city's Zodiac shooter. The "anatomy of the serial killer" was also the subject of the Mystery Writers in their annual symposium held in association with New York's John Jay College of Criminal Justice.

Books about serial killers on publishers' lists for 1990 included *From Cradle to Grave: The Short Lives and Strange Deaths of Marybeth Tinning's Nine Children* by Joyce Eggington; *Small Sacrifices: A True Story of Passion and Murder* by Ann Rule; *Death Shift: The True Story of Nurse Genene Jones and the Texas Baby Murders* by Peter Elkind; and *The Sleeping Lady: The Trailside Murders Above the Golden Gate* by Robert Graysmith. Graysmith was the author of 1986's best-selling *Zodiac*, about San Francisco's most elusive serial killer, which by coincidence was out in paperback when New York's Zodiac burst upon the scene, leading some crime observers to theorize that the New York Zodiac was using the book to copycat the original Zodiac.

In 1990, NCAVC staffers found themselves literally in the limelight as Orion Pictures descended on Quantico for the filming of *Silence of the Lambs*. It was based on the best-selling book by Thomas Harris, a novelist with an abiding interest in the subjects of mass murder (*Black Sunday*) and serial killers (*Red Dragon*, which became the movie *Manhunt*). During the shooting of *Silence of the Lambs*, in which the serial killer is fascinated by moths and driven to "hunt" large women so as to remove their skins (he calls them "hides") because he wants to convert himself into a woman, some NCAVC staffers became extras or were assigned small parts by the producers.

Perhaps the best-known FBI agent of 1989-1990 was smooth, cool-mannered, meticulous Dale Cooper, investigator of the murder of pretty young Laura Palmer in a remote lumbering-territory town.

However, there was no resemblance between Special Agents of the NCAVC and the rather bizarre fictional Agent Cooper featured in the decidedly quirky television series *Twin Peaks*. While Agent Cooper's made-up adventures were fascinating TV viewers, the BBC called at Quantico to conduct interviews with genuine-article agents for a TV special on serial killers and the Fox TV Network sent a film crew and actor Patrick Duffy to gather tape for its special on the Green River serial killer. A delegation of filmmakers also traveled up from Cordoba, Argentina, with many questions about serial killers.

History's most notorious serial murderer was on the minds of actor Peter Ustinov's writers and producers in seeking the help of the experts at NCAVC. The idea of their 1988 program was to sift through the details of the case of Jack the Ripper on the hundredth anniversary of his deadly doings. By going over the crimes, Ustinov hoped to settle upon the most likely suspect out of five men often listed as leading contenders for the title of Ripper. The roll call consisted of Sir William Gull, prominent doctor and consulting physician to the court of Queen Victoria; Prince Albert Victor, Duke of Clarence, the Queen's quite weird grandson; Montague John Druitt, a lawyer and teacher; another doctor, R. D'Onston, a Whitechapel resident and satanist; and a mysterious immigrant and loner by the name of Aaron Kosminski. The presentation of these suspects in the Ripper's crimes was a fascinating mixture of dramatized recreations of Jack's ghastly goings-on, actual evidence from the century-old puzzler—Saucy Jack's taunting letters and a knife used in one of the mutilation murders—and the views and analyses of leading "Ripperologists" and authors of books on the subject, as well as the ideas of an investigator from the "new" New Scotland Yard. Appearing on the live program to present the criminal personality profile of the Ripper worked up just for the Ustinov show were Special Agents John Douglas and Roy Hazelwood.

"Jack the Ripper was a white male, he was in his mid to late twenties, of average intelligence, and wasn't as clever as he was lucky," stated Douglas for openers. "Jack the Ripper was single," added Hazelwood. "He had never been married and probably had not socialized with women at all. He had a great difficulty interacting with people and women in particular. Also, the times when the crimes were committed—between midnight and six A.M.—indicate that he was not accountable to anyone; therefore, not married. We believe Jack lived very close to where the crimes were being committed, because these types of individuals generally start killing within very close proximity to their homes. If Jack was employed it would have been in a menial type of job requiring little or no contact with the public. He would not be employed in a profession. [So much for doctors Gull and D'Onston!] As far as his criminal history goes, as a child Jack would have set fires or abused animals. As an adult he would have been engaged in some erratic behavior, causing neighbors to call the police. Of more significance to his crime history would be his mental history."

Picking up that cue, Douglas explained, "Jack the Ripper was the product of a broken home. He was raised by a dominant female figure in his household who in all probability physically if not sexually abused him as a child. A way for potential offenders of this kind to cope with this is to internalize their feelings and withdraw from society, to become asocial, to become a loner and withdraw from the community. He would also be described as having very, very poor personal hygiene. He would be disheveled in his appearance and people would notice that he was nocturnal, meaning he preferred to go out in the evening hours under the cloak of darkness, stalking, walking many blocks, looking for victims."

"Jack hated and feared women at the same time," Hazelwood said, continuing with the profile. "He also was very intimidated by women. I'm sure everyone noted how quickly Jack subdued and killed his victims. This is very important in understanding Jack, because it tells us that taking of life was not of primary importance to him. It was secondary to the mutilation itself. That is actually the key to understanding Jack. The mutilations were sexually motivated. By displacing the victims' organs, he in fact neutered or desexed them and therefore they were no longer anything to be feared."

With a pixiesh look of astonishment, Peter Ustinov quipped, "It's perhaps British understatement to suggest that he killed five women because he felt *uncomfortable* in their company."

The opinion of Hazelwood and Douglas and the consensus of the show's panel was that Jack the Ripper had been the only man on the list of "suspects" that fit the profile, the mystery man Kosminski. Indeed, he had been high on the list of likelies in the offices of Scotland Yard and appeared to be the highest one in the mind of Sir Robert Anderson, head of the Yard's Criminal Investigation Division at the time of the murders. A Polish Jew and resident of Whitechapel, Kosminski certainly fit the latter-day profile of a potential serial killer. "This man became insane owing to many years of indulgence in solitary vices," wrote the noted Ripperologist Donald Rumbelow in *The Complete Jack the Ripper.* "He had a great hatred of women, especially of the prostitute class, and had strong homicidal tendencies: he was removed to a lunatic asylum about March 1889. There were many circumstances connected with this man which made him a strong suspect." Significantly, after Kosminski was taken off the street, Saucy Jack's killings stopped.

However, a TV drama dealing with the Ripper murders starring Michael Caine in the role of Scotland Yard's chief investigator Frederick Abberline did not see Kosminski as the culprit. This miniseries identified Dr. Gull as the Ripper, as had a much earlier film, *Murder by Decree,* in which Christopher Plummer was Sherlock Holmes. But Douglas and Hazelwood had dismissed Gull as unlikely, not only because he did not match their profile but because Gull was elderly and had suffered a stroke. Theories that Gull might have been the Ripper rested on the proposition that he was acting to protect the reputation of the royal family from a scandal involving Victoria's wacky grandson, the Prince. Why the Ustinov program listed Clarence as a suspect was a puzzle, inasmuch as there existed convincing evidence that His Highness the Prince Albert Victor was not in London at the time of some of the murders.

NCAVC personnel also were tapped for consultation on more recent crimes being portrayed by the producers of NBC-TV's show *Unsolved Mysteries.* But the television broadcast that relied most heavily on FBI cooperation was the Fox Network's highly rated Sunday-night *America's Most Wanted.* Anchored by John Walsh, whose commitment to capturing criminals that began with the murder of his son remained undiminished nearly a decade later, the broadcast was not based on the FBI's "Ten Most Wanted" program but on a wide variety of crimes from all over the nation, although some of those depicted were wanted by the FBI. Powerfully effective, Walsh's program led to the capture of well over one hundred individuals in its first year on the air.

The most spectacular of *America's Most Wanted*'s successes involved the locating and arrest of John List. Having planned and carried out the execution-style murders of his mother, wife, and three children, List had vanished from his Westfield, New Jersey, home in 1971 without a trace. Eighteen years later, on May 21, 1989, Walsh's program revived interest in the killings by staging a reenactment and then showing a bust of List as he might appear currently. Created by forensic sculptor Frank Bender, the head was that of a balding, jowly middle-aged man wearing horn-rimmed eyeglasses. More than 350 viewers called the program with tips. One of them was received by the FBI office in Richmond, Virginia, stating that List was living in Midlothian, Virginia, under the name Robert P. Clark. Confronted at his accounting office in Richmond, Clark denied he was John List, but in time, evidence was accumulated to persuade a jury in New Jersey that Clark and List were one and the same and that John List was guilty of the murders. When arrested, List in the flesh was an exact living version of the Bender sculpture.

The wedding of facial reconstruction, photography, and the publicity afforded by using the news media had been pioneered in a 1980 case in Miami, Florida. Using techniques described in an article by B. P. Gatliff and C. C. Snow, "From Skull to Visage," published in 1966 in the *Journal of Biocommunications*, medical examiners created a likeness from a badly decomposed body of a young black woman who'd been killed by a gunshot to the head. When the photograph of the reconstructed face was carried by the news media of Miami it produced no results, but a news story based on the case published in the *New York Times* ultimately led to an identification of the murdered woman. Writing about the case in the August 1983 *FBI Law Enforcement Bulletin*, physician Roger Mittleman, dentist Richard Souviron, and forensic photographers John Valor and Lynn Lugo of the Dade County, Florida, Medical Examiner Department noted that "persons skilled in the field of photography facial reconstruction, and the news media can all work hand in hand to solve the mystery of identification."

These emerging revolutionary forensic techniques also could work hand in hand with the work being done at the NCAVC in the field of missing persons and in cases of unidentified bodies that after identification might be connected to the profile of an elusive serial killer. There were plenty of them on the loose.

High on the wanted list in the Norfolk, Virginia, area was a person or persons who killed on an annual basis. Beginning in 1986, six young people were murdered in remote areas or lovers' lanes in the months of April, September, and October—one attack per year. While different methods of killing had been employed—stabbing, strangulation, and gun—the method of approach appeared to be the same—an unexpected appearance, gaining the confidence of the victims, perhaps representing an authority figure, maybe a police officer. After deliberating on the case, the FBI felt that the "Lovers' Lane Killer" was not hunting alone. Said FBI Special Agent Irvin Wells, "We believe that there are probably two people involved. One of the reasons we think so is that in each of the cases it appears that control of the victim was gained early on. There was no real struggle involved in any of the cases."

While the Norfolk area braced for the possibility of another lovers' lane killing in 1990, eight law enforcement agencies in central Virginia were concerned that the July disappearance of a Culpepper woman and the murder of another in Spotsylvania County might be related to the slaying of a woman in Orange County in 1989. Faced with the likelihood of a serial killer, the local law agencies met with representatives of the FBI to coordinate their investigators and to examine the NCAVC data banks to see if the murders corresponded to others reported to VICAP.

At the same time, people living and working along a dismal stretch of Frankford Avenue of Philadelphia had been witnesses to the savagery of a serial killer who'd trolled what the area's residents called "the Avenue" and reaped the lives of at least eight women. "Every one of his victims had some connection with this killing ground," wrote crime reporter Mike Mallowe in the August 1990 edition of *Philadelphia* magazine. He called them the "Nobody Murders" because the victims were the flotsam of society. "They call themselves prostitutes," he said, "but you have to look hard to tell. In the strictest sense, they don't seem to be people at all. More like *near*-people, as though the Creator made a few mistakes with the first batch: this one too pimply, that one too dirty, the one over there too emaciated, all of them with mucky hair and scarred arms and flimsy clothing that barely covers their ravaged bodies. But they are people; they are prostitutes. Victims in more ways than one. Pipe whores. Crack addicts. They are the latest fashion in sin on Frankford."

These murders were indicative of what a report of the U.S. Senate Judiciary Committee predicted would be "the bloodiest year in American history." Committee chairman Joseph Biden estimated there would be 23,220 murders in 1990—a rise of 8 percent over 1989. The previous record homicide year was 1980 (23,040). "The most ominous news we will hear today is that 1990 marks the beginning of a new crime wave as the children of the baby-boomers enter their 'high crime years,'" said Biden. "This baby-boomerang may mean that 1990 is but the first of many record murder years."

The Justice Department/FBI Crime Index report released in August 1990 by FBI Director William Sessions also portended an upsurge in violence crime. Data on crimes for all of 1989 showed that these were 5,741 criminal offenses per 100,000 inhabitants of the Untied States. Violent crime had risen by 5 percent since 1988. Of cases of violent crimes, only 46 percent had been cleared. Thus, more than half of the violent crimes in America in 1989 *were not solved* through arrests. The murder rate in 1989 had been nine per 100,000 people. Out of the estimated 21,500 murders in 1989, over half involved people who knew one another—which meant that many thousands had been committed by strangers. This was a continuation of a trend. "It used to be twenty-five years ago, if there was a homicide you looked for a spouse or a boyfriend or girlfriend," said Gerald Caplan, a professor of law at George Washington University and former director of the National Institute of Justice. "That's just not the case anymore."

EIGHTEEN

"*It Could Be Anyone*"

Stirring the Spanish moss and carrying the scent of tall pines, a gentle breeze wafted through the sundrenched courtyard of the Gatorwood Apartments as Wayland Clifton, police chief of Gainesville, Florida, stepped from his car. He found familiar faces: Deputy Chiefs Mike Jones and Ron Perkins; Lieutenant Dick Ward, head of the Criminal Investigation Division; Captain Norbert Thomas, patrol commander; and Lieutenant Sadie Darnell, public information officer.

If what awaited Clifton in a rear apartment was the same as what had been discovered in two other locations since Sunday, there was going to be a lot of press coverage.

Clifton also recognized men and women of the Alachuca County Sheriff's Department—Sheriff L. J. (Lu) Hindery, Captain R. W. Hamilton, and Lieutenant Spencer Mann of Public Affairs. They'd responded because the Gatorwood Apartments were just across the Gainesville line and in their jurisdiction.

From the University of Florida Police Department had come director Everett Stevens, investigator Major John Anderson, and public information specialist Angie Tipton. Three days ago, the biggest task facing Tipton was getting out the news of the start of the academic year and the forthcoming football season. As of now, her job was going to be a lot rougher. Three of the victims were University of Florida students. On Sunday afternoon, August 26, 1990, the bodies of two second-semester freshmen, seventeen-year-old Christina Powell of

Jacksonville and eighteen-year-old Sonya Larson of Deerfield Beach, were discovered butchered in the off-campus Williamsburg Village Apartments.

Eight hours later at an apartment about two miles away, sheriff's deputies discovered the body of eighteen-year-old Christa Hoyt. A student at nearby Santa Fe Community College and a full-time records clerk at the sheriff's department, she'd lived and died alone, sliced open from pelvis to chest and then decapitated.

Now, in the warm morning sunlight of Wednesday the 28th in blood-soaked rooms at the rear of the Gatorwood Apartments lay twenty-three-year-old Tracy Inez Paules, a Florida University student, and her friend twenty-three-year-old Manuel Toboada, a student and athlete at Santa Fe C.C., stabbed to death in bed.

By the time Chief Clifton arrived to survey the scene of the latest crime, stories had flourished in the local press about the nature of the first three murders, leaving him no option but to confirm that the bodies had been mutilated and that Gainesville harbored a serial killer. That afternoon he told reporters, "We have every reason to believe now that all five victims found beginning last Sunday afternoon about four o'clock and through this morning are probably all connected to one suspect or two suspects." University President John Lombardi was blunter: "It's clear this part of the country has some maniac on the loose."

In a futile attempt to head off panic and allay fears of students and parents, Clifton declared, "In the next few days, in the next few evenings, you will see more police coverage than in any city you've ever lived in." Despite that promise and the dispatch of Florida state police to the area, terror took over. In a state where buying a gun was always easy, stores sold out fast. Supplies of chemical Mace and other weapons were soon depleted, as were locksmiths' shelves of devices for securing doors and windows. Baseball bats were at a premium. Students abandoned off-campus quarters for the safety of dormitories hastily arranged in the university's athletic facilities. Many terrified young women left for their homes, willingly or at the demand of frightened parents.

One scared, fleeing student gasped, "It could be anyone."

As hundreds of students departed, reporters flocked to the campus from newspapers, magazines, and radio and TV networks and local stations across the country as their newscasts made room for the Gainesville serial killer in their exhaustive coverage of the possibility of a war between the United States and Iraq. Even the *New York Times* created space on its front page for the story under the headline "Panic on a Florida Campus After 5 Are Slain."

As the terror mounted, John Douglas was sent south from Quantico. Arriving a week before Labor Day and exactly ninety days after he'd been called upon to formulate a psychological profile of the killer who spent Memorial Day weekend selecting victims from the women of the stroll in Washington, D.C., he found the usually sunny and serene university community clouded by terror and buzzing with macabre remembrances of twentieth-century America's version of Jack the Ripper—Ted Bundy. However, except for the victims being young women who bore physical similarities to Ted Bundy's victims, the Gainesville murders were not at all like Bundy's. He'd trolled for most of his victims. Only his last had been college students in their homes.

In this case, the killer had surprised all his victims in their residences. Aspects of the crime scenes pointed to an organized killer. He'd gained control of the women immediately. That he knew where young women lived evidenced a familiarity with the area. It was likely that he'd stalked his victims and had scouted their homes looking for easy entry. The young women he'd stabbed to death were all pretty and petite and had dark hair, indicating that women of that type were part of the killer's plans. The attacks with a surgically sharp knife were brutally fierce but not frenzied. They appeared to be deliberate, calculated acts. The corpses were sexually mutilated and left where they'd died. One had been decapitated and the head prominently displayed. Police Captain R. B. Ward said, "In the scene, the setup, there was a message, to law enforcement, to whoever."

Chief Clifton declared, "We're not dealing with someone who gets into the scene and simply goes into a frenzy. It's not someone who does not know what he's doing. It looks like everything he does is methodical."

Although there was much about the crimes to remind police of the crimes of known serial killers, one of the FBI's pioneers in studying the subject did not believe that the Gainesville murders were the work of a serial killer. Appearing on CNN's "Larry King Show" on September 19, Robert Ressler, now retired from the FBI and working as a private consultant to law enforcement, described them as spree murders that were not likely to be repeated.

Indeed, months after the murders were committed they did appear to have ended. This was widely attributed to the fact that police had arrested 18-year-old Edward Humphrey. Jailed on a charge of assaulting his grandmother, Humphrey was held on a $1 million bond. Authorities considered Humphrey a prime suspect largely because he was a troubled youth with a history of mental disorders and violent behavior. But investigators did not unearth sufficient evidence to charge him.

A more promising suspect emerged in January 1991 with the arrest of Harold Rolling, a 36-year-old native of Shreveport, Louisiana. Arrested on a robbery charge in Ocala, Florida, at the time of the Gainesville killings, he was also suspected of three murders in his hometown.

Thus, Rolling's name was added to the long list of twisted men so familiar to agents Douglas, Ressler, and their colleagues: Edmund Kemper wondering what it would be like to shoot Grandma, Ted Bundy with a fetish for girls with long hair, Gacy and Corll with a lethal yen for youthful males, Albert DeSalvo working out his sexual maturation by progressing in his murders from old women to the young, Charles Manson on a power and mind-control trip, Henry Lee Lucas with an unquenchable thirst for blood, Chander Matta taking advantage of his parents' absence and finding holiday fun for himself by strangling hookers, and all the others whose bloody fingerprints stain the bulging files of the scientist/agents of the NCAVC, the pages of this book, and American history.

What about the future? Richard Ault says, "The changing image and mission of the FBI in the past ten years have provided the NCAVC with an unparalleled opportunity to dig into the foundations of violent and nonviolent crimes with the hope of discovering clues about the behavior of offenders that can be applied in a practical fashion to investigations. The future also holds promise for other research topics.

Using unique yet valid methods for research, members of the NCAVC can address such areas as public corruption, fugitives from justice, jury selection, child molestation, terrorism, and extortion. In fact, areas in the criminal justice system still needing research seem to be limitless."

Major fields of research being pursued by the NCAVC going into the 1990s were arson and bombing, assassin personality, child abductors and molesters, drug witnesses and violence associated with retaliation, homicide by poisoning, serial rape, sexual assault against the aging, sexual homicide, and sexual sadism. Other areas of interest included the use of hypnosis as an investigative tool and application of behavioral science by prosecutors in preparing and conducting murder trials. Of increasing interest and a possible area for intensive NCAVC research were the psychological and law enforcement implications of gangs and gang behavior.

In yet another area, Special Agent David Icove was teamed with Richard Ault and Kenneth Baker as principal investigators into computer crime with the goal of determining whether there were common characteristics of computer crimes; delving into the motivations for computer crime; delineating the personalities of computer criminals and "hackers" and how they manage to penetrate computer networks; developing techniques by which law enforcement might detect, predict, and prevent computer crimes; and devising means of training law enforcement agencies in these techniques.

Coinciding with the work being carried out in these high-tech crimes, the Behavioral Science Computer and Engineering Subunit (BSCES), established in May 1987, was at work creating an artificial intelligence (AI) system that would integrate the Automated Criminal Investigative Program (PROFILER) and the Arson Information Management System (AIMS). The unit also maintained the VICAP Computer System. To achieve all this, BSCES operated the NCAVC Computer Center, whose facilities matched those of an engineering corporation and used a Digital Equipment Corporation VAX 11/785 computer to network twenty-five workstations throughout the center. Pursuing this technological future, Roland Reboussin, David Icove, and William Tafoya were working to develop an AI system that would allow the NCAVC personnel to eliminate useless investigative paths that often proved fruitless in profiling; preserve and recall knowledge of similar cases, past profiles, and research studies; display complex criminal network hierarchies of organized crime and drug gangs; develop and use decision rules to speed up computer time; enhance the ability of NCAVC computers to "talk" to users and "advise and consult" with the user about what was available in the data bank; train new users; and create and preserve in a heavily used computer center a system that was not subject to human failings.

As the researchers of the NCAVC attempted to plumb the minds and methods of violent criminals, they devoted considerable time and effort to problems that confronted the human beings burdened with the task of policing a violent society. "A policeman's lot is not a happy one," noted operetta writers Gilbert and Sullivan a century ago. With perhaps less artful phrases but nonetheless succinctly, Dr. S. Al Somodevilla of the Dallas, Texas, police said in 1986: "It is an accepted fact that the police officer is under stress and pressure unequaled in any profession." In order to confront problems of burnout, coping, and stress and the overall mental health of men and women engaged in law enforcement, the NCAVC became engaged in counseling not only for FBI personnel but for all law enforcement managers and other professionals with respect to psychological services programs. In 1989, the center provided assistance to 135 FBI employees or academy students, counseling to more than 200 individuals regarding critical incidents or post-shooting trauma, and more than thirty consultations on setting up local law enforcement critical-incident and post-shooting trauma programs.

Leading the way in the center's studies of problems facing those who carry badges and guns was Dr. James T. Reese. "The problems inherent in being a police officer are innumerable," he said. "Aside from the boredom, there are times of sheer panic, when life-and-death decisions have to be made in a matter of seconds. While the 'action-oriented' stress may be more obvious, it is necessary to note that the boredom present in police work can provide as much stress as responding to and investigating crimes." On the job, the police officer routinely sees the worst manifestations of human behavior, continued Reese. "They deal with molested children, muggings of the elderly and defenseless, senseless beatings and murders, suicides, mutilated bodies, and rapes. The sum total of these experiences can lead to depression, despair, and discouragement." By researching these problems, Reese and others at the center hoped to assist the men and women of the nation's law enforcement community in dealing with the onslaught of more and more crime, especially violent crime, that all the barometers of human behavior were forecasting.

As serial killers were sure to force their way into our consciousness, so, too, we could count on being shocked by the explosive violence of troubled individuals who murder in mass. The years to come were likely to present us with horrors like those of Patrick Edward Purdy who in 1988 blasted his way onto the playground of the Cleveland Elementary School in Stockton, California, and mowed down everyone he saw. Firing 110 rounds from a Chinese-made AK-47 assault rifle, he killed five kids of Cambodian and Vietnamese descent and wounded twenty-nine others, along with a teacher, then killed himself. Why? The only clue seemed to be a statement Purdy had made that he resented the influx of immigrants from Southeast Asia into the Stockton area and the success they'd achieved. An assault weapon and several other guns were used in the mass murder that numbed the nation in September of 1989. In an attack at a Louisville, Kentucky, printing plant where he'd once worked, forty-seven-year-old Joseph T. Wesbecker walked in "looking for bosses" and promptly killed seven people and wounded fifteen others, then killed himself. An AK-47 rifle was in the hands of James E. Pough in Jacksonville, Florida, when he contributed to the 1990 murder rate by shooting eight people and committing suicide in an automobile loan office, apparently because his car had been repossessed.

Rage- or grudge-motivated apocalyptic mass murders such as these clear themselves—there's no doubt *who* killed, no one for the police to arrest. They leave society only with the task of finding out *why*. Those way go on these explosive public homicide sprees have little in common with Richard Ramirez, the "Night Stalker," who, six days after Wesbecker went hunting for bosses at his old place of employment, was convicted in California of thirteen murders and thirty other crimes that totaled eighteen "instances of special circumstances" that made him eligible for the gas chamber.

In mulling over the future of the NCAVC, Bruce Porter, the director of the journalism program at Brooklyn College and writer on crime issues, wrote in *Psychology Today*, "No one is willing to say how the computer can factor intuition and instinct into its analysis. But the day does not seem far off when the police will be able to identify a criminal by the psychic loops and whorls he left at the scene, just as quickly and as surely as if he had covered the wall with fingerprints."

Might the day dawn when the burgeoning computer capabilities of the NCAVC in its NCIC, VICAP, PROFILER and AI systems would be linked so that by hitting one key on a "supercomputer" keyboard a Special Agent at the NCAVC could produce not only a personality profile of a suspect in a violent crime but everything else about him? Asked to consider that prospect, Richard Ault stroked his trim mustache, smiled, rolled his eyes and said, "I think the civil liberties folks would have something to say about that—and rightly so." In fact, neither Ault, Roy Hazelwood, John Douglas, nor anyone else in the FBI expected that high-tech devices could or should replace human beings like the one whose poking around in the evidences of the crime for a clue as to who killed a girl called Precious came up with a credit card receipt—the hometown detective.

*B*ibliography

GENERAL

Abrahamsen, David. *Confessions of Son of Sam*. New York: Columbia University Press, 1985.

—. *The Mind of the Accused: A Psychiatrist in the Courtroom*. New York: Simon & Schuster, 1983.

Allen, William. *Starkweather: The Story of a Mass Murderer*. Boston: Houghton Mifflin, 1967.

Balmer, Edwin, and William MacHarg. *"The Eleventh Hour." The Achievements of Luther Trant*. 1910. Long out of print; quoted in Jane Horning, *The Mystery Lovers' Book of Quotations*. New York: Mysterious Press, 1988.

Black, David. *Murder at the Met*. Garden City, New York: Dial, 1984.

Breslin, Jack. *America's Most Wanted: How Television Catches Crooks*. New York: Harper Paperback, 1990.

Brodsky, Stanley L. *Psychologists in the Criminal Justice System*. Chicago: University of Illinois Press, 1973.

Brooks, Pierce R.; Michael J. Devine; Terrence J. Green; Barbara H. Hart; and Merlyn D. Moore. "Serial Murder: A Criminal Justice Response." *Police Chief*, June 1987.

Brussel, James A. *A Casebook of a Crime Psychiatrist*. New York: Bernard Geis, 1968.

Bugliosi, Vincent, and Curt Gentry. *Helter Skelter*. New York: Norton, 1974.

Cahill, Tim. *Buried Dreams.* New York: Bantam, 1985.

Campbell, Colin. "Portrait of a Mass Killer." *Psychology Today,* May 1976.

Cheney, Margaret. *The Co-Ed Killer.* New York: Walker, 1976.

Clarke, James W. *American Assassins: The Darker Side of Politics.* Princeton, N.J.: Princeton University Press, 1982.

Crockett, Art, ed., *Serial Murderers.* New York: Pinnacle, 1990. From the files of *True Detective Magazine.*

Douthwaite, L. C. *Mass Murder.* New York: Holt, 1929.

Doyle, Sir Arthur Conan. *The Complete Sherlock Holmes.* Garden City, N.Y.: Doubleday, 1930.

Farson, Dan. *Jack the Ripper.* London: M. Joseph, 1972.

"Federal Program Is Launched to Catch Serial Murderers." *Criminal Justice Newsletter,* Vol. 15, No. 15 (Aug. 1, 1984).

Frank, Gerold. *The Boston Strangler.* New York: New American Library, 1967.

Freeman, Lucy. *"Before I Kill More..."* New York: Crown, 1955.

Ganey, Terry. *St. Joseph's Children.* New York: Lyle Stuart, 1989.

Gollmar, Robert H. *Edward Gein.* New York: Charles Hallberg, 1981.

Graysmith, Robert. *Zodiac.* New York: St. Martin's Press, 1986.

———. *The Sleeping Lady: The Trailside Murders Above the Golden Gate Bridge.* New York: Dutton, 1990.

Gurwell, John K. *Mass Murder in Houston.* Houston: Cordovan Press, 1974.

Guttmacher, M. S. *The Mind of the Murderer.* New York: Farrar, Straus, 1960.

Harris, Thomas. *The Silence of the Lambs.* New York: St. Martin's Press, 1988. (Fiction.)

———. *Red Dragon.* New York: Putnam, 1981.

Howard, Clark. *Zebra.* New York: Berkley, 1980.

Howe, Cliff. *Scoundrels, Fiends and Human Monsters.* New York: Ace Books, 1958.

Klausner, Lawrence D. *Son of Sam.* New York: McGraw-Hill, 1981.

Larsen, Richard W. *Bundy—the Deliberate Stranger.* Englewood Cliffs, N.J.: Prentice-Hall, 1980.

Levin, Jack, and James Alan Fox. *Mass Murder: America's Growing Menace.* New York: Plenum, 1985.

Leyton, Elliott. *Compulsive Killers.* New York: New York University Press, 1986.

Lindecker, Clifford. *The Man Who Killed Boys.* New York: St. Martin's Press, 1980.

————. *Thrill Killers*. New York: Paperjacks, 1987.

Lindsay, David. *Mercy*. Garden City, New York: Doubleday, 1989. (Fiction.)

Livsey, Clara. *The Manson Women: A "Family" Portrait*. New York: Marek, 1980.

Lloyd, Robin. *For Money or Love: Boy Prostitution in America*. New York: Ballantine Books, 1976.

Manson, Charles, as told to Nuel Emmons. *Manson in His Own Words*. New York: Grove Press, 1986.

Michaud, Stepen G., and Hugh Aynesworth. *The Only Living Witness*. New York: Linden Press/Simon & Schuster, 1983.

Muir, Malcolm. *The Iowa Class Battleships: Iowa, New Jersey, Missouri and Wisconsin*. Poole, England: Blandford Press, 1987.

Nash, Jay Robert. *Almanac of World Crime*. Garden City, N.Y.: Anchor Press/Doubleday, 1981.

————. *Bloodletters and Badmen: A Narrative Encyclopedia of American Criminals from the Pilgrims to the Present*. New York: M. Evans, 1973.

Newton, Michael. *Hunting Humans: An Encyclopedia of Modern Serial Killers*. Port Townsend, Wash.: Loompanics Unlimited, 1990.

Norris, Joel. *Serial Killers: The Growing Menace*. New York: Dolphin/Doubleday, 1988.

O'Brien, Darcy. *Two of a Kind: The Hillside Stranglers*. New York: New American Library, 1985.

Olsen, Jack. *The Man with the Candy: The Story of the Houston Mass Murders*. New York: Simon & Schuster, 1974.

Palmer, Stuart. *The Psychology of Murder*. New York: Crowell, 1960.

Poe, Edgar Allan. "The Murders in the Rue Morgue." *Tales of Mystery and Imagination*. London: George C. Harrap, 1919.

Porter, Bruce. "Mind Hunters: Tracking Down Killers with the FBI's Psychological Profiling Team." *Psychology Today*, April 1983.

Reinhardt, James. *The Murderous Trail of Charles Starkweather*. Springfield, Ill.: C. C. Thomas, 1960.

Rule, Ann. *The I-5 Killer*. New York: New American Library, 1984.

————. *Lust Killer*. New York: New Ameican Library, 1983.

————. *The Stranger Beside Me*. New York: New American Library, 1984.

————. *The Want-Ad Killer*. New York: New American Library, 1983.

Rumbelow, Donald. *The Complete Jack the Ripper*. Boston: New York Graphic Society, 1975.

Samenow, Stanton E. *Inside the Criminal Mind*. New York: Times Books, 1984.

Sanders, Ed. *The Family.* New York: Dutton, 1971.

Sullivan, Terry, and Peter Maiken. *Killer Clown.* New York: Grosset & Dunlap, 1983.

Terry, Maury. *The Ultimate Evil.* Garden City, N.Y.: Doubleday, 1987.

Wilson, Colin. "The Serial Killer." *The Mammoth Book of True Crime 2.* New York: Carroll & Graf, 1990.

Winn, Steven, and David Merrill. *Ted Bundy: The Killer Next Door.* New York: Bantam, 1980.

FBI/NCAVC SOURCES

Ault, Richard L., Jr., and Robert R. Hazelwood. "Personality Assessment." Chapter 10 in *Practical Aspects of Rape Investigation, a Multidisciplinary Approach,* ed. Robert R. Hazelwood and Ann W. Burgess. New York: Elsevier Science Publishing Co., 1987.

———. "FBI Guidelines for Use of Hypnosis." *International Journal of Clinical and Experimental Hypnosis,* 1979.

Depue, Roger L. *Goals of the National Center for the Analysis of Violent Crime as Perceived and Preferred by Administrators, Faculty-Staff and Student-Users.* Doctoral dissertation, American University, Washington, D.C., 1986.

Douglas, John E.; Robert K. Ressler; Ann W. Burgess; and Carol R. Hartman. "Criminal Profiling from Crime Scene Analysis." *Behavioral Sciences and the Law,* Vol. 4, No. 4 (1986).

Hazelwood, Robert R. "Equivocal Deaths: A Case Study." *American Society of Criminology,* November 11, 1983.

———; Park E. Dietz; and Ann W. Burgess. "Sexual Fatalities: Behavioral Reconstruction in Equivocal Cases." *Journal of Forensic Science,* Vol. 27, No. 4 (October 1982).

Hazelwood, Robert R., and Ann W. Burgess, eds. *Practical Aspects of Rape Investigation: A Multidisciplinary Approach.* New York: Elsevier, 1987.

Lanning, K. V., and A. W. Burgess. "Child Pornography and Sex Rings." In D. Zillman and J. Bryant, eds., *Pornography: Research Advances & Policy Considerations.* Hillsdale, N.J.: Lawrence Erlbaum Associates, 1989.

Lanning, K. V. *Child Sex Rings: A Behavioral Analysis.* Arlington, Va.: National Center for Missing and Exploited Children, 1989.

National Center for the Analysis of Violent Crime. *National Center for the Analysis of Violent Crime.* Quantico, Va.: Behavioral Science Unit, FBI Academy, 1985.

——. *Annual Report, 1988*. Quantico, Va.: NCAVC, FBI Academy, 1988.

——. *Annual Report, 1989*. Quantico, Va.: NCAVC, FBI Academy, 1989.

Reese, James T. "Policing the Violent Society: The American Experience." *Stress Medicine*, Vol., 2, Surrey, England: 1986.

Ressler, Robert K.; Ann W. Burgess; and John E. Douglas. *Sexual Homicide: Patterns and Motives*. Lexington, Mass.: Lexington, 1988.

——. "Rape and Rape-Murder: One Offender and Twelve Victims." *American Journal of Psychiatry*, 1983.

Ressler, Robert K.; John E. Douglas; Ralph B. D'Agostino; and Ann W. Burgess. "Serial Murder: A New Phenomenon of Homicide." Paper presented at the 10th Triennial Meeting of the International Association of Forensic Sciences, Oxford, England, Sept. 18–25, 1984.

Sessions, William S. "From the Director: Violent Criminal Apprehension Program, Essential Link to Joint Investigations." *Police Chief*, June 1989.

PERTINENT ARTICLES FROM
FBI LAW ENFORCEMENT BULLETIN

Ault, Richard L., Jr. "Hypnosis: The FBI's Team Approach." January 1980.

——. "NCAVC's Research and Development Program." December 1986.

——, and James T. Reese. "A Psychological Assessment of Crime: Profiling." March 1980.

Deadman, Harold A. "Fiber Evidence and the Wayne Williams Trial." March and May 1984.

Depue, Roger L. "An American Response to an Era of Violence." December 1986.

Douglas, John E., and Murray S. Miron. "Threat Analysis: The Psycholinguistic Approach." September 1979.

Douglas, John E., and Anthony O. Rider. "FBI Psychological Profile Instrumental in Identifying Arson Suspect." February 1980.

Gladis, Stephen D. "The FBI National Academy's First 50 Years." July 1985.

Hazelwood, Robert R. "The Behavioral-Oriented Interview of Rape Victims: The Key to Profiling." September 1983.

——. "The NCAVC Training Program: A Commitment to Law Enforcement." December 1986.

——., and John E. Douglas. "The Lust Murderer." April 1980.

Hazelwood, Robert R., and Joseph A. Harpold. "Rape: The Dangers of Providing Confrontational Advice." June 1986.

Hazelwood, Robert R., and Ann W. Burgess. "An Introduction to the Serial Rapist: Research by the FBI." September 1987.

Hazelwood, Robert R., and Janet I. Warren. "The Serial Rapist: His Characteristics and Victims." January and February 1989.

Howlett, James B.; Kenneth A. Hanfland; and Robert K. Ressler. "The Violent Criminal Apprehension Program: VICAP: A Progress Report." December 1986.

Icove, David J. "Automated Crime Profiling." December 1986.

————, and M.H. Estepp. "Motive-Based Offender Profiles of Arson and Fire-Related Crimes." April 1987.

Lanning, Kenneth V., and Ann W. Burgess. "Child Pornography and Sex Rings." January 1984.

Lanning, Kenneth V., and Robert R. Hazelwood. "The Maligned Investigator of Criminal Sexuality." September 1988.

Lent, Cynthia J., and Joseph A. Harpold. "Violent Crime Against the Aging." July 1988.

Lyford, George, and Udy Wood, Jr. "National Crime Information Center: Your Silent Partner." March 1983.

NCAVC Staff. "Violent Crime." August 1985. (Special issue devoted entirely to the topic of violent crime.)

Ressler, Robert K.; John E. Douglas; Nicholas A. Groth; and Ann W. Burgess. "Offender Profiles: A Multi-Disciplinary Approach." September 1980.

Strentz, Thomas. "A Terrorist Psychosocial Profile: Past and Preent." April 1988.

Terry, Gary, and Michael P. Malone. "The 'Bobby Joe' Long Serial Murder Case: A Study in Cooperation." November and December 1987.

CONGRESSIONAL DOCUMENTS

Review of Navy Investigation of U.S.S. Iowa Explosion. Joint Hearings before the Investigations Subcommittee and the Defense Policy Panel of the Committee on Armed Services, House of Representatives, 1st Session, 101st Congress, December 12, 13, and 21, 1989. U.S. Government Printing Office, Washington, D.C.

Serial Murders: Patterns of murders committed by one person, in large numbers with no apparent rhyme, reason, or motivation. Subcommittee on Juvenile Justice of the Committee on the Judiciary, United States Senate, 1st Session, 99th Congress. July 12, 1983. U.S. Government Printing Office, Washington, D.C.

U.S.S. Iowa Tragedy: An Investigative Failure. Report of the Investigations Subcommittee and Defense Policy Panel of the Committee on Armed

Services, House of Representtaives, 2nd Session, 101st Congress. March 5, 1990. U.S. Government Printing Office, Washington, D.C.

MOVIES AND TELEVISION

Manhunter. 1986. Based upon Thomas Harris's novel *Red Dragon.*

The Secret Identity of Jack the Ripper. Harmony Gold Productions, 1988. Host: Peter Ustinov. NCAVC participants: John E. Douglas and Robert R. Hazelwood.

Silence of the Lambs. 1991. Based upon Thomas Harris's novel.

Index